The Butcher

"Behold the Man": Cumberland in 1746 as portrayed in the frontispiece of The Gentleman's Magazine. *The inset depicts Hercules after killing the Hydra, a many-headed monster, with his club.*

W. A. SPECK

The Butcher

The Duke of Cumberland and the Suppression of the 45

BASIL BLACKWELL · OXFORD

First published 1981
Basil Blackwell Publisher Limited
108 Cowley Road
Oxford OX4 1JF
England

British Library Cataloguing in Publication Data

Speck, W. A.
   The Butcher.
   1. Cumberland, William Augustus, *Duke of*
   2. Jacobite Rebellion, 1745—1746
   I. Title
   941.07'2   DA814.5

ISBN 0—631—10501—8

Typesetting by System 4 Associates Ltd, Gerrards Cross
Printed in Great Britain by Billing and Son Limited
Guildford, London, Oxford, Worcester

Contents

For
Caroline, Jackie and Kate

Maps

Note on Dates

Dates in the text are all Old Style,
with the year taken as starting on 1 January.

Acknowledgements

It is a great pleasure to acknowledge the many obligations which I have incurred while working on this book. Mr John Davey of Basil Blackwell Publisher Limited first suggested to me a life of Cumberland, and then agreed to my request to change it into a study of the suppression of the Forty-five. The Henry E. Huntington Library appointed me to a Visiting Fellowship in the summer of 1978, and the Twenty Seven Foundation financed my flight to Los Angeles. This enabled me to read the substantial Loudoun papers housed in the Huntington, where the staff spared no effort to make available the relevant letters in the Scottish correspondence of that collection. The University of Newcastle upon Tyne granted me study leave for the session 1979–80. Thanks to a grant from the British Academy I was able to spend the year in Cambridge, where I came to appreciate the facilities of the University Library, and particularly of the rare book and Manuscript rooms, where the staff were unfailingly obliging. The Master and Fellows of St John's College provided me with accommodation and otherwise extended their hospitality to me, and the President and governing body of Clare Hall made me an associate of that college. In consequence my year in Cambridge was extremely agreeable. For all his kindness in helping to make it so I am above all grateful to Dr Henry Pelling.

Since it began as a biography of the duke of Cumberland this book is based to a large extent on his papers, which I studied on the microfilm copy in Cambridge University Library. I acknowledge the gracious permission of Her Majesty the Queen to make use of this material from the Royal Archive at Windsor Castle. I also used extensively manuscripts in the British Library and in the Public Record Office, working in the convenient and congenial locations of the manuscript students room and the Round Room. When I changed the topic to an examination of the response to the Jacobite rebellion I investigated manuscript holdings in too many record offices and libraries to mention here. Those which yielded relevant material are cited in the notes; but I would like to thank all those who courteously and helpfully answered my requests for information. I am also pleased to acknowledge the grant which the Research Committee of Newcastle University gave me to help finance access to this material.

I am grateful to the Trustees of the Fitzwilliam Estates and to the Director of Sheffield City Libraries for permission to cite the Wentworth Woodhouse muniments. I am also indebted to Dr Eveline Cruickshanks, who generously lent me copies of documents and exchanged information with me. Miss Maureen Kavanagh patiently turned a rough draft into a fair typescript: my colleagues Tony Badger and John Cannon read this and made many perceptive observations, which greatly helped in the preparation of a final version. When this was completed it was typed by my wife, Sheila, who put up with much more than a copy-typing assignment while I was preparing this book. Nobody is responsible for any errors or infelicities which remain in it but myself; least of all my daughters, to whom it is dedicated.

The author and publisher are grateful to the following for permission to use photographs:

reproduced by Gracious Permission of Her Majesty the Queen: pages 16, 50, 104, 108, 134, 137, 138, 142, 150–1, 152, 154, 200; BBC Hulton Picture Library: page 132; Bodleian Library, Oxford: frontispiece; J. T. T. Fletcher Esq., and the National Galleries of Scotland: page 45; Library of Congress: pages 146, 172, 191; Mansell Collection: page 5, 160; Victor Montagu Esq., and the Naval Museum, Greenwich: page 8; National Galleries of Scotland: endpapers and pages 75, 167; National Portrait Gallery, London: pages 61, 65, 157; the National Trust: page 202.

Introduction

As every schoolboy knows, the Jacobite rebellion of 1745 was a failure. The story of how Charles Edward, the Young Pretender, failed to depose George II, and place his own father on the throne as James VIII of Scotland and III of England has been told so often, usually in a romantic glow which makes it a glorious rather than a dismal failure, that there is no point in telling it once again. This is not a tale of the losers, however, but a story of the winners. For the Hanoverians rather than the Stuarts the Forty-five was an undeniable success. Yet the success story has rarely been related. Though it is often complained that historians record successes and have little time for failures, the reverse is true of the Forty-five. Hardly a year goes by without the appearance of a new life of Bonnie Prince Charlie, or a Jacobite saga; but there has never been a full biography of Charles Edward's rival, the duke of Cumberland, or a detailed account of how Jacobitism was finally eliminated as a threat to the regime.

Perhaps the main reason why there has not been a thorough examination of how the British government dealt with the rebellion is that, until recently, it was not felt to be necessary to provide an explanation. Historians, especially those writing in the whig tradition, assumed that the Hanoverian kings and their ministers commanded the support of the bulk of the British, or at any rate the English, people. Although it was admitted that power was wielded by a whig oligarchy, it was nevertheless taken for granted that they could rely on the acquiescence of the landed, professional and commercial classes in their rule since, it was alleged, they ruled in the interests of those groups. Indeed it became commonplace to assert that the whigs, by their financial and commercial policies, had created a vested interest in their regime which ensured that it was too stable to be toppled by an adventurer whose credit-worthiness was considered shaky by those whose securities were tied up in government funds, and whose guarantee of their investments in the event of his victory could not be taken seriously. This view was admirably summed up by V. H. H. Green:

"The Hanoverian dynasty and the vested interests to which it was attached, the merchants, the clergy, the landed gentry, had so deep a stake in the country that even those who were most critical of the royal family and were romantically attached to Jacobite legends would not lightly uproot it."[1]

Consequently the Pretender was thought to have appealed only to a minority of misfits. Catholics who shared the Pretender's religion, and had therefore been second-class citizens since the Reformation except during the brief reign of James II, hoped to obtain a proper place in society from his son. Highland clans who could not share the benefits of an expanding, commercially-oriented economy resisted its threats to their ancient way of life by becoming Jacobites. Their counterparts in England, gentry families who were unable to adjust to the demands and opportunities of the agricultural revolution, sought in Jacobitism a desperate solution to impending bankruptcy.

These assumptions have been challenged of late from a variety of quarters. So far as Scotland is concerned, Dr Bruce Lenman has shown that Catholics, though they were staunchly Jacobites, could not give the Pretender substantial support since there, as in England, they constituted only a small minority. The religious mainstay of the Jacobite cause north of the border was the episcopal church, which had been disestablished in 1690. Thereafter most of its clergy had become nonjurors, that is they had refused to take the oaths of supremacy and allegiance to a regime which they regarded as illegitimate. The episcopalians were not confined to the highland zone, but drew considerable strength from the lowland coastal strip between St Andrews and Aberdeen. Nor was there a simple link between economic success and loyalty to the government on the one hand, and failure and disaffection on the other. Lord George Murray, the ablest general in the Young Pretender's army, who proved to be more than a match for some of the commanders on the other side, was an improving landlord, while Cameron of Lochiel, whose house was sacked and whose estate was devastated by government forces in May 1746, was a shrewd and successful businessman.[2]

As for England, Dr Eveline Cruickshanks has argued that a substantial section of the political nation, perhaps a majority — the tories, were so alienated from the Hanoverian kings and their whig ministers that they actively sought and even worked for the restoration of the direct Stuart line. Their years in the wilderness as political outcasts following the death of Queen Anne made Jacobitism attractive to them as a way back to the promised land. Dr Linda Colley, while doubting the degree of enthusiasm for the Stuarts among the tories, would agree that the government could not take for granted the support of the tory gentry, for they supported a political party which maintained an active and constant opposition to the whig ministers throughout the early eighteenth century. She has also shown that toryism was not confined to country gentlemen, but penetrated the professional and business communities. Tory candidates were returned from large urban constituencies, as well as from English and Welsh counties, where they drew on local middle-class support and even appealed to the 'popular' vote in their elections. Investigating more specifically the relationship between the whig oligarchy and the lower orders, E. P. Thompson has concluded that the regime was very narrowly based on a ruling clique which maintained its ascendancy over the great majority of Englishmen by ruthless exploitation of the law for its own ends. Walpole and his fellow whigs had grabbed power after the Hanoverian accession and clung to it by a variety of questionable means, even though they were bitterly opposed by the rest of the population outside the charmed circle of the Court. They particularly alienated the propertyless masses by stringently asserting the rights of the propertied few, provoking resistance which found expression in attacks upon property, in riots, and also in popular Jacobitism. The regime was thus a vulnerable and exposed gang of adventurers and free-booters whose collapse was ardently desired by most subjects of the first two Georges.[3]

These studies seriously challenge the views of those who have maintained that by the central decades of the eighteenth century Britain had achieved political stability, based on a consensus of public opinion that the Revolution settlement, secured by the Hanoverian accession, had established a regime which was preferable to any alternative which the Stuarts had to offer. As one who subscribes to those views, as the very title of my last book implied, I felt that this was a challenge which could not go unanswered.[4] This book is therefore a response to it. The first chapter attempts to assess the strengths and weaknesses of the government's position on the eve of the rebellion. The following narrative shows how the government gradually capitalised on its strength, while the Young Pretender failed to exploit its weaknesses, until the duke of Cumberland was able to crush Jacobitism once and for all at Culloden. The final chapter, drawing on the narrative, then tries to assess how serious a threat to the stability of the political system under George II the Forty-five had been.

The suppression of the rebellion might appear at first sight as a grim, sombre story by contrast with the romance of the Jacobites. Indeed there is a fairy tale quality about the uprising, with its handsome, dashing prince, the Young Chevalier, and even a heroine in Flora MacDonald. If the sober truth only helps to dissipate some of the myths created by Bonnie Prince Charlie's supporters then something will have been achieved. Nevertheless, as we shall see, the story of how he was opposed is not without its epic moments, while his main opponent, the duke of

Cumberland, also became a legendary figure as 'the Butcher'. Whether or not he deserved that title is fully investigated in the ensuing narrative.

While there is no intention whatsoever to whitewash Cumberland, it is only fair to stress at the outset that his reputation before the Forty-five was totally unsullied. Until allegations of atrocities committed at and after the battle of Culloden began to call his honour into question he was regarded as in every way a worthy opponent of the Young Pretender. Any account of the rebellion which sees it as a duel fought between a Prince Charming and a Monster uses hindsight literally with a vengeance.

Most accounts of Charles Edward's exploits in the Forty-five stress his youth, and yet William Augustus, duke of Cumberland, was in fact the younger of the two. The Young Pretender had been born in 1720, while William Augustus was born in April 1721. Cumberland was therefore only twenty-four when he commanded the forces raised to crush the rebellion. This was in marked contrast to other commanders of the British army who took part in the exercise. Sir John Cope must have been at least in his sixties, while George Wade was seventy-two, and Sir John Ligonier was sixty-five. Where Wade had fought in Flanders under William III, and Cope and Ligonier were veterans of Marlborough's campaigns in the War of the Spanish Succession, Cumberland had first seen action as recently as 1743, when he accompanied his father at the battle of Dettingen. It had, however, been a baptism of fire, in the course of which he was wounded in the leg. His bravery earned him the respect of James Wolfe, the future conqueror of Quebec, who wrote that "the soldiers were in high delight to have him so near to them". The duke of Richmond commented that "by his love of the service, by his generosity and compassion of prisoners, and by all the good qualities that ever a young Prince was endowed with, he has justly got the love and esteem of everybody".[5] He did not take part in the 1744 campaign, but was made Captain General of his Majesty's land forces in March 1745.

It was very much his Majesty's appointment. Ever since the breakdown of relations with his elder son Frederick in 1737 the king had become devoted to William Augustus. He had encouraged him to pursue the military career which was his own ruling passion, and had obtained for him the command of the Coldstream Guards in 1740, and promoted him to the rank of Lieutenant General after Dettingen. He finally gave his son a chance to lead his troops into action, as he himself had done in that battle. Cumberland did so at Fontenoy in May, with disastrous results. They marched straight into withering fire which thinned their ranks remorselessly, and yet they marched on under his command until he saw that further progress into the deadly barrage was hopeless, and ordered a retreat. The infantry then withdrew in perfect order, leaving over 1,500 of their number dead, and many more wounded, on the battlefield.

Cumberland learned the hard way how devastating sustained firing from cannon and musket could be, and was to apply the lesson to the rebels at Culloden.

WILLIAM DUKE OF CUMBERLAND.

Cumberland projecting his military image. Over his armour he wears the sash of the Order of the Garter, presented to him on his installation in 1730, at the age of nine. Around his neck is the insignia of the Most Honourable Military Order of the Bath. He had been installed as the first and principal Knight Companion of the Order upon its institution in 1725, when he was only four years old.

Despite this setback he earned the respect of the rank and file. His disregard for his own danger, and the discipline he managed to retain over the infantry, gave him a reputation which the event itself hardly justified. Although he could scarcely be called charismatic, he was an imposing figure, who commanded respect. He was tall, and had not yet put on the massive weight which was to help to carry him to an early grave. Indeed when he became colonel of the Coldstream Guards a hostile observer, who attributed the promotion to Sir Robert Walpole, claimed that the prime minister had hung military honours "on a post", which implies that his height was more noticeable than his girth at that time.[6]

The elder statesman was also associated with the young duke in an apocryphal story involving a contrivance to get him out of an undesirable marriage. When George II chose the deformed princess of Denmark for his son's bride Cumberland allegedly sought the advice of the former prime minister, now retired as earl of Orford and even within a few days of death. "After a moment's reflection, Orford advised him to give his consent to the marriage, on condition of receiving an ample and immediate establishment, 'and believe me' he added, 'when I say, that the match will be no longer pressed.' The duke followed his advice, and the event happened as the dying statesman had foretold."[7] Cumberland in fact remained a life-long bachelor, though he was no misogynist, for his name was linked with so many women that he acquired a reputation as a rake even in that permissive age. It could be that family life did not appeal to him after growing up in the strained household of George II and Queen Caroline, who smothered the young duke with affection and frequently wished his elder brother Frederick were dead. Cumberland contrived to stay on good terms with his brother despite this, though he was much closer to his sisters. On the other hand it was not unusual for military men to remain unmarried, and among his own colleagues in the high command, Cope, Hawley, Ligonier and Wade all remained bachelors.

Although they were all much older than him and his youth led him to be referred to as "the martial boy", his lack of years and military experience does not appear to have been a disadvantage to him. Being the king's son, of course, helped. His determination to live up to his father's expectations of his military career also made him fit the role of a commander. He projected the image of a military leader, with a stiff bearing enhanced by uniform, a confident demeanour and a forthright manner. In every way he looked the part for which he had been chosen when he led his father's troops against the Jacobites. During the ensuing campaign, however, Cumberland's nickname was to change from "the martial boy" to "the Butcher".

CHAPTER ONE

"The whole Nation was ripe for a revolt"

I shall not dissemble, that for some time before the breaking out of the Rebellion, the nation had been in a ferment, miserably divided into factions and parties. The many and heavy taxes laid upon the subjects, the scandalous corruption in the Parliament, the heats and contentions in Elections, the depredations committed on our trade by the Spaniards and the like, had laid the Government open to be continually pelted by every paultry scribbler, and the opposition made to the ministry and administration, was construed and loudly pronounced a disaffection to his Majesty, and an inclination towards the Pretender; And thus our enemies abroad, and the unthinking multitude at home, were made to believe, that the whole Nation was ripe for a revolt.

Anon, *The History of the Rebellion in the Years 1745 and 1746*

At about midday on Tuesday 9 July 1745, Captain Brett, commander of HMS *Lion*, sailing over 100 miles west of the Lizard, saw two ships to leeward. He ordered his crew to bear down on them and by three o'clock in the afternoon was able to make them out to be two French ships, the *Elisabeth*, a man of war with sixty-four guns, and the *Du Teillay*, a frigate of sixteen guns. An hour later, when he was less than two miles from them, they raised the French flag and prepared to engage. Battle commenced between the *Elisabeth* and the *Lion* at five o'clock, and they fired at each other until ten o'clock at night, by which time they had virtually reduced one another to wrecks. The *Lion* came off worse, for her rigging was cut to pieces, her masts were shot through, and forty-five of her men were killed in the action, so that eventually she was crippled. Although this enabled the *Elisabeth* to sail away and be out of sight within an hour, she could not continue her voyage, but had to return

An impression of the fight between the Lion *and the* Elisabeth *on 9 July
1745. While the two men of war engaged, the frigate* Du Teillay, *carrying
the Young Pretender and the "Seven Men of Moidart" to Scotland, looked
on, probably from a much safe distance than in this reconstruction.*

to France. Brett did not know it at the time, but he had deprived the
Jacobites of 700 men, 1,500 muskets, 1,800 broadswords and other
arms, ammunition and supplies, for that was what the French ship was
carrying. The *Du Teillay*, however, which lay off from the others at a
great distance while they were engaged, was able to sail on to its destination, carrying Charles Edward, the Young Pretender, and the legendary
"Seven Men of Moidart". They landed safely at Eriskay, an island in the
Outer Hebrides, on 23 July. Meanwhile the *Lion*, its captain wounded,
and its master missing an arm shot off during the fight, limped into
Plymouth.[1]

The Young Pretender had set out to remove George II from the British
throne and to replace him with his own father, James VIII of Scotland
and III of England as his supporters called him. To assess how realistic
this aim was we must try to set aside knowledge of his eventual failure,
and to gauge the situation in Britain on the eve of his voyage from France.
Such an assessment requires an examination of the government's person-
nel and policies, and the extent to which these were supported in Scotland
and in England.

By 1745 George II had reigned for eighteen years. His was therefore
already the longest reign since that of Charles II, who died in 1685. James
II had been king for less than four years, before the Revolution of 1688

obliged him to fly to France with his infant son James Edward. Had the Revolution not set aside the direct Stuart line, then James Edward would have reigned from his father's death in 1701 until 1766. Instead he spent his entire life in exile, dubbed 'the Old Pretender' because of his claim to the British throne, while his followers were called Jacobites from the Latin version of his first name. In 1689 the Bill of Rights named William of Orange as King in place of James II, and provided for the accession of his sister-in-law princess Anne if he left no heirs. As William III he reigned for thirteen years before a fall from his horse hastened his end. Anne managed to be Queen for another twelve years despite wretched health. George I who succeeded her in 1714, was King until 1727, when he died suddenly on a visit to his native Hanover.

George II had ruled long enough to make the Hanoverian dynasty seem permanently established on the British throne. Jacobites could entertain some hopes of the Stuarts regaining it naturally between 1688 and 1714, when first William and then Anne left no heirs. But when the Act of Settlement was passed in 1701, vesting the succession in the Protestant House of Hanover despite many more substantial hereditary claims, and George I came to the throne peacefully under its terms, there could be no prospect of the new line becoming extinct early, for the new royal family proved to be a very prolific dynasty. In 1745 George II had seven off-spring who had survived the perilous years of an eighteenth-century childhood to become adults: five girls; Frederick Louis the heir apparent, born in 1707; and William Augustus duke of Cumberland, born in 1721, who was destined to defeat the Jacobite rebels at the battle of Culloden. Frederick, the Prince of Wales, had married Augusta of Saxe Gotha in 1736, and by the time of the rebellion they had five children; one daughter and four sons, the youngest, Henry Frederick, being born on 27 October 1745.

If George II and his family exuded an air of permanency, so did his ministers. It is true that none emulated the feat of the earl of Orford, who died on the very eve of the Forty-five. As Sir Robert Walpole he had been prime minister for twenty years, from 1722 to 1742, and his tenure of power for so long had done more than even the first two Georges to give the regime an image of durability. Yet Henry Pelham, the Chancellor of the Exchequer and first Lord of the Treasury, who after 1744 was at least nominally Prime Minister, had been in government service since 1724; while his brother, the duke of Newcastle, had enjoyed high office since 1717, and for the past twenty-one years had been one of the two English secretaries of state. Lord Hardwicke, who became lord chancellor in 1737, had been a leading government lawyer since 1720. All three had risen under Walpole, and along with other former Walpolites in the administration were known by 1745 as the 'Old Corps'. The very

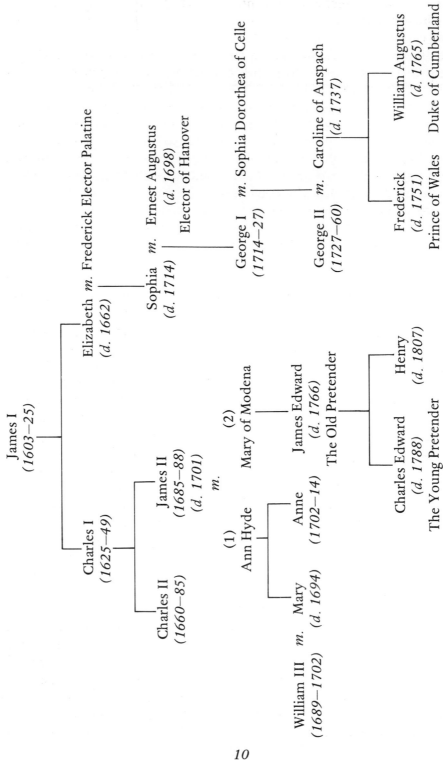

The Stuart and Hanoverian Dynasties

James I
(1603–25)

Charles I
(1625–49)

Elizabeth *m.* Frederick Elector Palatine
(d. 1662)

Charles II
(1660–85)

James II
(1685–88)
(d. 1701)
m.

Sophia *m.* Ernest Augustus
(d. 1714)   (d. 1698)
              Elector of Hanover

(1)
Ann Hyde

(2)
Mary of Modena

George I *m.* Sophia Dorothea of Celle
(1714–27)

William III *m.* Mary
(1689–1702)   (d. 1694)

Anne
(1702–14)

James Edward
(d. 1766)
The Old Pretender

George II *m.* Caroline of Anspach
(1727–60)   (d. 1737)

Charles Edward
(d. 1788)
The Young Pretender

Henry
(d. 1807)

Frederick
(d. 1751)
Prince of Wales

William Augustus
(d. 1765)
Duke of Cumberland

name indicated a measure of continuity which survived Walpole's fall, and which seemed to ensure permanency for the political system which he had established.

Yet there had been changes on the Great Man's downfall, which had obliged the Old Corps to work with politicians who had not been a part of his system. From 1742 until 1744 they had to share power with two men whose services Walpole had specifically rejected, the earls of Bath and Granville.[2] Lord Bath, who as William Pulteney had been Walpole's greatest rival, had not actually been appointed to office, but Granville replaced Lord Harrington as secretary of state. The Pelham brothers got on with them no better than Walpole had done, though when they managed to bring about Granville's resignation in November 1744, instead of reverting to his system they formed the so-called Broad Bottom Administration, since tories and dissident whigs were brought into the ministry. Among the tories given office for the first time since 1714 were Lord Gower, Sir John Hinde Cotton and Sir John Philips, who became respectively lord privy seal, treasurer of the chamber and a member of the Board of Trade. The dissident whigs, some of whom had been in opposition for over a decade, included the duke of Bedford, and the earl of Chesterfield, who were appointed to the posts of first lord of the admiralty and lord lieutenant of Ireland.

The Pelhamite victory of 1744, however, was only a partial one. George II refused to give it his blessing, insisting that he had been forced to abandon Granville, who in any case remained high in his favour. As a ministerial supporter put it, "the common vogue is that the outs are much caressed at Court, and the ins as remarkably disregarded, and that the broad bottom will soon be no bottom."[3] Among the 'outs' favoured by the king, besides Bath and Granville, was the earl of Winchilsea, who had been superseded at the admiralty by Bedford. Nor were all Granvillites purged from the ministry in 1744. Three men in particular continued to represent their views in the Cabinet: the duke of Bolton, the earl of Stair and the marquis of Tweeddale. Bolton held no office of national importance, being only warden of the New Forest and governor of the Isle of Wight; but Stair was commander of the armed forces in England, while Tweeddale was secretary of state for Scotland.

The Scottish-Secretaryship had been re-established in 1742, after a lapse of seventeen years. Since the abolition of the separate Privy Council in Edinburgh after the Act of Union in 1707, the government of the northern kingdom had been carried out almost on a makeshift basis.[4] Certain officials bore the brunt of the administrative tasks, particularly the leading legal and judicial officers, the lord president of the session, the lord justice clerk, the lord advocate and the solicitor general. The men who occupied these key posts in 1745 were Duncan Forbes of

11

Culloden, Andrew Fletcher of Milton, Robert Craigie and Robert Dundas. Forbes and Fletcher were to play a major role in maintaining the government's interests during the rebellion, the Lord President in Inverness, where he went as soon as he heard that the Young Pretender had landed, and the lord justice clerk in Edinburgh. Both owed their positions to the patronage of the third duke of Argyll, though Fletcher was more closely associated with him than was Forbes. The dukes of Argyll had usually taken upon themselves the political job of managing the government's affairs in Scotland, and the third duke had served an apprenticeship in this role under Walpole even before he succeeded to the title. The first thing he did when the rebellion broke out was to head south to London, which showed his appreciation of where power ultimately lay. The men who represented the government in Scotland functioned as a team no more than did their colleagues in England. Indeed they were divided more or less along the same lines. Lord President Forbes, Lord Justice Clerk Fletcher and the duke of Argyll tended to side with the Pelhams, while Lord Advocate Craigie and Solicitor Dundas were associated with Tweeddale.

When the king departed for Hanover in May 1745, therefore, he left behind very divided counsels. The body which exercised authority in his absence was known as the lords justices. This was effectively the Cabinet acting as a kind of regency, and therefore included the rival ministers, the Pelhamites, led by Newcastle and his brother Henry, and Lord Chancellor Hardwicke; and the Granvillites Bolton, Stair and Tweeddale. Although Granville himself was no longer one of their number, as a privy councillor his name features conspicuously upon Orders in Council which the lords justices issued while the king was away.

The characterisation of the conflict between the Pelhamites and the Granvillites as a struggle of 'ins' and 'outs' was to some extent true. The Pelhams, for instance, had pushed William Pitt's claims to office, but these had been unacceptable to the king. Thereafter Pitt was to make a thorough nuisance of himself until he was eventually given the post of paymaster. And it was a sign of Granville's continued influence with George II when he informed Henry Pelham that the king had bestowed a Tellership in the Exchequer on one of his own supporters, which infuriated the prime minister, who "said he would not bear it," since as Chancellor, "it was naturally under his office to dispose of".[5]

It was also a clash of personalities. The men who governed Britain during the crisis were all remarkably self-willed. George II above all liked to have his own way, and could be irritable, sarcastic and even violently bad tempered with anybody who stood in it. He had always been tetchy and impatient and age, now that he was over sixty, instead of mellowing him, had if anything made him worse. These characteristics come out clearly in Lord Hardwicke's well-known account of a somewhat strained audience he had with the King shortly after Granville's resignation.

> *King*:   I have done all you asked of me. I have put all power into your hands and I suppose you will make the most of it.
> *Hardwicke*:   The disposition of places is not enough, if your Majesty takes pains to show the world that you disapprove of your own work.
> *King*:   *My work!* I was forc'd: I was threatened.
> *Hardwicke*:   I am sorry to hear your Majesty use those expressions.

The conversation also emphasises the vital importance of the royal authority in government. George II was no cypher, either in theory or in practice. Limited monarchy might be an appropriate way of describing the Constitution which prevailed at the time; but it was a monarchy nonetheless. The king was expected to rule and not merely to reign. Moreover George II had no intention of doing anything else. He was not idle, and worked hard at the business of being king. His command of the army could not be questioned, even by his younger son the duke of Cumberland when he was captain general. Although George was very fond of Cumberland at this time, the duke could not take for granted his own recommendations for promotion. And while politicians could and did challenge his control of political appointments, they could not act independently without his co-operation. Getting rid of Granville was only a partial victory so long as George made it clear that he still preferred him, and refused to give the Pelhams his countenance.

He did so partly because Granville was polished, urbane and cosmopolitan, an able diplomat who could converse in the king's native German. He was also offensively arrogant to his fellow ministers, hardly bothering to keep Newcastle informed of diplomatic developments until the duke complained of his "insufferable silences", while he once referred contemptuously to Henry Pelham as being no more than "a chief clerk". His wit especially when warmed with wine, which was not infrequently, could be devastatingly mordant.

The Pelhams themselves, though brothers, could hardly have been more different. Newcastle, excitable and even neurotic, wore his heart on his sleeve, while Henry, reserved and timid, concealed his behind a phlegmatic exterior. Most contemporaries seem to have considered the duke to be something of an ass, while they respected Henry's formidable financial ability. Yet Newcastle tended to be under-rated and this has affected his reputation ever since. His capacity for sheer hard work, expecially in the crisis of the Forty-five, was astonishing. And there was more to his competence for high office than an appetite for drudgery, for throughout the rebellion he not only kept himself and many others well-informed about its progress, but could discern its pattern and supervise its containment and eventual suppression. He emerges as a presiding genius who co-ordinated naval operations around the coasts of the entire island, and military movements, both professional and amateur, in two kingdoms, which ultimately concluded in victory.

The dispute between these men, however, concerned more than places and personalities: it involved the whole question of Britain's international role. At the time of the Forty-five Europe was engaged in one of the most complex conflicts of modern history, the War of the Austrian Succession. As Sir Leslie Stephen put it "for what particular reason Englishmen were fighting at Dettingen or Fontenoy or Lauffeld is a question which a man can only answer when he has been specially crammed for examination and his knowledge has not begun to ooze out".[6] Basically the original reason was that Maria Theresa, daughter of the Holy Roman Emperor Charles VI, claimed her father's hereditary territories of Austria, Bohemia and Hungary, the Austrian Netherlands (modern Belgium) and some Italian possessions on his death in 1740. Although almost all the European powers, including Britain, had guaranteed her right to them, within weeks of her accession Prussia and Saxony were claiming parts of Bohemia, while Savoy and Spain were asserting claims to some of the Italian possessions. Behind these claimants stood the might of France, the greatest power in Europe. The French supported the election of the elector of Bavaria, who succeeded Charles VI as Emperor.

George II at first tried to keep out of the ensuing conflict, claiming that as elector of Hanover he was neutral. Granville, however, persuaded him to renounce Hanoverian neutrality, and to attempt to build up a system of alliances to assist Austria against her enemies. In the summer of 1743 a British contingent joined Hanoverian troops who were themselves in Britain's pay, and together with Austrian forces made up the Pragmatic Army under the command of George himself, who led it into battle at Dettingen. Although he defeated the French the action was much criticised, on the grounds that British resources were being squandered on continental campaigns which were of concern not to Britain but to Hanover. Later in 1743 Granville negotiated the treaty of Worms between Britain, Austria and Sardinia, and treated with the new Emperor Charles VII in an attempt to detach him from the side of France.

These diplomatic initiatives irritated the Pelhams for several reasons. The duke of Newcastle was chagrined because, although he was Granville's fellow secretary, he was scarcely consulted about them. Henry Pelham disliked them because they committed Britain to paying subsidies which he, as chancellor of the exchequer and first lord of the treasury, would have to raise in parliament. Extra financial burdens were not welcome at a time when government expenditure was already high on account of a war with Spain which had broken out in 1739. Both brothers became convinced that Granville was "making court to the king by preferring Hanoverian considerations to all others".[7]

The treaties also aroused the ire of the French, who retaliated by allying with Spain, pledging support for the reconquest of Gibraltar and Minorca, and by backing the Jacobite cause. Towards the end of 1743 formidable preparations for an invasion were started at Dunkirk, while in January 1744 Charles Edward, the Pretender's eldest son, made his way to France from Rome. On 24 February the British and French fleets lay off the coast of Kent to engage in a battle which, if the French had won it, would have cleared the way for the invasion. Then a violent storm broke out, and both fleets, badly damaged, made for home ports, while the transports in Dunkirk were destroyed. The invasion was called off, though France now formally declared war on Britain.[8]

The entry of France directly into the War of the Austrian Succession proved calamitous for George II and his allies. A French invasion of the Austrian Netherlands led the Pelhams to insist that the Dutch must be brought actively into the alliance. The Dutch were reluctant to participate, however, largely because the king refused to commit Hanover wholeheartedly to the cause, for which Granville was blamed. It was this which gave the Pelhams the pretext for insisting upon his removal from office in November 1744.

Throughout 1745, nevertheless, international concerns continued to create tension between the king and his ministers. George II was more committed to a major role in Europe than ever, and spent the summer on the continent in pursuit of it. In January the Emperor Charles VII had died, and George as elector of Hanover devoted his energies to securing the election of Maria Theresa's husband Francis as his successor, a campaign which was crowned with success in September. The only other good news for the British that summer was that an expeditionary force from New England had taken Cape Breton from the French in June. Meanwhile the duke of Cumberland at the head of the allied army had been defeated by Marshal Saxe at Fontenoy in May, after which the French forces had proceeded across the Low Countries, taking Tournai, Ghent, Oudenarde and, on 12 August, Ostend. It was in this dire situation, when Cumberland despaired of saving what was left of the Austrian Netherlands and feared for the security of the Dutch Republic, that news reached him that the Pretender's son had landed in Scotland.

When the Young Pretender raised his standard at Glenfinnan on 19 August, before perhaps 1,000 supporters, the duke of Cumberland had about 34,000 British troops under his command on the continent. There was an inevitable outcry that most if not all of these should be recalled to Britain to deal with the rebellion. As we shall see Cumberland was reluctant to jeopardise the campaign by detaching forces from his already overstretched army to deal with rebels, and he hoped that these would be crushed by available forces on the spot. His father took the same line, encouraged by Granville and his allies in the government, Bolton, Stair

An allegorical design by Lieutenant Wilhelm Schilling in 1748. It features scenes from the recently ended War of the Austrian Succession, including, top left, the battle of Culloden.

and Tweeddale. These played down the scale of the uprising, claiming that the rebels were "a despicable rabble" who could be "crushed with all the ease in the world", at the same time insisting that Britain should fulfill her European commitments or risk alienating the Dutch.[9] The Pelhams and their adherents, on the other hand, took the contrary view that top priority should be given to suppressing the rebellion, even if this would involve withdrawing British troops from the continent completely until the job was done.

The government, therefore, so far from presenting a united front during the Forty-five, was in serious disarray. Indeed the rebellion postponed until February 1746 the final showdown between the Pelhams and the king over the continuing influence of Lord Granville. Had the rebellion not broken out, it seems clear that the decision to force the king to show the world that he approved of his own work, to adapt Lord Hardwicke's nice way of putting it, would have been taken in September 1745 after George returned from Hanover.

Moreover, although it was called the Broad Bottom Administration, the ministry was not so broadly-based as this title suggests. On the contrary, it had several opponents besides the Granvillites. There was serious disaffection in Scotland, while in England not all tories or even dissident whigs had been reconciled to the Old Corps in the reconstruction of 1744.

Relations between Scotland and England had traditionally been strained. In many ways they had actually been at their worst just before the Union of Parliaments in 1707, which was regarded as a shot-gun marriage. It was widely resented in Scotland, where many came to believe that a majority of the last Scottish parliament had been blatantly bribed to accept a treaty which deprived the northern kingdom of its independence for dubious benefits. As one whig historian commented "they were apt to consider themselves degraded to a province of England".[10] The extent of disaffection had been revealed in the rebellion of 1715 when the earl of Mar rallied eighteen Scottish lords and 10,000 men to the Pretender's standard. Had he been a more skilful commander he might well have defeated the duke of Argyll at Sheriffmuir in November 1715, for even though he was militarily incompetent he managed to avoid a defeat. His failure to gain a victory spelled the end of the Fifteen as a military affair. Yet it had shown that Jacobitism was a formidable force north of the border. In the highlands, especially among the clans which shared the Pretender's Catholicism, and along the east coast where the episcopal church was strong, it was a positive preference for the house of Stuart based on ancient loyalties. In the lowlands, south of a line between the Firth of Forth and Loch Lomond, it was a negative dislike of the house of Hanover and rule from England, for there was little love lost between the dominant Presbyterians and the Catholic Stuarts. These regional distinctions were appreciated by parliament when it passed the Disarming Act of 1716, which forbade the carrying of weapons by Scots in a quite carefully defined highland zone. The government also spent a great deal of money and time constructing 260 miles of roads and reinforcing fortresses in the highlands in the years after 1715, in order to try to nip in the bud another uprising.

During those years there was little change in Scottish political preferences north of Glasgow and Edinburgh. If anything Jacobitism became more entrenched, as the politics of nostalgia for a mythical golden age when a cultured aristocracy had held sway, and before upstart whigs and Presbyterians had turned the world upside down.[11] The lowlands, on the other hand, became slowly resigned to, if not reconciled with, the Union, as they began at last to feel some economic benefits from it. Although it had been sold as a salvation for the ailing Scottish economy, the Union had not produced the immediate economic miracle which its more ardent advocates had prophesied. By the 1730s and 1740s, however, the integration of Scotland in the British imperial system was paying off. Glasgow in particular benefited from her involvement with the colonial trade.

Yet while these developments might have been expected to improve relations with England, Walpole learned to his cost that there was still considerable anti-Union sentiment in southern Scotland. The Porteous riots of 1736 demonstrated a marked degree of hostility to his government in the very capital. They were fomented by the trials of smugglers who had attempted to rob an excise officer, two of whom were sentenced to death. When one escaped, troops commanded by Captain Porteous were put in charge of the other. At the smuggler's execution a sympathetic crowd harassed these men until they retaliated by firing, killing six. As their commanding officer Porteous was arrested, tried for murder and condemned to death. Upon news of his being reprieved reaching Edinburgh from London, about 4,000 people took part in a raid on the prison where he was held, from which he was dragged and lynched. The murder of Captain Porteous by a mob might be popular in Scotland, but it could not be tolerated in England. Steps taken to impose sanctions on Edinburgh for the breakdown of law and order, however, alienated even government supporters in Scotland. The second duke of Argyll went into opposition, and used his extensive influence against the government in the parliamentary elections of 1741. Where normally the majority of Scottish seats were more or less guaranteed for the ministry, Walpole found that most MPs returned from Scotland in this election were against him, which was a crucial factor in his downfall.

After Walpole's resignation more harmonious relations were reestablished, at least with the Scottish whigs. Argyll died in 1743, and his

18

brother, the third duke, was, as we have seen, close to the Pelhams. Nevertheless events in Scotland in the years immediately prior to 1745 had demonstrated that the government could not take the support of the lowlands for granted. The Pretender, who could count on raising men in the highlands, could also calculate on exploiting the residual dissatisfaction with the king's ministers in the lowlands.

The English political scene also seemed promising for a Jacobite rebellion. Tory reaction to the modest relaxation of their long proscription, which the promotion of a few tories to national office, and their admission to commissions of the peace in the localities procured, was ambivalent. Some welcomed it as a foothold in the door of power which more pressure might widen. Thus when Sir Charles Kemys Tynte offered himself as a tory candidate at a by-election in Glamorganshire in December 1744 he was advised:[12]

> if you can venture on it without offending your real friends, I fancy it may not be improper for your agents to magnify the present coalition more than it deserves, and to intimate to the tools of power that by offending you and acting against your interest they may possibly disoblige a person who may soon be able to resent their behaviour in a manner that will be very disagreeable to them.

The 'real friends' whom Sir Charles risked offending by this tactic were those tories who were not prepared to change from opposing the Court to supporting it, just because some of their number had, in their eyes, sold out. They included such important magnates as the duke of Beaufort and Sir Watkin Williams Wynn, who had the reputation of being Jacobites.

How many Jacobites there were in the tory ranks is hard to determine. It has been estimated that in the last parliament of Queen Anne's reign "the committed supporters of the Pretender in the House of Commons numbered at least 80" and may have been as high as 100.[13] It is true that not many of these joined in the Jacobite rebellion of 1715, which led one who did to complain bitterly[14]

> That they do not care for venturing their carcases any further than the tavern. There indeed...they would make men believe...that they would overcome the greatest opposition in the world; but after having consulted their pillows, and the fume a little evaporated, it is to be observed of them that they generally become mighty tame, and are apt to look before they leap, and with the snail, if you touch their houses, shrink back, and pull in their horns. I have heard Mr Forster say, he was blustered into this

business by such people as these, but for the time to come he would never again believe a drunken tory.

Thomas Forster, however, the tory MP for Northumberland who led a forlorn band of men to Preston to surrender to General Carpenter in November 1715, patently never stood a chance. He was a poor military commander and minor politician, who could not inspire confidence in his leadership to make it seem worthwhile for men disinclined to fight to risk their lives. Things might be very different if a charismatic leader like Charles Edward, with competent generals and above all with aid from France, invaded the country to restore the Pretender. Certainly James Edward did not despair of tory assistance after the Fifteen. The names of nearly all tory MPs were sent to him during Walpole's long ministry as men whom he could rely on to support his cause if he landed with a sufficient force. Walpole too took the Jacobitism of the tories very seriously, and devoted a great deal of effort in attempts to expose it. During the invasion scare of late 1743 and early 1744 the Pretender's agents were in touch with prominent tories such as Beaufort and Wynn, and linked their names with thousands of alleged sympathisers in the country. Some had come under the government's suspicion at the time as being prepared to rise if the French invaded, one of those implicated being Sir John Hinde Cotton. He joined the government in 1744, however, as treasurer of the chamber, and during 1745, was not sending assistance to the Pretender but remitting money to George II in Hanover.[15] Yet there was a report, which the government intercepted, that he planned to signal the moment for the French to invade by resigning from office.[16] Clearly if Charles Edward was going to tap any support in England and Wales it would come from men like these.

Besides appealing to tories who indicated some inclination to support his father's cause, the Young Pretender also hoped to attract to his banner others, including even dissident whigs, who seemed to be disaffected towards the Hanoverian dynasty. These opposition politicians subscribed to views which contemporaries distinguished as Country rather than as tory or whig. That is they regarded governments in general, and the Hanoverian regime in particular, with suspicion as being bent on depriving Englishmen of their liberties. Governments were alleged to aim at this sinister end by a variety of means, both direct and indirect. Directly the growth of the standing army, with its attendant bureaucratic apparatus of officials, and incidence of taxes to sustain both, was an overt threat to liberty, as seen in absolute monarchies on the continent. Indirectly, and yet more insidiously, the executive conspired to reduce parliament to the status of its rubber stamp. The Septennial Act of 1716, which widened the statutory gap between elections from three to seven years, had allegedly been designed to give the executive more scope to infiltrate the legislature, by corrupting MPs with posts in the administration. Thus the number of placemen, as such members were called, had been greatly increased under Walpole until they made up nearly a third of the Commons. Septennial elections had also driven up the cost of contests and thereby corrupted the voters in hosts of small constituencies. These had been bribed, so the opposition claimed, to return placemen, rather than independent country gentlemen who would vote as their consciences and not as the Court dictated.

Corruption was thus seen as undermining the constitution and its guarantee of liberty and property. The only real antidote to it was 'Patriotism'. In this sense a 'Patriot' was a virtuous citizen who performed his civic duties by constant vigilance against the sinister corrupting forces operating at Court. It was mainly the dissident whigs in the opposition who prided themselves on their patriotism, though some tories also identified themselves as 'patriots'. Sir Walter Blackett, the tory member for Newcastle upon Tyne, for instance, was known as 'the patriot'.

The 'patriots' sought to purge corruption from the political system. The constant campaign of the opposition had therefore been to reduce the standing army, to replace the Septennial Act with the Triennial Act which it had superseded, and to eliminate placemen from the Commons and bribery from the constituencies.

They also argued that since the accession of George II English interests had been subordinated to those of the electorate of Hanover. Country politicians claimed that England's proper role in international affairs was as a naval power, since geography had separated her from the continent, and the sea was her natural element. The government, in their view, should devote its foreign policy to extending English trade in time of peace, and protecting it in time of war. England should not become involved as a major military power in Europe, but should assist her allies only as an auxiliary, making the navy her main instrument of policy. Instead of doing this, it was maintained, Walpole had scandalously neglected English trade, until Spanish reprisals against merchants trading in the New World inflicted serious damage on England's commerce and even more on her pride. At the same time he was keeping on foot an army in order to intervene on the continent in defence of the king's Hanoverian possessions. In 1739 the Country clamour against Spanish attacks on English merchant shipping forced the reluctant prime minister into war with Spain. At last, the opposition crowed, foreign policy was serving England's interests, and when Admiral Vernon attacked Porto Bello he became a Country hero overnight. In 1740, however, Britain became involved in the War of the Austrian succession, and taxes were increased to pay for a military adventure on the continent. When George II fought at Dettingen in the uniform of Hanover Country politicians claimed that the king was adding insult to injury. It was manifestly to serve a petty German principality that Englishmen were paying high taxes to sustain expensive commitments in Europe.

Such Country rhetoric had united tories and dissident whigs for years, even if attempts to fuse them into a single Country party had proved to be less durable. The polarisation into Court and Country rather than into tory and whig was sufficiently apparent, during the general elections of 1734 and 1741, for the press to report their outcomes in terms of gains and losses for the Court and Country interests rather than for tories and whigs. During the last election before the Forty-five, Sir John Hinde Cotton stood in Cambridgeshire not as a tory but as a Country candidate. He arranged to run off handbills which read, "at the repeated desires of great numbers of the gentlemen of this county in the Country interest I have been encouraged to offer myself as a candidate at the ensuing election." [17]

Among the dissident whigs who associated with tories in the Country interest at that election at least two types can be discerned. These were men such as William Pulteney and Samuel Sandys, who were little more than frustrated politicians using the Country platform to get themselves into power. Once they achieved this goal in 1742 it was to be of no more use to them than a railway station platform is to a man when he has boarded the train. With these could be included those MPs associated with Frederick Prince of Wales, who was in opposition at the time of the election, and was never entirely reconciled with his father until his death ten years later, though he did not rock the boat during the rebellion. Indeed some of his supporters formed part of the administration's Broad Bottom, none more so than George Bubb Dodington, who occupied the post of treasurer of the navy from 1744 to 1749. But alongside these were genuine Country whigs, who were concerned about the extent to which corruption was corroding political morality. They included knights of the shire such as George Bowes, MP for County Durham, and Sir James Lowther, who represented Cumberland, and even the respected member for the City of London, Sir John Barnard. These men deserved the title of 'Patriots'. [18]

The Country interest was far more broadly based than the Court, for many of its members were returned from counties and cities, while the bulk of minsterial supporters sat for small boroughs. Certainly, after the elections of 1734 and 1741, the Opposition could boast that it represented the overwhelming majority of the electorate, though, thanks to the prevalence of seats for constituencies with very few voters, the government had an actual majority in the House of Commons. Under Walpole, therefore, the Court could fairly be depicted as a narrow oligarchy, with the majority of the gentry, professional and business classes, and forty-shilling freeholders and urban freemen opposed to it. Even when the Pelhams broadened the base of the administration, it still left most of these politically-conscious classes outside its scope.

The Jacobites entertained the hope that those in the Country interest were so alienated from the Court that they would welcome the Young Pretender. As one of their number, James Maxwell of Kirkconnell, saw it, the changes following Walpole's fall had merely shored up his system, and "disappointed the real Patriots in their present expectations, and cut off all future hopes". In his view[19]

> It was now but too plain that parliamentary remedies were mere chimeras; it was not to be expected that at any period the spirit of patriotism would be more general and exert itself more vigorously than in these last elections, all which had availed nothing. There was no remedy left but a revolution of some kind or other, which would be the more difficult and dangerous the longer it was delayed...In these circumstances the Prince's project was by no means chimerical...it was highly probable, from the situation of England, that if the Prince landed anywhere in the island with arms, ammunition and a body of regular troops, he would be joined by a great many, and opposed by none but such as, being entirely devoted to the Court, were already becoming the object of the hatred and contempt of their fellow subjects. Abundance of the Tories had still a warm side for the family of Stewart; and as for the old staunch Whigs, their aversion to families had no other spring but their love of liberty, which they saw expiring under the family of Hanover; they had still this, and but this chance left to recover it.

The Pretender clearly held the notion that a substantial part of the nation was so disaffected that it would help him in his efforts to regain the throne. His manifestos, and Jacobite propaganda put out on his behalf, appealed not only to tories but also to dissident whigs. Indeed they virtually encapsulated Country grievances, and undertook to redress them when the rebellion succeeded. Thus the Declaration which James Edward issued in December 1743 emphasised the high taxes which Englishmen were paying to finance a war which could only benefit foreigners, inveighed against bribery and corruption, and lamented the decline of trade. At the same time the duke of Ormonde objected to the standing army, and promised to repeal the Septennial Act and to pass an Act reducing the number of placemen in parliament.[20] During the Forty-five Charles Edward published several proclamations which enlarged on the same themes.[21] On 10 October 1745 he issued a long declaration from Holyrood Palace, in which he asked "Why has the nation been so long crying out in vain for redress against the abuse of parliaments, upon account of their long duration, the multitude of place-men, which occasions their venality, the introduction of penal laws, and in general against the miserable situation of the kingdom at home and abroad?" More rhetorical questions were posed in the even longer *Considerations addressed to the Public*, which summed up its argument thus:

> How well the Usurper has loved you, let your blood, your treasure spent, the heavy taxes unknown to your forefathers, the decay of your trade, the bribery, the universal depravity of manners, the allowing puny Hanoverians, not long since content to dine on a turnip, to wallow in your riches, and fatten themselves with the spoils of your honest industry, bear witness: Are you men, and can you bear it?

An Address to the People of England likewise asked "Would you have your grievances redressed? Would you have your Constitution restored? Would you have your Liberties secured against all future encroachments? Would you be for ever disunited from Hanover? Would you be an island again? This is the critical juncture, NOW or NEVER." The Young Pretender's final appeal to the Country interest was by way of the inscriptions on the banners of the regiment raised in Manchester; one read, "Church and King", the other "Liberty and Property".

Besides appealing to alienated elements among the political elite, Charles Edward could also entertain hopes of attracting support from the mass of the English people. Relations between the regime and the bulk of its subjects appeared to have been strained ever since the accession of the house of Hanover. Immediately after the arrival of George I there had been a rash of riots demonstrating dissatisfaction with the new dynasty. On his coronation day there were disturbances in Birmingham, Bristol, Chippenham, Norwich and Reading. Throughout 1715 there was a constant spate of rioting, affecting several constituencies during the General Election held in February, flaring up throughout the summer, especially in the West Midlands, and recurring in Oxford and London. The Riot Act was rushed through parliament to deal with a problem which seemed to have become endemic. It made the riotous assembly of twelve or more people a felony if they did not disperse within an hour of the reading of a proclamation ordering their dispersal.

The Riot Act was the first of several statutes which the ascendant whigs passed to curb the activities of the lower orders. The great increase in capital offences which occurred in the eighteenth century began after the whigs came to power on the death of Queen Anne. In 1716 an Act stipulated the death penalty for those caught mutilating "rows and walks of young trees planted by gentlemen for ornament about their houses". The most notorious of these measures was the Waltham Black Act of 1723, provoked by organised poaching in game parks, which made some fifty associated crimes capital offences. Although allegedly to deal with an emergency, and therefore initially passed for only three years, it was periodically renewed long after the 'crisis' was over. It has been cogently argued that Walpole and his whig colleagues exploited the twin fears of Jacobitism and a 'crime wave' in the early 1720s to perpetuate their hegemony, and that the Act embodies the ideology of a new oligarchy which considered property to be sacrosanct, and threats to it from the propertyless as more heinous than crimes against the person.[22] Certainly the Waltham Black Act was seen as a political rather than as a judicial instrument, and was criticised along with the Riot Act in Country propaganda against Walpole for having infringed English liberties, while the opposition occasionally demanded the repeal of both as well as the Septennial Act.

Walpole's much vaunted fiscal policy was also regressive, since he tried to lift the burden of direct taxation from the landowners and compensate the Treasury with indirect taxes, especially excises, which fell more heavily on the poorer classes. Thus in 1732 he reduced the land tax by one shilling in the pound, making up the loss of revenue by a duty on salt. In 1733 the celebrated Excise scheme was introduced as a measure to abolish the land tax altogether, and replace it with inland duties on tobacco and wine. The salt duty caused murmurings, though the prime minister could claim that he was merely reviving a recently expired tax; but the Excise scheme provoked a popular outcry so fierce that it undoubtedly contributed to his withdrawal of the measure. The subsequent widespread rejoicing was said to have been exploited by Jacobites. "Can gentlemen imagine," Walpole himself asked the House of Commons a year later, "that in the spirit raised in the nation but about a twelvemonth since, Jacobitism and disaffection to the present government had no share?"[23] Indeed he was inclined to see any demonstration against the government as being inspired by the Pretender's agents. When there were riots in London on the occasion of his Gin Act in 1736, he observed that "these lower sorts of Jacobites appear at this time more busy than they have for a great while, they are very industrious and taking advantage of everything that offers, to raise tumult and disorders among the people."[24]

Where excises provoked popular resistance, Walpole's customs duties were blatantly flouted by a highly organised smuggling trade, especially along the coasts of Sussex, Kent, Essex and Suffolk.[25] The activities of smugglers were connived at and even encouraged by a wide section of the population. One of the more cogent reasons for the abortive Excise scheme was that it would eliminate losses to the customs service which were calculated to be enormous. Those smugglers in the south-east who illicitly traded with France were generally regarded as Jacobites. At the height of the Forty-five the duke of Newcastle received a report about their Jacobitism which claimed that "Suffolk and Essex are more pestered with this treason and villany than Kent or Sussex".[26]

Thus on the eve of the rebellion there appeared to be massive popular discontent with the regime. The harsher criminal code seemed to reveal the law nakedly as an instrument of the propertied classes, exposing the myth of the equality of all Englishmen before it. The regressive system of taxation shifted the fiscal burden from the shoulders of the rich to those of the poor, with Walpole playing Robin Hood in reverse. His habit of detecting Jacobitism behind any popular demonstration against his government showed a nervousness among the rulers of England about their relationship with the lower orders, indicating that they had alienated them to the point where they would rise up against them given a proper opportunity.

When Charles Edward persisted in sailing on to Scotland, therefore, despite the fact that the *Elisabeth* had been forced to retreat to France, he could be buoyed up with the thoughts that his arrival in Britain would be greeted by hosts of supporters. Not only did he expect most of the highlands to rise; he also believed that he would appeal to lowlanders who had been alienated in recent years, and even entertained hopes of attracting many Englishmen to his banner. Nor were these hopes confined to the tories, for he appealed as well to dissident whigs on a Country platform against the Hanoverian Court. He also anticipated a massive popular uprising in England in his favour. The Young Pretender had arrived at the same conclusion as one which some modern historians have reached, that the British government in the mid-eighteenth century rested on a very narrow base. A corrupt, divided and discredited oligarchy had lost the last vestiges of popular support which the Revolution Settlement could once boast. It was no more liked than the Republic had been on the eve of the Restoration. All that remained for him to do was to play Monck to his father's Charles II. The next few months were to reveal to what extent these expectations were realistic.

CHAPTER TWO

"This impotent attempt"

We doubt not but that, with the Divine Blessing on the Justice of your Cause, Your Majesty's known wisdom and fortitude, seconded by the hearts and hands of a free people, will with ease crush this impotent attempt.

Address of Exeter Corporation to the King, 13 September 1745

It was some time before the government was able to piece together the details of the Young Pretender's voyage in the *Du Teillay*. Although they picked up rumours that he had left Nantes early in July, the lords justices were not sufficiently convinced that he had indeed sailed until 1 August, when they issued a Proclamation offering a reward of £30,000 "to any person who shall seize and secure the eldest son of the Pretender, in case he shall land, or attempt to land, in any of his Majesty's Dominions".[1] They also urged George II, who was abroad in Hanover, to return as soon as possible. When the duke of Newcastle learned a few days later that he was about to set out, and required transportation across the North Sea to be made available for his return, he was very relieved, writing to his fellow secretary of state Lord Harrington, who was with the king, "never any news was more welcome to his Majesty's faithful servants," since the king's presence was needed "in this time of danger".[2]

Others, however, were not so convinced that it was a time of real danger. Lord Tweeddale, the secretary of state for Scotland, could scarcely credit that Charles Edward had landed, since he had received no intelligence from anybody in the government service. As late as 6 August he had no certain account of what had happened to the frigate which had accompanied the *Elisabeth*. "All accounts agree," he wrote, "that the Pretender's son was either on board the Elisabeth or the frigate. The Elisabeth is certainly forced back to Brest, and I can hardly believe the frigate would pursue her voyage to Scotland."[3]

On 7 August the duke of Argyll received the first hard information that Charles Edward had indeed landed, and was now on the mainland. His steward in Mull and Morvern had written to the sheriff deputy of Argyleshire on 5 August[4]

> This morning I had an express with very extraordinary news cou'd it be depended on, viz. that a vessel is landed in Arisaig with between two and three hundred men and two thousand stand of arms among whom are the Pretender's eldest son, General Keith and old Lochiel. That there was another vessel in company but was taken and this narrowly escaped...My authority I have for this news is not to be relyed on, so as to give it credit in the whole, but that some vessel is come to them parts with strangers on board is probable, tho not of the distinction my informer calls them...

The steward was right to be sceptical, for the number of men alleged to have landed was exaggerated, while the so-called General Keith was not among them. Nevertheless the sheriff deputy considered the news to be hot enough to send it to Andrew Fletcher, the lord justice clerk, who was staying with the duke of Argyll at Rosneath, between Glasgow and Inveraray. They immediately passed it on to the government, Argyll writing to the duke of Newcastle and Fletcher to the marquis of Tweeddale. Although they sent it by express it took from 7 to 13 August to get from Rosneath to London. Newcastle was immediately convinced. Overlooking some discrepancies, he wrote excitedly to the duke of Cumberland:[5]

> The description of the vessel; the number of men and arms said to be on board; and the circumstances reported, that they sailed in company with a man of war which had engaged an English ship and had either been taken or forced to put back to Brest; answer so exactly the accounts we have received of the frigate that was in company with the Elisabeth that there hardly can be any doubt but that it is the same; and that the Pretender's son is now actually landed in some part of Scotland.

Tweeddale, on the other hand, still remained doubtful, especially when contrary intelligence came to his hand about the Young Pretender's whereabouts. One memorandum actually stated that John Murray of Broughton, Charles Edward's secretary, "was laughing heartily at the ministry not knowing where the Young Pretender was, and said that the noise of this ship would put the Government off the scent of their real designs." [6]

Nonetheless, Newcastle's view prevailed with a majority of the lords justices, who immediately ordered Sir John Cope to "assemble as great a number of troops as he could get together and march directly to the place where the enemy were to rendezvous; and endeavour to attack and suppress them at once".[7] They also asked the Dutch to make available 6,000 men, which they had undertaken by treaty to provide should the Hanoverian dynasty be threatened. Although, for the moment, they did not request a detachment from the British forces under Cumberland's command on the continent, he was advised to prepare for such an eventuality. Cumberland, owning himself "surprised to see this Romantick expedition revived again, and that it had taken place as far as the landing any troops in Great Britain," hoped that this would never arise, as he was averse to sending a detachment at a time when the allies were desperately trying to stem the French advance across Europe.[8] Since defeating the duke at Fontenoy in May, Marshal Saxe had marched across the Austrian Netherlands and now threatened the Dutch Republic, who might well make her own terms with France if the allied army was seriously weakened in order to suppress the Jacobite rebellion. As Sir Everard Fawkener, Cumberland's private secretary, observed[9]

> one must be deprived of his senses not to see that France is at the bottom of all this. They throw off this squib, and care not if it bursts, or in whose hands, or about whose ears. If they can alarm us so far as to make a detachment they do everything; for if this allied army once comes to divide I am afraid all is irretrievably over.

On 20 August, however, the lords justices reappraised the situation, and sent "immediate orders for all the British troops that were in garrison at Ostend to be re-embarked forthwith and brought to Great Britain".[10] This decision represented the victory of the Pelhams, who considered the crisis to be too serious to be contained by the available armed forces, over those who felt that they were sufficient, without reinforcing them from the army abroad.

Explaining the need for the Ostend garrison the lords justices referred Cumberland to "the very small number of regular troops" in Great Britain. In Scotland Sir John Cope commanded at most 3,850 men. These comprised two regiments of horse, three and a half regiments of foot and nine "additional" companies. Colonel James Gardiner's dragoons were based on Stirling and those of Hamilton on Edinburgh. Most of the infantry were stationed in those centres, too; though there were men in various outposts, including in the Highlands the Forts with the quintessentially Hanoverian names of William, Augustus and George, and the barracks of Bernara, Ruthven and Inversnaid; and in the Lowlands, the borders, Glasgow, Aberdeen and the adjacent coast. In the north the earl of Loudoun was just beginning to raise a Highland regiment, having received a commission for that purpose in May, while there were garrisons of invalids in the castles of Edinburgh and Stirling. In England there were no more than 6,000 troops, the bulk of them in London, though the rest were scattered about the country, Lord Cobham's dragoons being at Kingston and Lord Mark Kerr's at Windsor, for example.

Scanty though these forces were, the earl of Stair, commander in chief of the army in England, considered them adequate to deal with the crisis. Thus some time in August he drew up a memorial on the state of the troops under his command.[11]

> Supposing...that the rebels should be masters of Edinburgh and march into England...even supposing that the highlanders should be joined by an invasion from France; it will be proper to consider what force there is in England to resist the enemy in that case.
>
> There are now in England four battallions of guards, four other battallions besides three battallions to be formed of the additional companies: there are now actually embarkt at Williamstadt five battallions of Dutch troops, of which one is to go to Scotland, the four battallions which come into England are to be instantly followed by three more battallions; with these seven battallions of Dutch added to the eleven British battallions, with two regiments of those and three regiments of dragoons Lord Stair thinks he can answer for the quelling of this rebellion.

The Pelhams were less sanguine. They agreed that there were sufficient men to crush the rebellion; but not to deal with an invasion from France. The duke of Richmond informed Newcastle on 16 August "I shall enjoy no ease till the troops are in England. I have not the least fear of the Young Gent in Scotland...but my great apprehensions are from a French invasion, which I look upon as certain if not timely prevented."[12] Richmond's apprehensions were shared by a majority of the lords justices. They thought it necessary to send for the Ostend garrison not only on account of "the defenceless state of the kingdom" but also "from the great reason there is to apprehend some desperate attempt against his Majesty's government".[13] They feared that the Young Pretender's expedition would be followed by an invasion from France and Spain, who had "a considerable naval strength in the western ports of France and in the Bay of Biscay", and were said to be preparing to repeat the designs of 1744 to invade England, which had only been aborted when bad weather destroyed their preparations. While Admiral Vernon was instructed to defend the coast, naval power alone could not be depended upon to prevent a French landing. Some did not even depend upon the Admiral. "That blundering beast Vernon cannot get out to sea," Lady Isabella Finch wrote to her brother Lord Malton on 5 September, "the wind's against him. For my part I dread his conduct, and have no opinion of his courage."[14] She emphatically agreed with those who urged the necessity of recalling troops from the continent.

The duke of Cumberland was uneasy about the request for the British troops who had garrisoned Ostend. He made excuses that they could not be sent immediately, and even asked his father who was at Helvoetsluys on his way to London, whether "just at this time I should make a detachment for England of any part of the British troops?" apparently in an attempt to have the orders from the lords justices countermanded by the king.[15] As he explained to Newcastle[16]

> I think the motives to this expedition of the Pretender's son are not altogether to be relied on, for in his circumstances nothing seems to me too hazardous or desperate for him to undertake; and France may have been induced to promise to support him (tho' possibly it never will) upon the single prospect of obliging us to make a detachment from this army.

When he learned that the rebellion had begun, Cumberland had no doubt "but Sir John Cope will be able to put a stop immediately to this affair".[17] Cope did not, however, do so. On the contrary, his attempt to intercept and defeat the rebels in the Highlands proved a disastrous failure. Far from forcing them to engage him in a battle which he set out convinced he could win, their strength and his weakness obliged him to avoid them by diverting his troops to Inverness, leaving the way clear for Charles Edward to march down through Scotland to Edinburgh.

The rebels at first made for the Great Glen between Inverness and Fort William, the strategic key to the control of the Highlands. A soldier stationed at Fort William in 1744 described the Glen as[18]

> one long vale that runs E.N.E. and W.S.West about 70 miles from sea to sea, nowhere above a mile broad, in many places much less…a very good level road is made, and cut thro' rocks at an immense expence the whole way. Here at the West end is Fort William built by King William, where I am quartered with 4 companies. It is the last of the 3 garrisons…in this chasm, for the vale deserves no other name. It is overlooked by vast high mountains. The sun will not shine on us in winter but 2 or 3 hours…midway to Inverness is Fort Augustus, a new thing where the public money

has been thrown away profusely. They say it cost £30,000 on spacious buildings, a governors house etc., but it is no fortress and one would be amazed at the folly and profusion that appears there. Twas this year erected into a Government with an establishment for gunners etc....half their garrison are left out of the new fort and quartered in a barrack a quarter of a mile from them. Fort George at Inverness is at the East end of this vale.

The government had constructed the chain of three forts in the Glen to subdue the Highlands, but it had its weak links. At Fort Augustus the acting governor, Hugh Wentworth, as late as 13 August could not find "one man that knows how to point a gun or even saw a shell fired out of a mortar".[19] Despite expecting "hourly to be attacked" he nevertheless hoped "to give a very good account of them", since the rebels were said to have no artillery, and that "we should all show ourselves true Englishmen, and fight boldly in a good cause".[20] Alexander Campbell, the governor of Fort William, had complained that the garrison was too small to hold out when he first heard of the rebels' movements, so Cope arranged for reinforcements to be sent to him, which he was confident would make it "as strong as the place can contain".[21] On 16 August two companies of foot soldiers were making their way there from Fort Augustus, when they were attacked by some rebels at Highbridge. Four or five were killed, the first government casualties on the mainland in the Forty-five, while the rest, some eighty-two men, were made prisoners.

From the first Cope determined to strengthen the government's hold in the Highland forts by going there himself at the head of an army. He did not have to wait for confirmation of the Young Pretender's landing, for in the morning of 9 August Lord President Forbes, who was leaving Edinburgh for Inverness, called on him "in his boots in his way northwards," and gave him the news that Charles Edward "came lately on the coast of Uist and Barrar".[22] His informant finally added the last piece to the puzzle of what had happened to the *Du Teillay* after it had sailed away on 9 July, for he reported that Charles had arrived in a small vessel that "came out in company with a large man of war, who meeting with an English ship of force was so disabled as to be obliged to return".

Cope immediately "ordered as many of the troops as with security can be spared from this part of the country to assemble with the utmost expedition, and I will march with them directly to oppose whatever enemys I shall meet with." Next day he informed Tweeddale that he was going to "march to the forts which form a chain from Inverness to Fort William", a proposal which met with the minstry's approval "as the most effectual method to disappoint any designs his Majesty's enemies may have to arise in favour of the Pretender."[23] It took until 20 August for

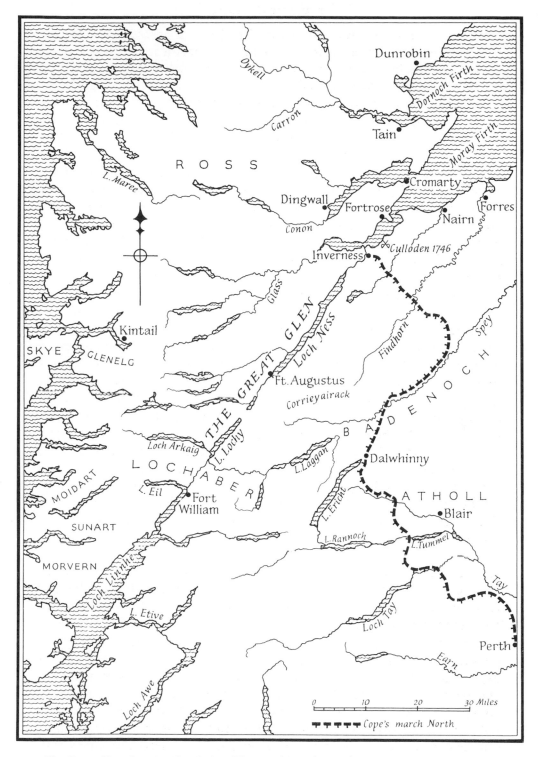

The Great Glen showing the chain of forts and Cope's march to Inverness, August 1745

sufficient biscuits and money to be provided for the expedition, though the ovens of Leith, Stirling and Perth "were kept at work day and night", while Cope had urged the necessity for funds to be made available as early as 3 August. Until the arrival of the duke of Cumberland the financing of military activities in Scotland was a major problem, largely because of the primitive method of arranging credit with the receiver general. If this official had not sufficient funds available he could refuse to assist the commander, who had then to go cap in hand to the merchants of Edinburgh for an advance in anticipation of monies from London. Cope did not receive authority from the central government to raise a loan until 17 August. He got the money on the 19th and went immediately to Stirling where his forces were assembled. Even though there were still some biscuits to be provided he set out next day for Crieff, where he had to stay overnight on the 21st until the last consignment came from the bakers.

Besides intending to secure the chain of forts Cope also hoped to make contact with loyal Highlanders, and had even arranged to meet two such, the duke of Athol and Lord Glenorchy, in Crieff. Glenorchy had complained that government supporters in the Highlands were handicapped by the Disarming Act of 1716, which had forbidden Scots in that zone to carry arms, while subsequent measures had forced many to surrender their weapons. Only Jacobites, therefore, who had disregarded the legislation, were armed. The government recognised that this was a drawback, and Tweeddale had hinted to Cope that he should offer arms surreptitiously to its chief supporter in Scotland, the duke of Argyll. The duke, however, had retorted "that till the Government had made it lawful for him to do such service as might be in his power, he durst not even defend himself." This attitude exasperated the government, which took the line that to defend oneself against rebels and traitors could not reasonably be regarded as illegal. Cope had therefore been encouraged to carry 1,000 weapons with him to give to the men whom, he was led to believe, would rush to join his army. In the event nobody came in spontaneously, while the commander found to his consternation that neither Athol nor Glenorchy turned up with a single man. He was so outraged by this that he shamed the duke at least into providing a dozen or so, though even these "after marching a day or so with the army, went home again". Dejected if not disgusted Cope sent 700 weapons back to Stirling, and carried on via Taybridge, Trinisuir and Dalnacardock through what was essentially hostile country. As he later complained "two hundred of the baggage horses deserted from Trinisuir in the night, which obliged us to leave so many bags of our bread there, with the Duke of Athol's steward, who promised to send them to us the next day," adding sourly, "but they never came." According to a fellow officer "the country people...

used to rip up the sacks, destroy the provisions and run off with horse loads entire into the woods."

Another incumbrance on the march was that the army had to rely on the civil authorities for transport.[24] One of the ways in which civilian suspicion of military activity had manifested itself, in the century-old debate on the merits of a standing army, was in insisting that the co-operation of magistrates was essential when moving troops about the country. Thus before Cope set out he "sent before expresses to the several sheriffs and justices of the peace, with the lord advocate's and solicitor's orders to them to provide carriages and other necessaries; at the same time acquainting them with the number of horses we should want, and the day and places they should meet the army." Unfortunately these local dignitaries were not so co-operative as the army officers expected them to be, either through disloyalty, which was suspected, or inefficiency, which seems more likely. At all events,

> by the delay of the country horses, which we were assured would be punctual, we were many hours endeavouring to get all the provisions carried with the army, yet were always obliged to leave part behind, with strong assurances from the Deputy Sheriffs that they should be sent to overtake us, which was never performed: so that, by what was left upon the road, by what was destroyed by the heavy rains and embezzlements during the march...at Dalwhinny there was not quite three days bread for the army.

It was consequently a very dispirited army which arrived at Dalwhinny on 26 August, only to find that the rebels were in control of the pass over the Corrieyairack which lay between them and their destination, Fort Augustus. To proceed was to risk disaster, for as a contemporary observed "the south side of the Corriarrick is of so very sharp an ascent, that the road traverses the whole breadth of the hill seventeen times before it arrives at the top...each traverse in ascending is commanded by that above it; so that even an unarmed rabble, who were posted on the higher ground, might, without exposing themselves, extremely harrass the troops in their march. Whence, the attempting to force seventeen traverses, every one of them capable of being thus defended, was an undertaking which it would have been madness to have engaged in." Cope's colleagues, whom he consulted about the predicament, expressed similar sentiments. To stay put, in order to engage the rebels on more favourable terrain, was also ruled out, since provisions were now too low to remain long, while the enemy could easily bypass them anyway. To retreat back to Stirling through territory which had already proved to be unfriendly, with a rebel army in pursuit, was too risky, and could dishearten any potential supporters in the region. Moreover, Cope stubbornly insisted that he had been ordered to proceed to the chain of forts, which could only be done now by making for Inverness, where there were said to be loyal High-landers. A diversion to Inverness therefore seemed to be the only prudent decision, and even this had to be undertaken by forced marches to avoid an ambush.

The march of Cope's army to Inverness, where he arrived on 29 August, left the way south open to the rebels. It was to take Cope nearly three weeks to get back to the vicinity of Edinburgh by way of the east coast. Meanwhile Charles Edward advanced on the Scottish capital by way of Blair Athol, Perth and Stirling, meeting no real resistance. This situation was still not known in London when the king arrived there on the 31st "in perfect health" and "very good humour", proud of the haste he had made to get back "when there was any apprehension of danger affecting this country".[25] The seriousness of the danger only became apparent a few days later, when the government learned that the rebels had "found means to steal by at a distance from the king's forces, which were moving on through the Highlands to give them battle, and were, when the last letters came away, in full march for Edinburgh, having left Sir John Cope by that motion two or three days behind them."[26] Even more alarming was the fear that the success of the rebellion would encourage the French to invade, and the news that they were preparing to do so. The apparently defenceless state of the country led an old soldier like Marshal Wade to state bluntly that "England is for the first comer".[27]

These considerations determined the duke of Newcastle, Henry Pelham and their adherents in the Cabinet to insist that the duke of Cumberland should be ordered to send over ten of his best battallions immediately, under the command of Sir John Ligonier. Although the king and Lord Harrington had shared Cumberland's reluctance to detach forces from his army when they were on the continent, after their return to England they came round to agreeing with the Pelhams' assessment of the gravity of the situation, and the need for reinforcements. On 4 September Harrington wrote to Cumberland "His Majesty having been determined to avoid, if possible, drawing any detachment from your army...I am much con-cerned to find myself so soon obliged to acquaint your Royal Highness with the absolute necessity which His Majesty now sees of altering what was then settled."[28]

This counsel "prevailed with the greatest difficulty,...as it was opposed by Lord Tweeddale."[29] The Granvillites refused to accept that it was absolutely necessary, arguing that it was "deserting our allies, and giving up the common cause; and the ministry should be impeached for it".[30] Such language infuriated the duke of Richmond, who protested to Newcastle "Our Master is so blind to his own interest that he will put his

36

whole government into the hands of my Lord Granville and others, who I am persuaded will bring immediate destruction to him and his Government, perhaps by rashness of measures, perhaps by design to bring in the Pretender."[31] He went on to urge that all British forces should be returned home, with the duke of Cumberland at their head: "In this point I am as positive as a mule...every one of you singly have always seem'd to be of my opinion; yet when you are all together, the advising the king to send for the whole army home has never been thought expedient."

When he received his instructions Cumberland was downcast, writing to Newcastle "I am heartily sorry for the occasion of this great detachment from our army, but will do our utmost not to be devoured by the enemy...I hope that Great Britain is not to be conquered by 3,000 rabble ...but should they dare to advance I will answer man for man for the 10 battallions Sir John Ligonier will bring you."[32] A similar letter to the duke of Richmond elicited the forthright reply:[33]

> I must beg your indulgence, Sir, for two words for myself, for fear you should look upon me as an idle adviser in the late measures of withdrawing so many troops from your Royal Highness's army. I plead guilty to it at once, and what is more I have been of opinion for these last two months that your Royal Highness, with your whole British army, should be sent for to save this kingdom, and have declared this my opinion to the king your father...in the name of God, Sir, what is all Europe to us, if your royal father loses his crown, and we consequently all our liberty and everything that is dear to us?

"The ten battallions I have named for this service," Cumberland informed Lord Harrington, "are the three battallions of guards, Sowle's, Pulteney's, Charles Howard's, Braggs, Douglas's, Johnson's and Cholmondley's, which will be put under the command of Lieutenant General Sir John Ligonier according to his Majesty's orders."[34] He assured the king that he had seen the whole army, and could with confidence say that they were all in good order, "but if there were any preference to be given it was to these ten, which I have picked out for that very reason." Before they sailed, part of the Dutch contingent, which included three Swiss battallions, arrived in London, and on 19 September 2,200 of these, together with the duke of Montagu's and Brigadier St George's cavalry regiments and five companies of Blakeney's regiment, were ordered to prepare to march under General Wentworth towards Lancashire, "or any other county in England where he shall hear the rebels are."[35]

Meanwhile the government authorised the mobilisation of civilians to augment the regular forces it was deploying against the rebels. The normal machinery for doing this was the militia. Since Tudor times all able-bodied men had been required to serve in this force, raised in each county and commanded by the lord lieutenant. The rise of a professional army, however, had led to the neglect of the amateur county militias, which had become a very rusty and unreliable military machine. Indeed vital pieces were missing in some counties in Scotland, which did not have lords lieutenant, the essential heads of the militia, in office at the time. Instead of calling out the militia in the north of Scotland the government sent twenty blank commissions to the lord president at Inverness, "to be distributed among the well affected clans, as your Lordship shall think proper".[36] These were to be used to raise independent companies, a method of mobilisation which was employed elsewhere, even in places where the militia could also be mustered. Thus although the militiamen, or fencibles as they were called, were eventually called out in Argyllshire, they were augmented by three such companies.[37]

In England the situation was not quite so desperate, and on 5 September the lords lieutenant of the four northernmost counties were ordered to put their militias into readiness for immediate service.[38] Even so there were difficulties in implementing the Order. The lords lieutenant of Durham and Northumberland both expressed concern about their ability to raise money locally to sustain their forces. The problem was not an unwillingness to pay, but genuinely held doubts about the legality of levying local taxes for the purpose.[39] The law stipulated that county funds should maintain the militia for one month, but thereafter national revenues ought to be employed. If counties paid their militiamen for more than a month, then they were entitled to refunds from the government for the extra expenditure. Until these refunds were paid, no further calls could be made upon local resources. By 1745 this was not a theoretical concern, since many counties had previously paid their militias for longer than the statutory month, and had not been reimbursed. Until they were, or parliament changed the law, then it was argued that there was no legal obligation to pay for the upkeep of the county levies. This difficulty could not be surmounted until parliament met, so that it was not until November that a bill was passed to try to remedy the situation.

When some counties mustered their militias notwithstanding these legal technicalities, the result scarcely inspired confidence. From Cumberland it was reported that " 'Tis so long since the militia was raised that we are apprehensive the arms are either lost or in bad order."[40] Lord Lonsdale, their lord lieutenant, warned Newcastle "I am afraid your Grace will find the militia in the other Northern counties much in the same way."[41]

Besides calling out the northern militias, the government also tried to ensure that any fifth column of potential rebels was disarmed. On 5 September the king issued a Proclamation "for putting the laws in execution against Papists and Nonjurors".[42] Six such laws were cited in the Proclamation itself. An Act of 1689 "for better securing the government by disarming papists and reputed papists" stipulated that anybody who refused to subscribe to the Declaration in the second Test Act of 1678 against specific Catholic beliefs, such as transubstantiation, was not to be allowed to keep any arms or ammunition, beyond what was necessary for self defence, or a horse or horses worth more than £5. Another Act of the same year extended disabilities placed upon Roman Catholics, which included the liability to payments of double taxation, to those who would not take the oath of allegiance and supremacy. This would include nonjurors, who by definition were those who would not take these oaths because they refused to recognise the regime, as well as Catholics. Moreover by a statute of 1715 such persons were to have their refusals recorded among the rolls of quarter sessions, while clerks of the peace were to certify these enrolments to Chancery or King's Bench. An Elizabethan statute confined Catholic recusants convict to within five miles of their homes, while one passed under James I forbade them to live within ten miles of London. Again in 1689 this latter law was stiffened by empowering justices of the peace within that area to arrest suspected Catholics and tender them the Test Act Declaration. Those who refused it and still remained inside the ten mile district were to be treated as convict recusants, and to have their names registered. This legislation in effect lapsed during normal times, for as Lord Chancellor Hardwicke himself admitted, "the laws against Papists, as they stand in the statute book, are so severe that they are the cause of their own non-execution."[43] Crises like the Forty-five, however, saw attempts made to enforce them. The Proclamation commanded "all our justices of the peace, and all others whom it may concern, that they do, with the utmost diligence and application, put the said laws strictly in execution against Papists and Nonjurors, and that they tender to them the said oaths and Declaration, and take from the refusers thereof their horses and arms." It also gave specific directions for its implementation in London, Westminster and Southwark. Catholics were ordered to leave the area ten miles round the capital on or before 19 September. After that date parish officers were to search from house to house, making lists of any Catholics they encountered, and to communicate these to two justices of the peace to take the appropriate action. In consequence Catholics in and around London were subjected to considerable harrassment, though not enough as far as Lady Isabella Finch was concerned. When the Proclamation came out she expressed scepticism about how effective it would be:[44]

how will our epicures and coxcombs part with their cooks and valet de chambres? Were I in parliament I'd immediately propose a round tax upon every family according to the number of their French servants to the full as great as the wages they give them, and what they might have an English one in the same place for, very sure the French cooks valet de chambres maitres d'hotel and footmen would of themselves be no inconsiderable army if they were to turn soldiers, when they could be no longer spies. Therefore I am for shipping them out sans ceremonie by an Act of Parliament to take place from this day forward. There's no common sense in harbouring such wretches in the heart of our island at a time when they will have such opportunities of doing mischief.

To implement the Proclamation elsewhere Orders in Council were sent to the lords lieutenants of all English and Welsh counties "to cause all arms belonging to Papists, nonjurors or other persons that shall be judged dangerous to the peace of the kingdom within your Lieutenancy to be seized and secured." This was a job that fell mainly on the justices of the peace, though they could ask for help from the militia if they felt that they would be resisted in their execution of it. It was a distasteful task which only a zealous anti-Catholic could perform with any enthusiasm, and the degree to which the order was implemented varied from place to place. In Lancashire, where there were probably more Catholics than in any other county except Middlesex, there was a correspondingly strong response to the Order by the more heavily committed government supporters. None was more so than the whig Sir Henry Hoghton, who tried to organise a witch hunt of papists in the county. On 18 September he wrote to Henry Pelham, the prime minister, to complain that although over 3,000 Catholics were convicted in the previous year, the clerk of the peace had neglected to record their convictions in Chancery or King's Bench, which prevented the justices from proceeding against them, or at least gave most of them a good excuse for not doing so.[45] He persisted in accusing the clerk of wilful neglect until he had him removed from his post.

The earl of Gainsborough was another whig zealot who tried to implement the order in Rutland. Unfortunately he discovered only two active justices in that small county, one of whom, Sir John Heathcote, refused to join in searching the house of the only Roman Catholic family which Gainsborough could find. His lordship, however, procured an order from the government obliging Heathcote to co-operate, and together with his fellow justice he duly visited "the three Roman Catholic houses which are all that we are apprised of in this county". It must have given him some satisfaction to report that they had found "neither arms nor horses nor any correspondence", and could only seize a chest of drawers from one cottage which had surplices "as we suppose used by the priests saying mass, together with pictures, mass books, beads, crosses and other things", a contemptible kernel for such a sledgehammer to unshell.[46] The results of similar investigations elsewhere were negligible. A thorough search of Lord Petre's seat in Essex found no more arms "than might be expected in the house of a country gentleman".[47] When Lord Fairfax's house at Gilling was searched no arms at all were discovered, "nor any the least appearance of mischief".[48]

Away from Lancashire and London there does not seem to have been severe harassment of Catholics in the Forty-five. A survey of the "Papists, reputed Papists and nonjurors" in Westmorland disclosed only twelve in all, half of them women, and two of them "a very poor industrious man" and "a poor lame man".[49] A search through the soke of Peterborough unearthed no Catholics "other than two or three labouring persons of no consideration".[50] In Shropshire Lord Herbert, the lord lieutenant, passed on the Order in Council with the advice that he did "not apprehend it is expected to be put rigorously in execution provided they live quietly at home and behave as they ought towards the government."[51] Although he was a staunch whig, he did not hold with harassing Catholics, advising justices "who live in the neighbourhood of or in friendship with any Popish families to mention the substance of these instructions in the most civil and agreeable manner it can be done." His attitude was probably far more typical than that of Sir Henry Hoghton. For their part, too, most Catholics seem to have shared the sentiments of the leader of their community, the duke of Norfolk, who wrote to Newcastle[52]

> if the Catholics are debarr'd from meeting and acting with the most loyal of his Majesty's subjects for the defence of the country, the only proof they can give of their loyalty is their peaceable behaviour, which I hope may obtain the protection of the Government and save them from conviction. I doubt not but your Grace is satisfied of my honest and peaceable dispositions and will not regard any idle insinuations contrary to truth, and I desire you will do me the honour to represent me to the king as a faithful subject and as one no way wanting to the duty I owe to his Majesty.

The readiness of other subjects to show their loyalty was publicised in the official *London Gazette*. George II's return to London on 31 August was made an occasion for demonstrations of support by various bodies up and down the country. The lord mayor and court of aldermen of the City set the example on 5 September when they waited upon the king to congratulate him on his safe return, their Recorder taking the opportunity to assure him that

41

the many and great blessings we enjoy under your Majesty's mild, just and prudent Administration must, at all times, on our part, excite and demand the highest expressions of loyalty and gratitude; but more especially at this, when we find ourselves alarm'd with repeated insults and most unjustifiable attempts against your Crown and Dignity.

Warm'd, Royal Sir, with these just and equitable principles, these your faithful subjects esteem it an indispensable duty to omit no opportunity of tendering your Majesty the sincerest assurances of their affection and zeal for your Majesty's person and government, of their steady and invariable attachment to our present most happy Establishment in Church and State; and of their unshaken resolution to support and defend them at the hazard of their lives and fortunes.

Inspired by the City's example, others addressed the king with similar sentiments. Between the 3rd and 21st of September the *Gazette* carried twenty-four from various bodies including: one from "the merchants of London", their names filling nearly three columns of the paper; the universities of Oxford and Cambridge; the cathedral clergy of Canterbury and Worcester; and the corporations of Berwick, Bristol, Canterbury, Exeter, Glasgow, Hull, Newcastle, Nottingham, Portsmouth, Rochester, Warwick and Great Yarmouth. Some waxed almost embarrassingly eloquent, that from Rochester, for example, extolling "the many Prince-like and endearing qualities which we daily experience in your Majesty". It went on to assert that "the Protestant Succession is our great Palladium: if this is lost, we are no more a nation, at least not a nation of free people".

Yet, while such expressions might have warmed the cockles of George II's heart, if not that of his ministers, it could hardly be said that there was a groundswell of loyalty in the three weeks immediately following the king's return. For one thing, surprisingly few addresses were presented. For another, many were not spontaneous expressions of thanks for the favour of the royal presence, but were carefully orchestrated by the government. When Lord Malton asked the duke of Newcastle for directions "as to the proper manner" in which the Yorkshire gentry could express their loyalty, he replied "in this conjuncture it must be very proper for all counties and especially in so considerable a one as the county of York, to express their zeal and affection for his Majesty and his Government by Addresses and all other proofs they can give of it."[53] It was hard to read anything into words thus elicited. As Charles Yorke commented "the Gazettes about the time of the Revolution were filled with handsome ones to King James".[54]

In this respect it was ominous that one of the addresses came from the lord provost, magistrates and Council of Edinburgh. Although they boasted that "this City has always distinguished herself by a firm and steady attachment to Revolution and Whig Principles and a hearty abhorrence of all Popish and Arbitrary Governments", in the event they appeared to distinguish themselves more by the alacrity with which they opened the City gates for the Young Pretender on 17 September. If actions speak louder than words, then this address at least appears not to have been worth the paper it was written on.

Yet such a verdict is unfair to the colleagues of Archibald Stewart, the lord provost, even if he was himself later charged with neglect of duty.[55] In the month between Cope's march north and the surrender of the Scottish capital to the rebels they did what they could to put the City into a posture of defence. They immediately set in motion the machinery for raising the City's militia, the trained bands. As in England this was a cumbersome operation, while in Edinburgh it ran the additional hazard that many disaffected men would inevitably be mobilised by it. The lord advocate reported on 10 September "both the volunteering and the levies go on with great spirit and success and the people in the suburbs have also taken courage."[56] At a meeting of the Council and substantial citizens, therefore, a joint committee was set up to consider more efficient means of defending themselves. This recommended raising a regiment of 1,000 men to be maintained for three months by the subscriptions of those who were willing to sign an association, for which purpose the provost applied to the king for a warrant, which was granted. The provost and Council also appointed Colin MacLaurin, professor of mathematics at the university, to take charge of making good the city walls. Although the work went slowly at first, with only a handful of workmen employed at it, by dint of hectic activity in the days just before the rebels arrived the walls were put into tolerable repair. By 15 September, too, there were over 1,000 men in arms ready to defend the city in addition to the trained bands, consisting of the new regiment, companies of volunteers, and the town guard.[57]

The fateful decisions which led to the fall of Edinburgh to the rebels were not taken by the civil authorities, but by the military officers. Cope left in charge of the City, General Guest, and of the Castle General Preston, both octogenarians. When the main body of the regular infantry marched to the Highlands, the only professional forces left behind were the garrison of the castle and Gardiner's dragoons at Stirling, and a garrison of invalids in the castle, together with Hamilton's dragoons in Edinburgh. A Dutch battalion, however, was expected to join these early in September, and Brigadier General Thomas Fowkes was sent to Edinburgh to take command of these and the dragoons. He arrived in the City on 15 September, and attended a meeting at the lord chief justice's house where General Guest, the lord advocate and the provost were present. There they debated what could be done to resist the rebels, who were advancing on Edinburgh and were then no further away than Linlithgow. As they approached Stirling, Gardiner's regiment had retreated to Edinburgh. A proposal to bring the dragoons into town was discussed, but was turned down, according to the provost by the military men, while Fowkes claimed that Stewart had objected that there was not enough food for the inhabitants for more than two days, let alone for two regiments as well. Early next morning Fowkes went to inspect the dragoons, who were camped at Colt Bridge to the west of the city, and "found many of the horses backs not fit to receive the riders, many of the men's and some of the officers' legs so swelled, that they could not wear boots; and those who really were to be depended upon, in a manner overcome for want of sleep." Colonel Gardiner recommended that the regiments should be moved to Leith, to await Cope's arrival there, to which Fowkes consented. Moreover, although Fowkes later claimed that their removal was orderly, it was not only the rebels who asserted that it was effected with undue haste to get out of their way. The 'colt-brigg canter', as they described it, was executed so "very hastily" that the provost claimed the dragoons "had run away". Their hasty departure broke any remaining will to fight in those left to their fate. As the lord justice clerk bitterly observed "This afternoon the two regiments of dragoons retired before, I may say fled before, the rebel army in the sight of the City of Edinburgh, where so many loyal gentlemen volunteers stood armed ready to defend the city, which so dispirited and struck with consternation the inhabitants that they resolved to open their gates to the rebels, despairing of speedy relief and unable to make a long defence."[58]

The abandoning of Edinburgh, not only by the dragoons but also by the chief civil authorities, the lord justice clerk, the lord advocate and the solicitor, left Provost Stewart responsible for the safety of its inhabitants, and he was consequently made the scapegoat for the surrender of the City. The confusion which engulfed it during the hours between the departure of the dragoons on 16 September, and the arrival of the rebels early on the 17th, also clearly overwhelmed him. "Monday the 16th of September 1745," Provost Archibald Stewart later recalled, "was a day of universal distraction in Edinburgh." On that day he was up at six o'clock having had less than two hours rest. After organising the supply of provisions to the dragoons, he went to Lock's coffee house at about ten o'clock. There one Andrew Alves delivered a message to him and his fellow magistrates from the rebels, that "if they would let them enter

Andrew Fletcher, Lord Justice Clerk of Scotland. He left Edinburgh on 16 September 1745, shortly before the rebels entered, complaining that it had been abandoned by the troops sent to protect it.

quietly, their privileges and possessions should be preserved: But otherwise they must expect military execution: or words to that effect." The provost thereupon went to Goldsmith's hall to confer with his colleagues about how they should respond to this message. They decided that the best thing to do was to ignore it. Alves, however, went around the town repeating it, until about noon Solicitor Dundas heard him and took him before the lord advocate. They discussed the matter with the lord justice clerk and General Guest, and agreed that Alves should be placed in custody for abetting rebellion. The provost was sent for and, after being upbraided for ignoring the message, was prevailed upon to commit the messenger to prison.

While General Guest stayed with the advocate a commotion started on the streets, probably by the organisers of a petition asking the Council to call a meeting of the principal inhabitants to discuss ways of dealing with the threat from the rebels. This persuaded both to ask for a hundred of Gardiner's dragoons "to suppress disorderly people, and to encourage those who were in arms for the government in the city". Guest therefore sent an oral request for this military aid, and then retired to the castle before two o'clock. Within an hour General Fowkes sent a message that he was unwilling to send in the dragoons unless he had written orders from the governor, who in turn was prepared to issue them only if the advocate, the solicitor and the provost also put it in writing that they felt such assistance was necessary. These bureaucratic proceedings took until nearly four o'clock, by which time the dragoons were on their march from Colt Bridge to Leith. The provost, who had meanwhile been presented with the petition, now heard cries of "would he have them all murdered, by defending the town after the dragoons had run away?" He therefore returned to Goldsmith's hall and sent for the lord justice clerk, the advocate and the solicitor to give him their advice, only to find that they had all left town. They had, however, sent a messenger, Walter Grosett, to ask Stewart to order Fowkes to post at least some of the dragoons in the city; but he refused, saying he had no authority to do so, although they were welcome to come in if they wished. As he explained his dilemma, "a thorn had been put into his foot; for if he should accept that offer, and the town should be taken, he might be charged with having ensnared so many of his Majesty's troops. On the other hand, if he should refuse to accept the offer, he might be blamed, if the town was taken, for having lost it by not receiving that succour." Grosett therefore took a negative answer back.

By this time it was between four and five o'clock, and there was such a crowd in the hall that an adjournment to a large auditorium, New Church Isle, was proposed. Upon this the fire bell rang, the signal for the volunteers, city regiment and trained bands to take up their posts, as a result of which few of them attended the mass meeting, while it was said that many disaffected men were present at it. As they were making their way from Goldsmith's hall to New Church Isle, a Mr Cunningham, who had been sent by the dragoons to get their baggage, rode up and blurted out that the rebels were now thought to be 8,000 strong. This news frightened the crowd into insisting that it was madness to oppose so many.

New Church Isle was "chop full of people" from about five o'clock to six. Amid the pandemonium "the general cry was for giving up the City." When the provost put it to the meeting that the dragoons might be ordered back there were shouts of "No dragoons. No dragoons. They were gone, they were fled." He then asked whether they wanted to surrender the City to the rebels, at which Dr William Wishart, principal of the university, objected that before such a question was put, the meeting should be purged of Jacobites; whereupon one wit said "then you should be amongst the first that should be put out of it; which raised a great laugh". Despite other objections the majority were clearly in favour of giving up without a fight.

Towards six o'clock a letter, addressed to the provost, magistrates and Town Council, was handed in by one Charles Fraser. Fraser had taken it from a man in the street, who claimed to have been given it by "a man dressed in black clothes" in the Luckenbooths. It was passed through the crowd to the provost, who "could not read it, being then almost dark...he gave it into the hands of a person sitting above him, nearer the window." This person announced that it was signed "Charles P(rince) R(egent)", which produced an uproar, some shouting, "read, read", while others objected that it was treason to read it. The provost promptly closed the meeting, and forced his way through the crush back to Goldsmith's hall. When some magistrates and others joined him there, the contents of the letter were divulged, which required them to prepare for the Young Pretender's reception, warning them that if they allowed the dragoons in, or sent arms and ammunition out, it would be regarded as a heinous offence. After promising to preserve the city's rights and liberties, and the property of its inhabitants, Charles Edward concluded "but if any opposition be made to us, we cannot answer for the consequences, being firmly resolved at any rate to enter the city; and in that case, if any of the inhabitants are found in arms against us, they must not expect to be treated as prisoners of war." According to General Guest this was taken to mean that "if they did not suffer them to enter peaceably, they would first plunder, and then burn" the city.[59] Stewart sought legal advice from the four city assessors about how to handle this situation, but only one could be found, and he refused to give an opinion, prompting the provost to exclaim "Good God! I am deserted by my arms and by my assessors." The city fathers then agreed to send a deputation of three of their number to the rebel camp, "to beg they would not attempt to enter the town in an hostile manner, for that the Council were deliberating what answer to send to the summons." About this time, and apparently in reaction to this decision, the volunteers and the city regiment marched up to the castle, deposited their arms in it for safe keeping, and dismissed themselves. The militia, by contrast, kept theirs, since after Charles's message they held that sending them to the castle was the surest way to get their throats cut. The provost was later blamed for not ordering the trained bands to hand in their weapons, since they fell into the hands of the rebels, but he insisted that "they were in themselves of very little value, being generally old guns without bayonets, bought at half a crown or three shillings a piece, more for shew than use, as they were never otherwise employed than at a birthday parade."

The councillors moved from Goldsmith's hall to the council house to await the return of their deputation. While they were awaiting, at about seven o'clock Walter Grosett returned with the news that Sir John Cope was off Dunbar, and would soon be coming to their relief. Immediately two messengers were sent to stop the deputation going to the rebel camp, while Governor Guest was asked to provide arms and to send for the dragoons. But when the messengers returned, having failed to catch up with the deputies, while Guest expressed the opinion that it was better for the dragoons to await Cope's arrival, the momentary rallying of the will to resist was dissipated. Grosett tried to keep it alive by departing at about eleven o'clock at night, promising to return with the dragoons in two hours.

Shortly after he left the deputation returned, with the Young Pretender's demand "to be received into the City as the son and representative of his father", insisting on an answer by two o'clock in the morning. The magistrates waited until that time, but when Grosett failed to return they sent another deputation to try to obtain a delay until nine or ten o'clock, with the lame excuse that "the burghers were all in bed, and could not be convened for several hours". Realising that they were playing for time, Charles sent them back in a hackney coach at about four o'clock on 17 September, with the answer that they "perhaps might have half an hour to deliberate after their return". In fact they had less, for the coach brought them back in at the West port, and when the Netherbrow port was opened to let it out, a body of rebels rushed the gate, entered the city, "and became at once masters of the capital".

As Provost Stewart's defending counsel observed at his subsequent trial (which found him not guilty of negligence): "It is proper to consider, in this case, the uncertainty of the situation to which the magistrates and council were reduced, during the last and most distressing scene of this unlucky affair; sometimes terrified with the immediate approach of the rebels, at other times encouraged with some prospect of relief. Even towards the end of this period, there were some hopes of the return of the dragoons…Mr Grosett had gone in quest of them: nor was that expectation quite over in the meeting of the council, until they heard that the rebels had entered the town."

The dragoons whose return the loyal magistrates forlornly awaited were in fact encamped at Prestonpans and Tranent. They had made

48

their way there when it was realised that the wind would keep Sir John Cope out of the Forth, and oblige him to land at Dunbar.

Cope had returned south from Inverness as soon as he could. At first he had hoped to make his way overland, but this was dependent upon reinforcements of friendly Highlanders, which, apart from about 200 Monroes, was not forthcoming. The alternative was to march down to Aberdeen, having sent urgent messages ahead to General Guest to provide shipping there for transporting the troops to Leith. The governor and the lord justice clerk responded with alacrity to these requests, sending the *Fox* man-of-war to accompany the transports, which actually arrived in Aberdeen before Cope's army. Even though he left Inverness on 4 September it took until the 11th to reach Aberdeen. Jacobites who saw his troops on the march reported that "there was never such a parcel of poor mean fatigued creatures under heaven...they don't march above eight miles a day."[60] Contrary winds delayed their sailing south until the 15th, and prevented them sailing up the Firth of Forth, so that they finally landed at Dunbar on the 17th. It was not until the 18th that all the artillery was got ashore, and the remainder of that day was spent resting the men whom Cope had brought with him, and the horses of the dragoons who had joined them. By the time they set out to the relief of Edinburgh on the 19th, therefore, the rebel army had marched from the city to oppose them.

They met at Prestonpans. Cope took up position there on 20 September in expectation of an encounter with the enemy. Some criticised his choice of ground, saying it "let the enemy keep the hills and rising grounds" while the royal army "drew up on a flat plain", but others were as adamant that "Sir John Cope chose an excellent field of battle", an opinion with which even his opponents concurred.[61] He expected them to attack from the west, and drew up his troops accordingly to face that way. However, they moved south of his camp during the day, obliging him to turn his formation towards them again. During the night they moved east, looking in the darkness "like a black hedge moving towards us", and forcing Cope to about face his toops once more.[62] According to Captain Singleton "such different movements with an harrast little body of an army helped to add to our fatigue very much", while General Guest thought that "they must put him in some little disorder". Nevertheless, Cope managed to get his men into battle formation before the rebels attacked, so that, as Singleton admitted "we had compleated our new change and formed a front directly to receive them." The only difficulty experienced in this manoeuvre was that the cavalry on the right wing found it "impossible either to advance or wheel" between the infantry and the artillery, a problem which was still being sorted out when the rebels charged, just as dawn broke on the 21st.

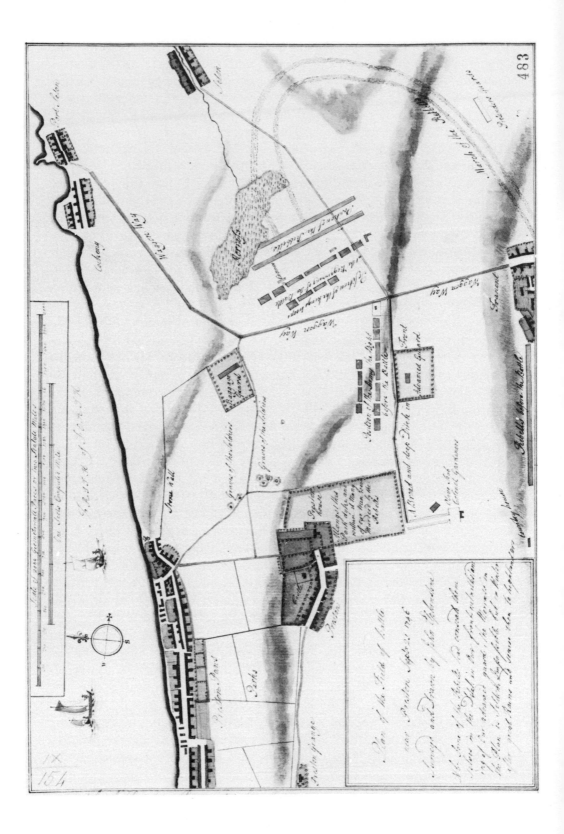

483

General Wightman, who was an onlooker at the battlefield, along with "many officers and country gentlemen who were spectators", observed then that "the scuffle began (I say scuffle for battle it was not) which lasted 4 minutes and no longer."[63] Certainly in less than ten minutes, by every account, Cope's forces fled from the field in panic.[64] The first to fly were the gunners, after firing two or three times, leaving only one officer and a private to man the guns. The rebels even captured some cannon and turned it on their opponents, though they were "slow in charging and not good marksmen with great guns". Meanwhile Gardiner's dragoons on the right and Hamilton's on the left had both turned tail and galloped away without firing a shot. At this the rebels threw down their muskets and went for the infantry broadswords in hand. They too ran for dear life: "it may be fitly called the chase of Cockenzie or Tranent rather than the battle," wrote another observer, "for never deer run faster before hounds than these poor betrayed men run before the rabble. Disciplined they were, but had no head and no confidence in their leaders."[65] This was not to be the opinion of the board of officers who inquired into the battle a year later, and concluded "that the misfortune on the day of action, was owing to the shameful behaviour of the private men and not to any misconduct or misbehaviour of Sir John Cope, or any of the officers under his command."

What unnerved Cope's men was the rapidity with which the Highlanders charged, their bloodcurdling cries, and above all the havoc effected by their broadswords, which left the battlefield "one scene of horror", in which "noses, arms, hands and legs were promiscuously strewed."[66] Even surgeons said "they never saw such terrible gashes as the Highlanders made with their broadswords."[67] At least 300 royal troops were killed that day, including the gallant Colonel James Gardiner, who stayed to fight after his regiment fled. "I believe he prayed for it," commented General Wightman, "and got his desire; for his state of health was bad, and his heart broken with the behaviour of the Irish dogs whom he commanded."[68] Some 1,500 were taken prisoner, many of them fearfully wounded. The rest, including Cope, headed south as fast as they could.

How many fought on each side became a matter of dispute. Some

(Opposite) *Plan of the battle of Prestonpans, fought 21 September 1745. Note the government compiler's claim that the rebels murdered many of their opponents in the grounds of Preston House, an unfounded allegation which encouraged savage reprisals when the boot was on the other foot at Culloden. Sir John Cope fled from the battlefield along a road due South of Preston which became known as "Johnnie Cope's road". The story that upon reaching Berwick he was sarcastically greeted by the Governor with the remark that he was the first general to bring the news of his own defeat is apocryphal.*

claimed that the royal army was heavily outnumbered. "Was it right to meet the rebels with so small a force?" asked Captain Singleton, claiming that "we had not that day above seventeen hundred fighting men to their six thousand."[69] Cope and supporting witnesses at his examination the following year maintained that the rebels were 5,500 strong. On the other hand Richard Jack, a teacher of mathematics who later boasted that he took charge of the royal artillery virtually single handed, and was the most outspoken of Cope's critics at the examination, concluded that "the king's forces, which consisted of two thousand and five hundred men, by not above fifteen hundred raw, undisciplined and despicable highlanders, no better than a mob, were completely routed."[70] In fact the armies were roughly equal, with approximately 2,500 men in each.[71]

The story of the butchering of the royal forces as they ran from the field lost nothing in the telling. A contemporary historian dwelt on "the more than Turkish inhumanity of the commonalty among the enemy", insisting that most of those slain "were killed in cold blood...the foot seeing themselves naked and defenceless, and the enemy rushing impetuously upon them sword in hand, they threw down their arms and surrendered prisoners. But the merciless enemy would grant no quarters, 'till they were compelled by their superior officers. The unheard of manner in which the dead were mangled and the wounded disfigured was a great evidence of the truth of this."[72] Such accounts of the battle of Prestonpans doubtless contributed to the more dreadful slaughter at Culloden.

CHAPTER THREE

"This thing is now grown very serious"

This thing is now grown very serious, the rebels to the great dishonour of Scotland having taken possession of it with three or 4,000 beggarly bandity.

Sir John Ligonier to Sir Everard Fawkener, 28 September 1745

The taking of Edinburgh and Cope's defeat at Prestonpans sent seismic shocks through the nation, the first causing a tremor, the second an earthquake. Fortunately any disposition to panic was dispelled by the "providential arrival" of Sir John Ligonier, with the ten battallions sent over from Flanders, the day before news of the battle reached London.[1] Their presence, in Lord Hardwicke's words, "furnished a kind of armour to us in London against the first shock of the bad news."[2] Otherwise, thought the duke of Newcastle, "the confusion in the City of London would not have been to be described; and the King's crown (I will venture to say) in the utmost danger."[3] Moreover after their victory the rebels retired to the Scottish capital and remained there, or in its vicinity, until 1 November. This interval gave the government's supporters a breathing space which they used to advantage. "Whatever advantages they may propose to themselves by such a proceeding," the Secretary of State was convinced, "it will certainly give us time which I hope we shall make the right use of by forming such a strength as may, by the blessing of God, at once put an end to this rebellion."[4]

Before the humiliation of Prestonpans the reaction to the rebellion had been curiously muted and even ambiguous. At first many refused to take it seriously. "The present rising...is looked upon here in very different lights," a correspondent in London informed Lord Loudoun on 27 August, "for in one company it is treated as a serious affair; in another it is exposed as a ridiculous invention of our governors."[5] In general people

noticed a "profound ignorance and deep lethargy", a "universal uncon-
cernedness", "an indifference and deadness", and a "general supineness".[6]
The earl of Halifax, in an after dinner speech at the George Inn at
Northampton on 25 September, urged that "if vigorous methods do not
immediately prevent it, we may pay dear for that unaccountable indolence, and pardon me if I say stupid insensibility which has so generally
prevailed in the nation."[7] The Dean of Raphoe, having tried to rouse the
inhabitants of Stratford upon Avon, concluded that "there was no disaffection among them to his Majesty's person or government; but there is
such a stupid indolence as may amount to pretty near the same thing. I
have endeavoured to awaken them with the notion of their religion, their
laws, their liberties and properties being at stake; at which they yawn, and
ask if they do not pay soldiers to fight for them."[8] Some took this to
mean that there was a passive unwillingness to assist the regime. "Between
you and I," Henry Pelham confided to Robert Trevor on 10 September, "I
don't find that zeal to venture purses and lives that I formerly remember."[9]
Pelham did not think that there was an active inclination to aid the
Pretender, being satisfied that "the dispositions of the people" were
"far different" from what they had been in 1715.[10] Others were not so
sanguine. "Nobody here knows any of the schemes formed by the Pretender
and his adherents," wrote Lady Isabella Finch from Court early in September. "I shan't be surprised if they burst forth on a sudden (as I've
apprehended even since he landed) in different parts of the king's
dominion, which will be very perplexing." Sir Rowland Winn was worried
that "the nature of the rebellion is such...that many people take their
measures from success."[11]

There was little of such talk after the fall of Edinburgh and the ensuing
battle. On the contrary, as one government supporter put it[12]

> when the news of the surrender of the City and the defeat of the
> army reached them, it spread an universal consternation and con-
> cern. It awakened them out of their stupidity. They saw their
> Religion, Liberty, and Lives, in the utmost danger; and Popery
> and Slavery approaching near to their borders. It must be own'd
> that then a spirit of Liberty and Loyalty appear'd amongst them
> which cannot be too much applauded by friends, and which struck
> terror into the enemy...It soon appear'd, by the behaviour of all
> ranks, that their Addresses were not empty compliments, but
> expressions of unfeigned loyalty, seconded with vigorous endea-
> vours to defend his Majesty against all violence and maintain their
> Religion and Liberties.

While a more objective observer might not have been quite so swept away by it, there was undeniably a new mood in the country towards the end of September. The first major indication of it was manifested at a meeting held in York on the 24th. This had in fact been arranged for several weeks, so the timing was merely fortuitous. Dissatisfaction with the militia led the duke of Newcastle to propose the alternative of raising troops and companies by means of local associations and subscriptions at a private dinner attended by his political allies on 3 September.[13] Lord Irwin responded to the idea by suggesting an Association to leading Yorkshire whigs at Wakefield races on 6 September, and it was agreed at a more formal gathering at Sir John Ramsden's house on the 11th to call a general meeting of the nobility, gentry and clergy of the county at York castle on 24 September to propose a loyal Association, volunteer companies in each of the three Ridings, and a county subscription.[14] The archbishop of York insisted that it should be a representative meeting, including tories and opposition whigs as well as Court supporters, so invitations were sent out to a great many people.[15] Nevertheless the news of Prestonpans, which arrived in Yorkshire on 23 September, ensured an almost complete turnout of the county elite the following day, when "about two thousand gentlemen and clergy met at York".[16]

The archbishop made a speech "to the assembled county that had as much true spirit, honesty and bravery in it," according to Horace Walpole, "as ever was penned by an historian for an ancient hero."[17] Putting on the whole armour of righteousness, he said[18]

> It was some time before it was believed (I would to God it had gained credit sooner) but now every child knows it, that the Pretender's son is in Scotland...is in possession of the capital city there; has defeated a small part of the king's forces...these commotions in the North are but part of a great plan concerted for our ruin — They have begun under the countenance, and will be supported by the forces of France and Spain... If these designs should succeed, and Popery and arbitrary power come in upon us, under the influence and direction of these two tyrannical and corrupted Courts, I leave you to reflect what would become of every thing that is valuable to us.... Let us unite, then, gentlemen, as one man, to stop this dangerous mischief, from which union no man surely can withdraw, or withold his assistance, who is not listed into the wicked service of a French or Spanish invasion, or wholly unconcerned for the fate of his bleeding country.

Thus cajoled, those there unanimously agreed to form an Association almost as soon as the archbishop stopped speaking. A suitably worded form, echoing the loyal sentiments of the speech, had been cobbled together by the main organisers of the meeting at Bishopthorpe, the archbishop's seat, the previous day. Under its terms those who signed associated themselves "in the support and defence of his Majesty's sacred person and government", undertaking to "withstand, offend, and pursue, as well by force of arms, as by all other means, the said Popish Pretender and traitors." They also dipped into their pockets to swell the subscription started at Bishopthorpe on the 23rd to £20,000. Subsequent collections all over the county raised a total of £32,844.[19] The response from all shades of political opinion in the county was prodigious. Besides Court whigs there were offerings from opposition whigs like William Aislabie, who had been alienated from the Court for years, from tories, and even from Roman Catholics.

The government was overwhelmed by these events. Lord Hardwicke rehearsed them to the king, who personally insisted that the archbishop's speech should be printed in the *Gazette*, and when the lord chancellor asked whether he could inform its author that his Majesty approved of "his zeal and activity", George insisted that this was not enough: "you must also tell the Archbishop that I heartily thank him for it." Informing Herring of this, Hardwicke wrote how the news had partly dispelled the gloom and melancholy following Prestonpans, adding "God grant that the glorious example they have set may be followed by other counties."[20]

It was. As Henry Finch wrote on 3 October "the Archbishop sure had a prophetic spirit when he made his speech. 'You are' says he 'the largest county in England, and consequently what you do will be in a great measure an example to all the other counties in England.' Shropshire and Suffolk have made it their pattern."[21] During the following weeks similar Associations were formed in several counties, while many towns also associated voluntarily. These registered the transformation from lethargy to frenzy which Prestonpans had galvanised. It even inspired a verse "upon the late Associations" which proclaimed[22]

> Secure in native strength, we slept a while
> Nor fear'd the rash Disturbers of our Isle;
> 'Till from Impunity Presumption grew,
> And arm'd in hostile Ranks the Rebel crew:
> But rouz'd at length, the Genius of the Land
> Arises glorious with a mighty Hand.

As in Yorkshire these demonstrations of loyalty were not confined to the ruling oligarchies. Undoubtedly Court whigs took the lead in organising them, which led a tory MP "to look upon these subscriptions and association, rather as methods taken by the busy promoters to recommend themselves to posts under the government, than as testimonies of the people's satisfaction."[23] The presiding magistrate at the assizes held at Hertford on 7 October recommended the formation of one at the end of a charge to the Grand Jury, which dealt rather luridly on the dreadful fate which awaited freeborn Englishmen if the rebellion achieved its aims, "to destroy this most excellent Constitution and...to dethrone, if not worse" King George.[24] But having initiated Associations, the government's supporters took pains to make them as representative as possible of political opinion in their localities. County Associations were generally drawn up in the names of "the nobility, gentlemen, clergy and freeholders", while some descended even lower, that from Suffolk, for instance, adding "etc" after this formula. It is true that some tories complained that they were being coerced into joining Associations to show that they were not Jacobites, while in three counties, Middlesex, Oxfordshire and Shropshire, they refused, for which they came under suspicion of favouring the Pretender. As Dr Linda Colley has shown, however, "an examination of their conduct suggests that they were motivated less by Jacobite sympathies than by a characteristic concern for constitutional proprieties". In Middlesex Sir Roger Newdigate refused to subscribe because he thought the subscriptions "contravened the principle of parliamentary supply", while George Cooke, a tory MP who owned land in the county, agreed and would only subscribe "into the Exchequer".[25] The view that Associations and subscriptions were of dubious legal status was not confined to tories. Lord Bath expressed misgivings in a letter he wrote to the duke of Newcastle on 25 October:[26]

> Before the meeting of Parliament I thought these Associations and subscriptions might be of service to his Majesty, in as much as they were demonstrations of his subjects' zeal and furnished money which might at that time be wanted. But now that a parliament is sitting I think them not only unnecessary but even wrong. The parliament is the best judge of what is proper to be done, and will no doubt provide every thing that may be necessary for the defence of the king and preservation of our Constitution, and by proper taxes lay the load (and heavy I fear it will be) equally upon all his Majesty's subjects: whereas by this way of subscription, the Jacobites and disaffected are eased and exonerated from any share of that expence which they alone have been the cause of bringing on the nation.

Of course constitutional scruples could cloak political objections, though opposition whigs could hold these as well as tories. In Shropshire both seem to have been opposed to the Association because of the clumsy way in which the Lord Lieutenant confined Deputy Lieutenancies to Court whigs. As a local tory observed: "the Gentlemen of this county greatly disagree upon the Association scheme. The C[ountr]y party think themselves ill used by ye L[or]d L[ieutenan]t taking no notice of 'em in his deputation, and they totally decline from that slight coming into any measures with ye C[our]t party."[27] Huntingdonshire even experienced difficulties in organising an Association because of the local rivalry of two Court whigs, the duke of Manchester and the earl of Sandwich. Manchester arranged a meeting at the George Inn at Huntingdon to "follow the laudable example of some...Northern countys", only to find that Sandwich had called a rival gathering at another inn.[28] Sandwich claimed that the county was too small to go it alone, and suggested that they co-operate with the arrangements which his friend the duke of Bedford was making to put Bedfordshire on a military footing. On the whole, however, county Associations appear to have spanned the political spectrum, apart from a handful of committed Jacobites.

Associations in some towns also resolved political differences. In Bristol, for instance, "people were so unanimous that even those that had not spoke to one another for years are all reconciled, and...have formed themselves into an Association for the defence of their country."[29] Some urban associations also penetrated below the civic elites. In Exeter, along with the bishop and cathedral clergy, the mayor aldermen and magistrates, were associated the gentlemen, "other clergy", merchants and inhabitants. Nottingham's Association combined the "mayor, aldermen, gentlemen, freeholders, burgesses, etc." There was even an Association of the manufacturers and others inhabiting in or near Spitalfields, who undertook to induce their several workmen, servants and dependants, who numbered no fewer than 2,919, "to take up arms with us whenever called thereto." [30] The most remarkable Association of all was that reported from Sussex, where nearly 1,000 smugglers were alleged to have associated "to oppose the French in case of an invasion", despite their notorious reputation for being militant Jacobites.[31]

Yorkshire's example was followed not only by the forming of Associations, but also, in most cases, by the raising of subscriptions. Indeed it was surpassed in Norfolk, where, Lord Malton was informed, "Lords Orford, Townsend, Johnny Hobart and his father have subscribed one thousand pounds apiece and old Horace five hundred, in short everybody has outdone the Yorkshire Lords."[32] In Hertfordshire 504 people subscribed a total of £10,194 15s.[33] A subscription began at Lincoln Castle on 1 October raised £6,013 from the 143 people then present.[34] Lancashire collected "a handsome subscription" of over £11,000 after a disappointing start.[35] The principal subscribers, as in Yorkshire, were the prominent Court whigs in the counties. Thus the dukes of Kingston and Newcastle got the Nottinghamshire subscription off to a good start with donations of £1,000 each. But also as in Yorkshire the political opponents of the Court whigs were involved. For example, Robert Vyner, the Country whig knight of the shire, subscribed £100 in Lincolnshire, while William Levinz, a tory who had previously represented Nottinghamshire, also gave £100 there.

Towns and even parishes collected subscriptions too. A collection in Chester on 2 October realised £3,885 18s.[36] Liverpool began one which raised £3,000 on the first day, and rose eventually to £5,000.[37] York subscribed £2,600, Bath £2,465 and Nottingham over £2,200.[38] Cambridge University collected £1,000, though £600 of this came out of the pocket of the Chancellor, who on finding that the dons had only contributed £400, made it up to a sum he thought "more suitable to the honour and dignity of such a body".[39] "The little town of Sheffield" raised £800.[40] But Bristol surpassed all others in its efforts, raising over £30,000.[41]

Most of the money subscribed was spent on local military preparations, though a sum raised in Peterborough was offered as a gift to the Crown as "contributing more effectually to advance his Majesty's service in this time of imminent danger than any other method of applying such money". Unfortunately the organisers had to find another method, since, as the prime minister tactfully pointed out to them, it was against the law for subjects to give money to the king "by way of benevolence".[42]

These activities were apparently genuine demonstrations of a determination to crush the rebellion which, especially after the apathy which marked its initial stage, seem to have taken observers by surprise. Certainly they were regarded as an index of loyalty to the regime. Thus an address to the king from the tory corporation of Marlborough observed that "the Associations that are forming in every corner of the kingdom in defence of your Royal person and Government, are an undeniable proof how much you reign in the affections of your people."

Where there had been a trickle of addresses in the month before Prestonpans, now there was a flood. Many of them were presented to the king by members of parliament, and this also served to advertise the broad spectrum of support for the administration. Along with staunch members of the Old Corps, like Martin Balden, David Polhill and Sir Charles Hanbury Williams, were opposition whigs like John Bance, Sir John Chapman and William Moore, who all presented addresses from their constituencies. Even more significant was the number of tories who did likewise, including Sir John Hinde Cotton, Sir Robert Grosvenor, Philip Herbert and Thomas Rowney. According to Lord Egmont, Rowney was "always reputed a rank Jacobite and has drunk the Pretender's health 500 times" yet "when the Pretender's son came into England he was frightened out of his wits, and ordered his chaplain to pray for king George which he had never suffered him to do in his life before."[43] If his presentation of the

Oxford City address is anything to go by, however, Rowney's conversion occurred before Charles Edward had left Scotland. That such presentations were taken seriously is indicated by the fact that a report of the Glamorganshire address being presented by the tory Bussey Mansel was corrected, "as inserted by mistake in the...*Gazette*", the presenter having been the whig Sir Edmund Thomas. Of course it could be argued that a tory MP could hardly refuse to present his own constituency's address. Yet that does not hold for Pensiton Powney and Sir Miles Stapylton, who took it upon themselves to present addresses from Maidenhead and Leeds, which were not even parliamentary boroughs.

As with the Associations, although most addresses were doubtless organised by Court supporters, pains were taken to try to ensure that they represented a cross-section of political opinion. Bishop Hoadly of Winchester sent one round his diocese, and when it came back he noted that it contained the "names of many to it at which I am greatly surprised, and which I never thought to see".[44] The Staffordshire address was presented to a very full meeting of justices of the peace, no fewer than sixty-two being present, which was virtually all the gentlemen in the county. One who was there but did not know who had drawn it up, was pleased to get an amendment made to it, "so," he could inform his brother "the address is a common performance".[45] Many addresses stressed the wide support which they had obtained. The mayor and commonalty of York, "forgetful of all little party distinctions and private animosities," assured the king that they would, "with our lives and fortunes, heartily unite in support of our Government and Constitution." It was "with the utmost pleasure" that the Oxfordshire addressers saw "that unanimity which prevails in persons of all parties to join their endeavours to frustrate the designs of our enemies...laying aside all party distinctions and private prejudices, and activated as well by the principles of duty and allegiance, as by interest, we will heartily unite in the support of your Majesty's person and government."

Although Lord Irwin was "very glad to observe...most of the southern counties...following the example of Yorkshire", and felt a warm zeal being openly professed throughout the whole kingdom, the government detected varying responses from different regions.[46] Looking at the pattern of the reaction to Yorkshire's lead the duke of Newcastle observed to Lord Lonsdale that "there is a great zeal almost universal in your northern counties; and I hope, and believe, that example will be followed by most of the Midland counties and some of the maritime ones: But I doubt the Western counties and Welsh counties will not behave so well."[47]

Newcastle was particularly concerned about the west country, where the French could be expected to land, which as he pointed out to the

Thomas Pelham-Holles, first duke of Newcastle, who was Secretary of State during the Forty-five. Although his many critics characterised him as an inept politician, his handling of the crisis was remarkably competent.

61

duke of Devonshire, "would create a great deal of trouble; for I am much afraid those counties are by no means so well affected as the Northern ones."[48] His suspicions, apart from reflecting the prejudices of a Court whig to areas which were markedly tory in their politics, were no doubt based on the fact that, while Cornwall and Devon formed Associations, neither raised subscriptions, while Somerset failed even to associate. In consequence they could not form local companies, but had to rely for their defence either on the county militias or on regular troops. In Cornwall the militia was even more of a broken reed than elsewhere, for Lord Edgecombe admitted that raising it would be "not only the most dilatory and difficult but the most ineffectual [method] of any other", as it was so long since it had last been mustered that he hardly knew how to go about it. He nevertheless was convinced that Cornish people were "as well intentioned as any others".[49] Even the apprehensive Lady Isabella Finch was inclined to agree. "In general, tho' the West has been reckoned disaffected," she wrote on 19 October, "I hear there appears now a proper zeal and detestation of the present rebellion."[50]

Judging by the experience of Somerset, moreover, the response to the idea of Associations in these western counties was not due to disaffection, as Newcastle feared, but to a failure of the local Court supporters to give a positive lead. Lord Poulet, the lord lieutenant, complained that he had been virtually abandoned by the leading whigs in the county when, under pressure from Newcastle, he held a meeting at Bridgwater to try to organise an Association. Since he himself was averse to the idea, and would have preferred mustering the militia, it is scarcely surprising that he failed to sell the Nottinghamshire model which Henry Pelham had recommended to him. All he could get the predominantly tory gentry who turned up to do was to join in an address to the king. He hoped, however, that "the names of so many gentlemen of such fortune and characters in this country to so strong an address will have a very great weight and effect on the county in general." "As to the temper of this county," he went on to inform Newcastle, "all the tory gentlemen run down and blame the present measures very much, but affect to talk zealously for the king, and warmly against the Rebellion."[51] For the duke, who wanted an Association rather than an address, this was not enough.

Nor can he have been any more impressed with the Welsh reaction. North Wales was particularly suspect, since its leading magnate, Sir Watkin Williams Wynn, was rightly regarded as a potential rebel. The government had picked up evidence in December 1744 that he was actively encouraging the Pretender to launch an invasion, while in October 1745 Newcastle was informed that the rebels "flatter themselves with a great assistance from Sr W...ns W...m Wh...n".[52] In the event, however, Wynn organised an Association in Denbighshire, though the response to the subscription launched afterwards was admittedly poor, while Flintshire failed either to associate or to subscribe, which was seen as an indication that the tory gentry in this region were disaffected. Further confirmation appeared when Lord Cholmondley started to raise a regiment in Cheshire and North Wales, for though he had no difficulty finding officers from "young gentlemen of the best estates in the whigg interest" he complained that "so far from having the assistance of the Tory gentlemen they have done all in their power in a clandestine manner to prevent their tenants and dependants from entering."[53] Yet the only positive lead that the government was given about Jacobite plotting in Flintshire proved to be insubstantial, while Sir Thomas Mostyn, a local tory renowned for his loyalty, was "persuaded the greater part of the country are well affected."[54] Elsewhere in Wales the tories showed themselves to be ready to support the government. In Glamorganshire "tory justices and Deputy lieutenants like Herbert Mackworth met to suppress disturbances and to put into effect the laws against Papists and Nonjurors", while the Association in Pembrokeshire "was 'unanimously' signed by the gentry, many of whom were no doubt sea serjeants", as the members of an allegedly Jacobite Club were called.[55]

Apart from the west country and Wales the only other district south of Scotland which was regarded as being potentially rebellious was Lancashire. When it was known that the rebels were heading for England it was immediately assumed that they were making for Lancashire, and there was even a rumour that the Brest fleet was sailing for Liverpool.[56] A "Letter from Manchester" dated 14 September claimed "that the disaffection of some in this part of the country is but too notorious" and predicted that "should the rebels march this way...they will meet with too many friends".[57] In the event, however, this prediction was confounded. The rebel army was only able to raise at most 200 men in Manchester. Otherwise the only demonstration in the Pretender's favour to occur in the county was an uprising of Catholics, said to number nearly 200, at Ormskirk on 25 November. Although they proclaimed him king they were quickly suppressed by the Protestants in the town without outside help.[58] Apart from these incidents, as the duke of Cumberland acknowledged, "there has not appeared any mark of disaffection even in that county".[59]

Indeed the basic message coming in to the government from all parts of England and Wales was that the overwhelming majority, at least of the political elite, was not only opposed to the Pretender but actively loyal to George II.

Judging by performance rather than promise the degree of commitment to a Stuart restoration even on the part of acknowledged Jacobite leaders among the tories was negligible. Late in September Lord Gower saw the king and "assured him that he had formerly been his enemy and a Jacobite, but he saw the folly of it and should be so no more."[60] Not long after, Gower was given a commission to raise a regiment to oppose the rebels, and made a very loyal speech promoting it in Staffordshire, in which he "treated the rebellious villains properly, and spoke of the king handsomely".[61] Lord Ailesbury followed his example of going to town to reassure the king of his loyalty. "Ailesbury you know I always said did not mean a Popish Pretender," Lady Isabella Finch informed her brother on 12 October, adding "without foreign forces the Pretender's son will do but little here, and indeed all the people reckoned Jacobites have loudly declaimed against him."[62] Perhaps the most ostentatious way in which the tories showed their loyalty was in their reaction to Charles Edward's proclamation of 9 October, which declared that those who attended the "Elector of Hanover's" parliament, summoned to meet on the 17th, would be engaged in "an overt Act of Treason and Rebellion".[63] The tories almost fell over themselves to get to Westminster for the opening of parliament, when, as Lord Perceval observed, "notwithstanding the Pretender's Declaration the Parliament met and above 400 members appeared".[64] The overwhelming majority of tories manifestly preferred George II to the Pretender.

So far as it can be ascertained, the mass of the population below the elite was similarly disposed. Some addresses stressed the union not only of all parties but also of all people in support of the Constitution. The Devon address looked "upon it as a most happy circumstance, that the main body of your people, of all ranks and orders whatsoever, should be voluntarily rising up at once (as they now actually are) in defence of your Majesty's just rights." Those in Staffordshire drew the king's attention to "the general union which appears among all your English subjects". This was manifestly not true of his Scottish subjects, yet even in Scotland the provincial Synod of Glasgow informed George II that

> tho an indelible stain of disloyalty and of the vilest ingratitude must be upon some parts of our country, yet it is with pleasure we can assure your Majesty that almost the whole people in these Western shires wherein we live still preserve a steady fidelity and affection to your Royal person and Government: so that a very small and inconsiderable number from these parts have joined in this daring and wicked attempt against your Majesty and their country; and of these few, none of them, so far as we know, are members of our Presbyterian communion.

In England, too, the Presbyterians were apparently loyal to a man. They followed the lead from the Committee of Protestant dissenters in

Henry Pelham, the duke of Newcastle's brother, as prime minister headed the so-called Broadbottom administration at the time of the Rebellion. The Pelhamites faced opposition not only from the Jacobites but also from colleagues in the Cabinet. These internal tensions created friction throughout the Forty-five, reaching a climax in February 1746 when the Pelhamites resigned en masse, *forcing George II to reinstate them on their own terms. This resolved a political conflict which had handicapped the government's ability to respond to the Young Pretender's challenge.*

and about London, which in September advised its co-religionists to be active in support of the king and his government.[65] The Quakers in their meeting for sufferers also advised Friends on 20 September to show "the most steady adherence to the present government".[66] Although they did not like to subscribe to specific military funds, Quakers "furnished woolen waistcoats to enable the troops to go through the winter campaign", and "thus assisted, without spilling the blood of any man".[67] The Methodists came under suspicion of disloyalty in Cornwall, and were even reported to the government for allegedly preparing the ground for a French invasion during their peregrinations. However the government which usually followed up any lead, ignored this report, presumably convinced that it came from a crank, since in fact the Methodists were staunchly loyal during the rebellion.[68]

"The middling sort" also came out strongly in support of the government. When the news of Prestonpans arrived in London, public credit was badly affected, and the stock market fell. This was widely regarded as a response to the Pretender's ambiguous attitude towards the national debt. The Jacobites claimed that the whole machinery of public credit set up in what has been called the Financial Revolution was an unjustified diversion of economic resources from productive investments into an artificial debt raised to finance Hanoverian interests. This led their opponents to insist that a Stuart restoration would lead to a repudiation of the debt. Charles Edward, appreciating that this gave the regime a propaganda advantage, tried to reassure stockholders that their investments were secure. Publishing his father's "sentiments with regard to the National debt" he proclaimed "that it has been contracted under an unlawful Government, no Body can disown, no more than that it is now a most heavy load upon the nation; yet in regard that it is for the greater part due to those very subjects whom he promises to protect, cherish and defend, he is resolved to take the Advice of his Parliament concerning it, in which he thinks he acts the part of a just Prince, who makes the good of his people the sole rule of his actions."[69] Such reassurances convinced nobody, and whenever the Jacobite cause achieved a success in the autumn of 1745, the money market reacted nervously. During the last week of September some stocks fell by five or six per cent, while there was a run on the Bank of England, the very symbol of the Financial Revolution which had succeeded the Glorious Revolution. Some attributed the panic to the political uncertainty caused by the divided counsels in the Cabinet as well as by the battle of Prestonpans. "Tis hoped the pannick will subside," a whig MP wrote to his brother, "and that people will get the better of their fears, which would certainly happen if an administration could once be settled that the people as well as the Crown could have confidence in."[70] The panic did subside when a substantial number of business men restored confidence by declaring that they would not refuse to receive Bank notes in payment of any sum of money. The scheme did not start until 26 September, yet the list of names took over six columns in the *London Gazette* for 24—28 September, which noted that it had not been able to publish the names of those who had signed after five o'clock on the 27th because of its printing deadline. The next issue published a further column and a half of the names of those who had signed since. "It is a step that never was taken before," Lord Hardwicke informed the archbishop of York, "and has had a prodigious effect to stop the run which was begun."[71] Addresses from corporations across the country, and subscriptions in several trading towns, indicate that the 'middling sort' elsewhere were equally zealous. When the army marched through Yorkshire to Newcastle, it was observed that "the zeal and loyalty of all the people wherever we pass is almost incredible. The gentlemen invite the officers and the middling people the soldiers to their houses."[72]

As for the lower orders, we know more about what their social superiors thought they ought to feel than about how they actually felt towards the rebellion. It seems to have been taken for granted that they should be at least indifferent, since the exchange of King James for King George would not change their lot, and at best ardently loyal, since they stood to lose life and liberty, if not property, too. "Montanus", an essayist in the *Newcastle Journal*, subscribed to the former view. He contributed "A letter from the Drapier to the people of Ireland" to the paper on 19 October, incidentally the very day after the death of Jonathan Swift, author of the original *Drapier's Letters.* It was in fact addressed not to the Irish but to "the common people, the labourers, farmers, artificers and journeymen of this nation", pointing out to them that if the labourer "must dig and delve when the Pretender is settled on the throne, he had as good stick to it now, for any difference I can see."[73] "Popularis", writing "an address to the common people" in the rival *Newcastle Courant*, disagreed. He did not want them to "be led away with a false notion that they have nothing to lose when the Government is overturned, the course of Justice stoop'd, the Laws trampled upon, and when Peace, Liberty and Property are invaded, which is undeniably the Design of the present Rebellion, and must be the consequence of its success." On the contrary, the overthrow of George II and his replacement by the Pretender would affect them most of all: "For when Oppression and Tyranny load a nation with their weight, they that are undermost must feel the greatest share; it must evidently fall heaviest upon them, and grind them to powder."[74] A refreshingly frank, if somewhat cynical, view was expressed by Henry Fielding in the *True Patriot*.[75] He conceded that, had the Young Pretender landed in England, the "rabble" might have entertained hopes of gaining from his success. But since he came via Scotland

The Highlanders are those to whom he must owe any success he may attain; these are therefore to be served before you; and I easily refer to your consideration, when Rome, and France, and Spain are repaid their demands, when a vast army of hungry Highlanders and a larger army of as hungry priests, are satisfied, how miserable a pittance will remain to your share.

The more common view, however, appears to have been that the lower orders shared in the blessings which the Constitution bestowed on those above them. As the Somerset address asserted, "in the Religion and Liberties of this country every one has an equal interest with persons of the greatest property."

These varying viewpoints indicate a degree of uncertainty and even insecurity about what the lower orders were actually thinking. This uneasiness is most discernible at the outbreak of the rebellion. In mid September John Banks, a Wakefield man, was apprehensive that "many thousands...of the vulgar unthinking people would flock to them could it be said the rebels was the strongest side."[76] Another Yorkshireman was "afraid much cannot be hoped for from the common people about London, I rather doubt they would be disposed to join in plundering than defending the property of other people." Lady Isabella Finch argued that, even if "the mob were well affected (the contrary of which I believed) there was no depending on them. Success would turn them on any side, and all the desperate people who had either ruined their affairs or never had estates...would be for confusion." Those that had no property would "endeavour to get some, as thieves do plunder in a fire".[77]

Yet by the end of September Lord Malton did not "think the mobs of the trading towns will presume to stir, or indeed are inclined to it", while a little later he could "see no danger of any rising in this county [Yorkshire] nor can imagine any formidable ones either in Lancashire or elsewhere since the country people are hearty."[78] Early in October "the common people" of Staffordshire were observed to be "steady for the Protestant religion", while Lord Poulet could assure the duke of Newcastle that those in Somerset were "expressing a desire to distinguish themselves in support of his Majesty's person and government".[79] Lord Tyrawly, on his way from London to Plymouth "with great pleasure observed the...good dispositions in those of a lower rank, having been stopped on the road at the doors of public houses to drink the king's health."[80]

There were two more formal occasions during October on which people could demonstrate their loyalty by drinking a toast to his Majesty: the anniversary of his coronation on the 11th; and his birthday on the 30th. Both were celebrated with great zeal throughout the country, with all levels of society joining conspicuously in the celebrations. At Newcastle upon Tyne on coronation day the noblemen, gentlemen, clergy and army officers attended the mayor at his house to drink many loyal healths, while "at night there were bonfires in several parts of the streets, and beer given to the common people, when the foresaid healths were likewise drank". The *Newcastle Courant* reporting the day's events, assured its readers that "the night concluded with the greatest peace, unity, love and friendship amongst all ranks." One of the more spectacular celebrations of the king's birthday occurred at Deptford, which witnessed an elaborate procession.[81]

> Viz. 1. a highlander in his proper dress carrying on a pole a pair of wooden shoes with this motto, *The Newest make from Paris.* 2. A Jesuit, in his proper dress, carrying on the point of a long sword, a banner, with this Inscription in large letters Inquisition, Flames and Damnation. 3. Two Capuchin Friars, properly shaved habited and accoutred with flogging ropes, beads, crucifixes etc. One of them bore on a high pole a bell, mass book and candles to curse the British nation with; the other carried a large standard, with this Inscription, INDULGENCES cheap as dirt, viz. murder, 9d. Adultery, 9½d. Reading the bible, 1000£. Fornication, 4¾d. Perjury, 0. Rebellion, a reward or drawback of 13½d Scots money. 4. The Pretender, with a green ribband a nosegay of Thistle etc. riding upon an ass, supported by a Frenchman on the right and a Spaniard on the left, each dressed to the height of the newest modes. 5. The Pope riding on his Bull...the Pope and the Pretender were in the evening committed to the flames, according to custom ...the whole concluded with Illuminations and grand fire works and the song of God save the King.

The National Anthem first made its appearance at this time, beginning "God save great George our King". As 'Lilliburlero' was said to have whistled James II out of three kingdoms, so this sang his grandson out of two.

The pope-burning procession was an old standby of whig propaganda, and seems to have tapped a genuine stream of popular anti-Catholicism. Shortly after the battle of Prestonpans "the brave ship carpenters of Whitby...being informed that the papists of Egton in the moors made great rejoycings for the defeat of the king's forces...took their axes and cleavers...to hack and hew the said papists in pieces, and were with extreme difficulty brought back to Whitby after they had marched two miles towards their enemies."[82] This was the first serious manifestation of an anti-Catholic sentiment among the "lower orders" which was to be their chief active contribution during the rebellion. As Francis Eld observed in Staffordshire early in October, "we are extremely quiet at present, and I apprehend no tumult unless the common people should attack the papists which they show some inclination to do, and should that ungovernable monster awake he must be fed. If so it would be prudent to direct his head toward the cause of these our troubles."[83]

The best way of directing the common people towards the enemy was to recruit them into the various forces that were being raised throughout the country. There appears to have been no reluctance to join up. The earl of Halifax recruited 500 men in Northampton in eight days.[84] Yorkshire raised forty-one companies, most of which were fully recruited by early October. "It would have been easy to have increased our numbers," claimed Lord Malton, "the common people being furious in the cause."[85] The drive for recruits was so successful in some places by the end of October that there were complaints of a shortage of men to fill up the ranks. An attempt by Lord Fitzwilliam to raise a company in Peterborough ran into difficulties because, as an agent explained to his lordship on 3 November, "our Liberty and Towns adjacent have been by the Dukes of Bedford and Mountague, Lord Gainsborough, Burghley etc. so culled of all men who could be procured that 20 would not be raised in two months."[86]

There had in fact been a plethora of military preparations in the seven weeks since the fall of Edinburgh. In some counties the militia was mustered, but its generally admitted inadequacy had inspired a variety of schemes to mobilise the country more efficiently. Indeed some were of the opinion that there were too many schemes. "It had been happy if at first one general plan for the whole nation had been fixed upon by the Government," Lord Derby complained to Newcastle, to which the duke replied that he agreed entirely, "but as the subscriptions made on this occasion have been purely voluntary, and an effect of the zeal of the nation for the support of his Majesty's government, it was judged advisable not to prescribe any rule as to the method of raising the troops, but to leave it to the discretion of the several counties and towns to form such plans as should be agreeable to themselves."[87]

Those local Associations which had raised subscriptions formed troops and companies which the subscribers undertook to pay and clothe, but which the government agreed to arm. The Liverpool subscribers, for example, arranged "to form eight hundred or a thousand men into companies of one hundred each, to find them with new blue frocks, hatts, shoes and stockings and to maintain them for two months certain".[88] It took time for the Ordnance to furnish the necessary arms; too much time so far as Lord Malton was concerned. He was protesting by mid October that "the Yorkshire companies have not yet got a single firelock amonst them, except a few old rusty musquests," which "put him in a violent passion".[89] Archbishop Herring, more temperately but no less firmly, warned Lord Hardwicke that "if this affair is not *instantly* attended to…this uneasiness will grow up into a rank and strong indignation," since the king's friends were very "shamed and vexed…that men are forced to exercise with broomstaffs".[90] General Wentworth wrote from Doncaster to urge that arms should be sent as soon as possible to encourage the spirit he found in Yorkshire. Meanwhile he had recommended using "scythes fixed upon poles in the manner of pikes, which would make them formidable; and such a weapon in a good hand may very well deal with a highland broadsword."[91] Newcastle put pressure on the Master of the Ordnance to expedite the shipping of arms to the north, only to be told that if the lords lieutenants there had gone about it the right way they could have received them sooner. Malton muttered that bureaucratic forms might have been set aside in a crisis, but by early November the Yorkshire companies were fully armed. Eventually twenty-two other counties and several towns were to raise forces by this method of voluntary association.

Besides taking a leading part in the county effort, Lord Malton formed a company of his own, recruiting his domestic servants into its ranks. At his own expense he had regularly armed sixty foot who appeared in uniform on Sundays at Wentworth church. He also had about fourteen horse, and together these men practised manoeuvres in his grounds from the top of the slope near his bowling green down to the parterre.[92] Similar private armies were mobilised elsewhere during the crisis. "Sir Gregory Page muster'd a body of 500 men on Blackheath, rais'd and cloth'd at his own expence."[93] Thomas Ridge, a Portsmouth ropemaker, enlisted seventy of his workmen.[94] The men of Penrith "collected all the arms this place will afford us, and have assembled ourselves in the field three days severally, to learn the military exercise and to form ourselves into a troop of light horse and a company of foot."[95]

Along with these improvisations a more regular force was raised by granting commissions to several noblemen to raise their own regiments. The idea was first mooted at Court by the duke of Bedford in late September. Initially the king demurred, saying "he would do the business with his regular troops".[96] Although the Pelhams were not sold on the scheme either, it appealed to such influential colleagues as Bedford, and his father-in-law Lord Gower, sufficient for them to push it in Cabinet. On 20 September therefore George agreed that several Lords should raise regiments. Eventually fifteen peers undertook to recruit them, "besides several who have been thanked for their good intentions and the offer declined."[97] In view of the unsatisfactory response of the gentry in Cornwall to the threat posed by the rebellion, two Cornish lords, Edgecombe and Falmouth, were granted such commissions. Even then they had difficulty in raising recruits, since Cornishmen were reluctant to be enlisted for service outside their own county.[98] Initially the "new regiments", as they were called, were raised at the expense of their Colonels, but when they came up to half strength they were put on the military establishment, and paid, clothed and armed by the government.

These arrangements came under attack shortly after parliament met on 17 October.[99] In his opening speech the king expressed "the firmest assurance that you are met together resolved to act with a spirit becoming a time of common danger, and with such vigour as will end in the confusion of all those who have engaged in or fomented this rebellion." However, as Lord Fitzwilliam gloomily noted "instead of the strict unanimity and the greatest harmony which ought to reign amongst them," the Commons met "in an ill humour".[100] There was even an attempt by two tory MPs to include a clause, in the address of thanks for the speech, committing the House to pass bills to eliminate corruption in elections and abuses in the administration, but this was left to lie on the table. The suspension of Habeas Corpus for a year was also agreed without a division. But critics of the government soon attacked its handling of the rebellion. On 23 October William Pitt moved an address to recall all British troops from the continent, which was defeated by only twelve votes. Five days later he seconded a call for an inquiry into the causes of the progress of the rebellion, which one member attributed to "the utmost neglect, or the blackest treachery" in the ministry. Such a savage attack was comfortably staved off by eighty-two votes. "The great argument of the ministry was this, that if a man's house was on fire, he would apply himself to extinguish it first before he enquired by whose negligence it happened" reported a disgruntled member of the minority.[101]

An attack upon the new regiments, however, posed a more serious threat, especially since some of the ministry's supporters disliked them. They were widely regarded as having created *"jobs for the boys"*. As Horace Walpole put it, "one of the great grievances of this is, that these most disinterested colonels, have named none but their own relations and dependents for the officers who are to have rank."[102] "I'm afraid the new rais'd regiments will occasion a very warm debate in the House," Lord Hartington informed the duke of Devonshire on 29 October, "and I much doubt whether they will pass, which as the king has given his consent to them, and some of them are almost complete, will be a very ugly affair, and I am afraid occasion great confusion, for which reason I believe I shall vote for them, tho I think there is a great deal to be said on the other side."[103] There was, and Lord Fitzwilliam, good Court Whig that he was, said it, writing to Lord Malton on 31 October:[104]

72

Tomorrow the English army in general is to be debated, when it is expected there will be hot work, as ever was known in that House, upon the 15 new rais'd regiments. I don't in the least deny but it is one of the most vile, low, dirty groveling schemes that ever was set on foot by a parcel of people who have taken advantage of the distress of the Government to fill their own pockets, which to be sure, is literally the case, and a greater clamour never was rais'd against any set of men than against these new Job Colonels as they are called. But at the same time I would appeal to any man in his senses, whether this is a time to be quarrelling amongst ourselves; when our all is at stake; for my own part, I can't help thinking but those that join in these factious measures are either Jacobites in their hearts, or to think in the most candid manner of them, are very indifferent who reigns over us.

In fact some of the Old Corps, including Henry Fox, one of Pelham's colleagues on the Treasury Board, and Thomas Winnington, the paymaster, voted against the regiments, indicating objections in some minsterial circles to their expense. Pitt, perversely, voted for them, which led Lady Isabella Finch to comment that "the divisions this session have been (if possible) more motley than ever."[105] "To be sure," she continued

all divisions are of bad consequence at this juncture, tho' I can't say in any one the Pretender's son has met with any encouragement more than what he and his friends may draw from a disagreement in parliament, which may create confusion, and upon that account I heartily wish no notice had been taken of those regiments after the king had signed the commissions, because addressing now is only making bad worse.

The outcome was that the new regiments were approved on 1 November by 235 votes to sixty-seven, though only for four months. Another motion, to address the king that their officers should not have ranks equivalent to those in the regular army, was rejected by only two votes on that day. The principal argument against giving ranks to the commissioned officers of the new regiments was that if they transferred to the regular army they would be put into unfair competition for promotion with those who had long experience of the military life. As one member expressed it "with what hope...can a man, who has nothing to plead but that he has done his duty, stand in competition with him who is supported by the power of the greatest of the nobility, and whose solicitations are assisted by the high officers of state, whose constant access to the sovereign gives them an irresistible superiority to all other petitioners?" The narrowness of the majority was partly due to the fact that George II himself approved of the address. John Tucker, who was mortified to learn the result, since he had left the House early with another member who supported the motion, informed his brother that "you will be surprised to hear that Mr Winnington and Mr Fox voted in the minority of this question, and many of the courtiers, or else the numbers could not have come to near a parity."[106] He added that the debate indicated "but a short reign to Mr P[elham] unless he take some immediate assistance from among the opposition." Instead the prime minister persuaded the king to change his mind, and when another address to the same purpose was proposed on 4 November it was defeated by 155 votes to 133.

After all the pains taken to save them from parliamentary censure, the new regiments, with the exception of the duke of Kingston's light horse, did not make a major contribution to the suppression of the rebellion. When Marshal Wade was offered their services at the end of October, he suggested that the only duty they were fit for was the suppressing of any insurrections which might take place in their localities. If the rebels were to approach he advised them to divide into small parties to impede their progress by firing from behind hedges.[107] As late as 30 November, when the duke of Cumberland inspected the duke of Bedford's regiment, his professional eye was not impressed. "I am sorry to speak my fears that they will rather be a hindrance than a service to me," he wrote to Newcastle, "for this regiment was represented to be the forward regiment of them, yet neither men nor officers know what they are about, so how they will do before an enemy God alone knows."[108] He preferred to rely on regular soldiers.

The Pelhams, though they had gone along with the raising of them, were inclined to agree with him. "I have a very good opinion of the zeal and good countenance of your volunteer corps," Lord Hardwicke informed the archbishop of York, "but I own my reliance is, under God, on regular troops."[109] All along he and his colleagues preferred to bring over forces from the army on the continent, but had to fight a constant battle with the king, backed by the Granvillites, who insisted on the necessity for a strong military presence in the Low Countries, and on the capacity of the forces in Britain to deal with the rebels, whose strength they played down. "When the ministers propose anything with regard to the rebellion," Horace Walpole claimed on 13 September, the king "cries 'Pho! Don't talk to me of that stuff!'"[110] As late as 21 September, the very day of Prestonpans, "Lord Stair and Lord Winchilsea ridiculed the rebellion as nothing."[111] When the news of Cope's defeat reached London, however, public opinion came out strongly on the side of the Pelhams. Sir John Ligonier reported to Cumberland, on the 28th, that

Marshal George Wade, here portrayed with a view of the military roads whose construction he supervised as commander-in-chief in Scotland after 1726. The portrait indicates why he had the reputation of being a dandy. His career ended under a cloud when, at the age of 72, he led the forces sent to Newcastle to intercept the Young Pretender after the battle of Prestonpans. His army marched fruitlessly about the North of England, never meeting its enemy.

"the cry of all here, great and small, is for all our forces coming home, and who dares resist the torrent when every man seems to think the king's person and crown in eminent danger?"[112] The cry was echoed in the Cabinet, which resolved that six battallions of foot and nine squadrons of dragoons should be sent over from Flanders as soon as possible, though Stair and Tweeddale opposed the resolution. Henry Pelham privately expostulated "that Winchilsea, Tweeddale, Stair, Bolton under Granville's influence were the wickedest of men to flatter the king with false security."[113] Harrington, who had previously been inclined to go along with the king to the extent that on 17 September George actually offered him the prime ministership if he would break with the Pelhams, now agreed that "things grow very serious, and...all other considerations must give way to that of the preservation of this country, which I really think is now in the most imminent danger. The most effectual means of providing for our security seem to me...the sending immediately for all the troops we can get from Flanders."[114]

George II was apparently coming to the same conclusion. The day after the Cabinet met Lord Perceval noted in his diary: "The king begins to be alarmed. This morning consented to the resolution of the Council to call over more troops."[115] Indeed he seems to have gone even further than the majority of the Cabinet, for he instructed Cumberland to send eight battalions of foot immediately to Newcastle upon Tyne, and to hold the dragoons in readiness for embarkation. This was followed on 1 October with orders to send over all the British foot remaining in the Duke's army. When Pitt moved in the Commons that all British forces should be recalled, therefore, only the cavalry remained to be summoned, and even they were ordered over in November.

Although the king was alarmed, he did not panic. Arthur Onslow, the Speaker of the House of Commons, saw him at Kensington on 26 September, at his first public audience since the arrival of the news of the battle of Prestonpans. Onslow found that "he looked as became him on the occasion, with a composedness that showed attention to what had happened, but void of the least appearance of fear or dejection, and just with cheerfulness enough to give spirit to others. I never saw him I think show so much of true greatness as he did then."[116] George could even indulge in an ironic joke: seeing Lord Hay at his levée, and recalling that his Lordship had assured him before the battle that the rebels would disperse if a magistrate read the Riot Act, he said "Well, Lord Hays, I think you had best go down and read the proclamation to the rebels."[117]

Instead of sending down Lord Hay the king sent Marshal Wade north to deal with the rebels, and with him the Dutch and four British regiments which General Wentworth had been preparing to march to Lancashire. Two battalions from Ireland were ordered to join them, and this was expected to make the army up to 10,000 men. Wade instructed these forces to rendezvous at Doncaster, whence he was to "proceed to Scotland or into Lancashire as the motions of the rebels shall make it necessary". On learning of his appointment to head an army against the rebels "a certain countess, remarkable for her wit" was reported to have said that "since we could not COPE with our present difficulties, we must WADE through them".[118] Wade was seventy-two, and had relinquished a command in Flanders because of his poor health. Yet though he was ill on the road, Lord Malton found him in good health and spirits when he reached Doncaster, reporting that he ate some venison, "which he commended and said it was the only fresh meat he had tasted of some days. It agreed well with him."[119]

At Doncaster Wade decided to continue to Newcastle, since the rebels remained in Edinburgh. By the time he got there on 29 October the forces from the continent had already arrived, under Lord Albermarle. Albermarle reckoned that the only way to deal with the rebels was "to march up to them, to drive them before us and to shew them no mercy".[120] Wade agreed, and proposed marching immediately northwards. He warned that progress might be slow in view of the exhaustion of his troops after their long march to the Tyne, not to mention his own condition, his "age and infirmities" now beginning to take their toll, making him incapable of even writing with his own hand.[121]

As he was on the road from Newcastle to Morpeth on 3 November, however, he received intelligence that the rebels had left Edinburgh and were heading south. He therefore countermanded the orders to march to Berwick, and returned to Newcastle. There he held a Council of War on 6 November, where "two different plans were proposed: the one to move towards the rebels; the other to receive them in our present camp."[122] The second plan was adopted, since "it would take time to make the roads practicable for the march and that the difficulty of carrying provisions forwards was great; and the designs of the rebels not certainly known".

They had in fact designed to march down into Cumberland, but by a cunning disposition of their forces kept Wade guessing that they might be making for Newcastle. On 8 November the Young Pretender crossed the Esk. The rebellion had been brought onto English soil.

CHAPTER FOUR

"*Flushed with success these lawless vagrants come*"

Flushed with success these lawless vagrants come
From France their maxims, and their Gods from Rome,
Ruffians, who fight not in fair Honour's cause,
For injur'd Rights, or violated Laws;
But, like the savage race, they roam for prey,
And where they pass Destruction makes their way.

O! Thou who dost o'er human Arts preside,
If Britain is thy care, be William's Guide;
The noble youth, whom ev'ry eye approves,
Each tongue applauds, and ev'ry soldier loves;
In the dire conflict may thy Pow'r afford
Strength to his arm, and vict'ry to his sword;
On Freedom's basis may he fix the Throne,
And add new Lustre to his Father's Crown.

New Prologue to The Beggar's Opera, *City subscription production,*
December 1745

The sense of security into which England had been lulled by the Young Pretender's sojourn in Edinburgh after the battle of Prestonpans was soon dispelled by the news that he was heading south. Fears that he might make his way down the west side of the country, thereby avoiding Wade, led the king to send most of the troops left behind by the Marshal, including some of the new regiments, towards Chester under Sir John Ligonier. His instructions were to arrest the progress of the rebels, either to the south of England or to North Wales, preferably by establishing control of the river Mersey, but "in all events to stop them between the Trent and the Severn near Shrewsbury".[1] They had scarcely been issued before news arrived that the rebels had indeed crossed the border some sixty miles west of Wade's army.

The first obstacle in their path was Carlisle.[2] At the outbreak of the rebellion both town and castle had been in no state to defend themselves. The governor was absent, the garrison consisted of at most eighty veteran invalids, and the walls were in a sad state of repair. Since the news of the Young Pretender's landing, however, something had been done to put them in a better posture of defence. The inhabitants mustered the town militia, and nine additional companies which the government authorised them to raise. They even paid and maintained about forty soldiers who fled there from Prestonpans. Lieutenant Colonel James Durand was sent down to take command in the absence of the governor. When he arrived on 11 October he estimated that 570 men had been mobilised, which in his opinion was not sufficient. He therefore prevailed upon Lord Lonsdale, the lord lieutenant of both Cumberland and Westmorland, to instruct the militias of those counties to enter the town. Durand also did what he could to repair the walls and other fortifications before the rebels arrived.

When an advance party of the rebel army arrived on 9 November it demanded quarters for 13,000 foot and 3,000 cavalry, threatening to burn the town down if they were not provided. The defiant answer was to fire cannon at them, whereupon they retreated. Next day a larger body appeared before Carlisle with a letter from the Young Pretender promising protection to all if he were admitted, but if not "he could not be answerable for the consequences that must attend the entering the town by force". Once more the garrison replied with cannon fire, "but if any execution was done it must have been by chance, for there was such a thick fog all the time that they could not see 100 yards over the walls".[3] Again the rebels retreated, to the surprise of the inhabitants, who concluded that their defiance was responsible for the withdrawal. The deputy mayor actually sent a letter to London, which was printed in the newspapers, boasting that Carlisle had "done his Majesty more service than the great City of Edinburgh or than all Scotland together."[4]

The rebels had not, however, withdrawn because of the resistance they had encountered, but upon receiving a report that Wade was marching to meet them. Durand, too, hoped that relief was coming from that quarter, and on 9 November had sent a letter to Newcastle requesting help. When the rebels ascertained that Wade was not in fact coming, they returned to the siege on the 13th. The same day Durand received a letter from the Marshal to the effect that he intended to intercept the rebels not at Carlisle but in Lancashire, since the only route to the west passable for his artillery lay through Yorkshire. This reply totally dispirited the militia, whose morale had already been lowered by what they considered to be arduous watches beyond the call of duty, since their month's tour

79

was already up, to defend a town which showed no gratitude for their presence. On the contrary, although "some were 8 some 7 and all 6 nights and days under arms upon the walls, they would not even allow straw for the poor men to lay upon."[5] Several of them began to desert over the walls. When their officers met on the 14th, therefore, to take stock of the situation, by a vote of eighteen to three they resolved to capitulate, despite Durand's pleading with them that the rebels could not possibly take the town if they held firm. As they explained to Lord Lonsdale[6]

> The hopes of being relieved by Marshal Wade made our men exert themselves and hold out longer than was required or could be expected from them, and for the last seven days neither the officers nor men had scarce an hour's rest being perpetually alarmed by the rebels and many of them being so sick by this great fatigue, and at last being out of all hopes of relief from his Majesty's forces, absolutely refused to hold out any longer.

The deputy mayor then assembled the corporation in the town hall to decide how to react to the decision taken by the militia officers. They decided by twenty-four votes to fiteen to capitulate. Although he was much scorned for his boastful letter when this decision became widely known, the deputy mayor to his credit voted with the minority.

Leaving the town to surrender, Durand joined the invalid garrison in the castle with about 400 of the militia, determined to hold out until relief arrived. But, although Wade at last set out from Newcastle to go to Carlisle's aid on 16 November, it was too late. The day before he left the castle surrendered too. Overnight the nerve of the militiamen had failed, and on the 15th they abandoned their posts. Durand, deserted by nearly all except the invalids, then learned that the rebels threatened to destroy the town if he did not give up the castle. He thereupon summoned a Council of War, which decided that "the castle being not tenable, it is for his Majesty's service that it be abandoned, as it will be absolutely necessary for the preservation of the lives of his Majesty's subjects, who would otherwise be exposed to inevitable ruin."

The militia, the deputy mayor and corporation, and even Durand, were much criticised for surrendering Carlisle to the rebels. There were not wanting accusations at the time that treachery was afoot, and allegations of Jacobite sympathies among some of the defenders of the town have been echoed by historians. The mutual recriminations between those involved did not help to dispel suspicion. Yet for all their shortcomings, their protestations of loyalty to the regime need not be discounted; for there can be little doubt that the town would have held out longer, had Wade given grounds for hope rather than despair about the prospects of relief.

When he reached Hexham on 17 November Wade learned of the "very scandalous and shameful, if not treacherous" surrender. A Council of War decided on the 19th to return to Newcastle, for several reasons. Even if they should get across to Carlisle they could not take artillery heavy enough to retake it, because of the bad condition of the roads. Pursuit of the rebels, either back to Scotland or down into England, would be hampered by their destruction of supplies behind them. Wade was having grave difficulties supplying his men anyway. A heavy snowfall and severe frost were hindering transport, so that there was not even enough straw for the men to sleep on, and in their first camp at Bywell, "many of the soldiers were obliged to lye on the ground tho' covered with snow".[7] Some actually froze to death. Others "could get nothing to eat after marching 13 hours", and when they reached Hexham next day there was no food provided there either. Brigadier Cholmondley was so appalled by their distress that each morning he filled his pockets with sixpences to give the men.[8] As the news of the situation travelled south it aroused the greatest consternation. The vicar of Hitchin was disturbed to learn that "both men and horses suffer beyond expression. They are pinched by cold and have neither money nor victuals nor comfortable drink to support and cheer their spirits. They are always fatigued and empty bellied. Yet these are the men on whose strength and well being all that is dear to us depends."[9] Though conditions clearly were terrible, Wade, who confessed that he "never saw more distress than what the officers and soldiers suffer at this time", cannot be altogether absolved from responsibility for the calamitous deficiencies of supply. General Lord Tyrawley complained that[10]

> there was not bread provided to go one mile further than Hexham.
> ...when we should have had at least ten days bread to have gone
> to Carlisle and have subsisted there, till more could be got. In
> every march that we make we labour under the same incon-
> venience. Bread, carriages, straw, firing and even coals for our men
> I have known wanting...All this for want of common forecast
> and a parsimony ill judged for the publick, that he cannot lay out
> half a crown tho ever so necessary...

Nor did the severe weather seem to hamper the movements of the rebel army, despite General Wentworth's speculation that "as the rebels are flesh and blood as well as us (tho perhaps something more inured to hardship) I take it for granted they must, while this bad season lasts, suspend all operations."[11] In fact they marched expeditiously south. On 21 November they were reported from Penrith to be "swarming in here all this day like bees".[12] By the 24th their whole army was at Kendal, where they proclaimed the Pretender king before setting out for Lancaster next day.

Meanwhile the army under Sir John Ligonier had only managed to advance as far as Lichfield. Ligonier himself had fallen gravely ill since appointed to its command, and the duke of Richmond had temporarily taken over. When his recovery was delayed Sir John himself suggested that General Hawley should be brought over from Flanders to replace him. Instead, on 21 November the king appointed his son, the duke of Cumberland, to the command. His appointment was extremely popular. Although the twenty-four year old duke had only commanded for one campaign, in the course of which he had actually been defeated at Fontenoy, his reputation as a general ran high. He had somehow managed to turn the military setback into a personal triumph. After the rebellion began his return to head an army against the rebels was widely demanded. When Sir John Ligonier returned to England in September he noted that "the people all roar for the duke", and he had joined in the cry.[13] Cumberland himself was very eager to answer their call, begging Lord Harrington to use his "utmost interest that his Majesty may permit me to return to England where there is now the greatest prospect of my being able to render him service," whereas "it would be the last mortification to me when so much is at stake at home, and brought to the decision of arms, to be out of the way of doing my duty."[14] He could not leave the continent until the allied army went into winter quarters, which in turn was dependent upon the French going into theirs, but at the earliest opportunity he returned to England, arriving there on 19 October. His father had given him a prominent role in the mobilisation of Ligonier's army, and now he had been put in charge of it. This step immediately boosted the morale of the troops. "It is certain that the army adore the Duke," Horace Walpole observed upon his departure from London, while it was reported in Lichfield that "all the soldiers leaped and skipped about like wild things that the Duke was to command them"[15] "He no sooner appeared among them," wrote his first biographer "than the hills and valleys repeated their huzzas; his heroic and unaffected mein, his easy greatness and martial countenance, revived them, and raised in them a confidence of victory."[16]

When Cumberland arrived at Lichfield on 27 November the rebels were already at Preston. They even marched south of the town and back again to dispel the superstition that they would get no further than they had done in the Fifteen. This conceit had inspired a Yorkshire vicar to coin the dreadful pun that "tho' they succeeded at Preston Pans they may perhaps go to Pot at Preston in Lancashire", albeit he did excuse it by adding "this is a joke in the taste of Cope and Wade".[17]

In fact the only potential obstacle to the rebel army in Lancashire was the militia, which the Privy Council on 26 September ordered to be put in a state of readiness for immediate service. There had been a subscription in the county, but this had not, as elsewhere, been spent on troops and companies. The organisers had wanted regular officers to command troops raised by it, and had even requested uniforms from the government. The duke of Newcastle had pointed out that neither could be supplied, and suggested that the money raised should be spent on paying recruits to join the regular army.

In the event nothing was done. Even mustering the militia caused problems, as they were still owed a month's pay since the Revolution, and could therefore claim legal exemption from liability to serve. It was not until 14 November that an Act was passed to rectify this and enable the early of Derby, their lord lieutenant, to muster them. Meanwhile Henry Pelham expressed the hope that Derby would raise militiamen anyway, as though the Act was already on the Statute book. The lord lieutenant was somewhat chagrined at this, complaining to Sir Henry Hoghton: "if I remember his words aright he only says he hoped we shall not scruple doing it for our defence. Why then do they scruple ordering us to do it, as they know that in strictness without such an order it cannot be done?"[18] Despite these legal niceties he and Hoghton managed to muster the militia, though when it assembled it was so raw and ill-equipped they decided that, while it might be suitable for suppressing local insurrections, it could not offer even token resistance to the rebel army. Derby scorned Wade's advice that they might harass the rebels by sniping at them from behind hedges, which he thought would "be to little purpose, and sure destruction to the undertakers".[19] When the Young Pretender marched into Lancashire, therefore, the militia was moved out of his way to Liverpool. There it was disarmed, the arms being stored on board ships to prevent them falling into enemy hands, and dismissed. Hoghton made his way to Hull, while Derby fled to London, which he called "the common asylum of the nation".[20]

There was some truth in Lord Derby's observation, at least as far as the social elite was concerned. The aristocracy and gentry fled in such numbers before the rebels that they caused morale to fall, and even left a vacuum of leadership in some parts of the country. A defence of the militia's behaviour at Carlisle claimed that "from their own country and neighbours, no assistance could be hoped for, for all the Gentlemen, all the substantial inhabitants, both of Town and Country, had secured their effects and fled for safety."[21] The earl of Cholmondley thought that "the pannick of the people" was caught "from others of higher rank, having observed, that, ever since they (the rebels) left Scotland, that in the several counties they have passed through, those who have called themselves the king's friends have been the first to fly, and have by that means spread terror and apprehensions in all parts."[22] This was no less true of his own command in Chester. A Cambridge tutor, commenting on a letter he had received from a student who had enlisted with Lord Gower's regiment and was stationed there, wrote "I cannot wonder to hear you have no time for books. Mars has no fellowship with the Muses: nor I find with Venus according to the account you give me, for the ladies as well as learning are fled from Chester."[23] Similarly leading Yorkshire families "sent all their females to London for safety."[24]

On 28 November the duke of Cumberland took stock of the situation which faced him in his new command. His infantry was in a line from Tamworth to Stafford, while the cavalry was between Lichfield and Newcastle under Lyme. As there were still some forces en route to join him he decided to stay put until they arrived, and asked Wade meanwhile to send his cavalry forward to harass the enemy until "either your whole force could come up or this army move forward".[25] Seeing that Wade had only moved forty miles from Newcastle to Piercebridge, the duke was being unduly optimistic in thinking that they could trap the rebels in a pincer movement between their two armies. Indeed the Marshal's behaviour was beginning to arouse critical comment. Before his army left Newcastle upon Tyne one of his own officers complained to the duke of Newcastle that "the Marshall is infirm and peevish...both in body and mind, forgetful, irresolute and perplext, snappish and positive sometime at the expence of good breeding."[26] A Council of War unanimously agreed to march south in three equal divisions, so that they could more readily find indoor accommodation and shelter from the severe weather. Yet Wade overruled them, and on 26 November they marched in a body, prepared to camp at night; "so that I suppose by the time we get to Wetherby," remarked Tyrawley, "we shall have no army, for there is not the least care taken to provide either straw, forage or meat to be killed for our men." Wade was making for Wetherby so that he could take his artillery to Lancashire through Leeds, Halifax, Rochdale and Manchester. When he got to Ripon on 30 November, however, the rebels had already reached Manchester themselves.

Their rapid progress through Lancashire made the duke of Cumberland apprehensive about the safety of Chester, fearing that they might make their way there en route for North Wales. The town and castle of Chester, and the county Palatine of Cheshire, were little better prepared for an invasion than Carlisle and the counties of Cumberland, Westmorland and Lancashire had been. The third earl of Cholmondley, who was both governor of the castle and lord lieutenant of the county, had gone there from London at the end of September to supervise the military preparations in both. During October the government decided to give him a commission to raise a new regiment rather than muster the militia, which pleased Cholmondley, who thought it out of the question to call out the latter "as the rolls are lost and no arms to be found".[27] By early November he had raised nearly 600 men, and was himself satisfied that the great effort put into repairing the walls and fortifications for the town and castle made them defensible for a few days, provided that the rebels brought no artillery with them. When Brigadier General Douglas arrived on the 17th to supervise these preparations, however, he sent back a very critical report to the duke of Cumberland:[28]

> with the tools we have to work with I pronounce the place quite
> defenceless. The ramparts, walls I should call 'em, are commanded
> in many places by the best houses in the suburbs and are to be got
> over by several others. The castle is a very weak place, and tho'
> it has some guns, not a gunner that can point one. The regiment
> here a parcel of ragged youths and some old men. The first of 'em
> have got arms but on Wednesday last, and the last of 'em Saturday,
> so as they don't know the use of 'em. I am thoroughly convinced
> if an enemy should appear they would throw them away.

Although Lord Gower's new regiment had been ordered to join Cholmondley's, Douglas was no more impressed by its military capability. Fortunately for Cumberland's peace of mind he had already sent 220 regular troops to Chester under Lieutenant Colonel Cornwallis, even commandeering horses to get them there as quickly as possible.[29] He thought that their arrival would put Chester out of danger of an immediate capitulation, and enable it to hold out until he could get there. They were certainly made very welcome, being met a mile from the town by a torchlight procession some 1,000 strong, having had free entertainment at every town they passed through on their way.

The route the rebels would take if they did advance to Chester, either from Wigan or Manchester, would be across the Mersey at Warrington or Crossford bridges.[30] At first Cholmondley was ordered to hold these bridges until Ligonier's army could relieve him. When it became obvious that the rebels could be there before the regular army, he was commanded to render them unpassable, a task which he performed with the help of a company raised in Liverpool.

The apparent concern of the rebels to repair Crossford bridge at Stretford misled Cumberland into thinking that they were heading for Wales. In fact they intended to proceed to Derby, and marched to Macclesfield on 1 December. Even there they managed to deceive the duke as to their intentions, for while the Young Pretender went straight to Leek, Lord George Murray diverted to Congleton, apparently making still for Wales, and then deftly rejoined his commander at Leek on 3

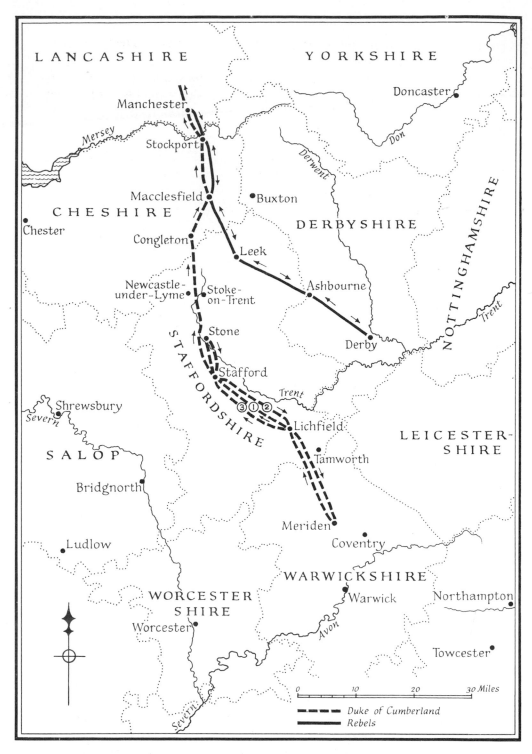

The movements of Cumberland's army and of the rebels in the Midlands,
November to December 1745

86

December. The reunited rebel army then marched towards Derby, arriving there on the 4th.

These manoeuvres forced Cumberland to keep his army ready either to follow them into Wales or to intercept them in the Midlands. As Sir John Ligonier explained on 28 November, when he was at Lichfield with the duke,[31]

> our situation in regard to forbidding them Wales and Derbyshire is very difficult because from Stockport to 8 to 10 miles on this side of Macclesfield is a ridge of impracticable hills called Bow hills which separate this part from Derbyshire. On the other side of the mountain is the great road from Lancashire by Buxton to Derby. If we move up to the Mersey, they may behind that mountain march into Derbyshire; if we remain here in order to prevent that I fear they may get into Wales.

Cumberland decided to move forward, hoping that the breaking up of the turnpike between Buxton and Derby, which the duke of Devonshire undertook, would slow down the rebel advance if they tried to elude him by heading towards Derby. By the 29th his cavalry was dispersed in billets from Stone to Stoke on Trent, and his infantry from Stafford to Warwick. Such scattered billeting had its inconveniences, but without it Cumberland was convinced that "half the battalions would have been at the hospital already".[32] He was roughing it himself, not sleeping in a bed but "upon straw in his clothes".[33] On 1 December some of the cavalry was moved to Congleton, where they encountered Lord George Murray's men and retreated, while part of the infantry advanced to Stone, and actually pitched on a battlefield there on 2 December. The same day the duke of Richmond informed Cumberland of "a fine champ-de-bataille" near Newcastle under Lyme, being convinced that the rebels were either marching to meet the royal forces or else making for Wales: "as for the Derby road, I think they have quitted that by coming to Congleton."[34] Sir Everard Fawkener, forwarding this information to London from Stafford later that day, admitted that "to this hour we can't judge with any certainty whether they really intend to try to slip by us into Derbyshire or to march to Wales through Cheshire."[35]   He continued

> It is a very difficult point to secure both the passes, for if by staying at Lichfield His Royal Highness had resolved to provide against their reaching Derby, he must have left them at liberty to have got into Wales without any difficulty or opposition, which it is hoped cannot now be done...if the motion Westward was a feint, then indeed we shall by our advancing be less in reach of keeping them out of Derbyshire.

The king was worried that it was a feint. "His Majesty is persuaded your Royal Highness will not depend upon the roads in Derbyshire or any others being rendered impracticable or impassable for Highlanders," the duke of Newcastle warned Cumberland, "but will make it your first object to prevent the rebels getting between you and London."[36] George was right to be concerned, for the rebels did indeed gain a day's march between Cumberland and the capital by getting to Derby on 4 December. The duke was made aware of this after waiting in vain for their arrival on his battlefield at Stone in the early hours of the 3rd. "Had the troops been as able as they seemed to be willing I should have marched directly for Derby," he told Newcastle[37]

> but troops that had scarcely halted six hours these ten days, had been without victuals for twenty four hours, and had been exposed to the coldest nights I ever felt without any shelter, for the country produced not straw sufficient for two battalions, were not able to march without halt or provisions.

He therefore resolved to stay at Stone overnight, and then to move to Northampton. His march route shows that he hoped to get the cavalry there on the 6th and 7th, and the infantry between the 8th and the 10th which led him to hope that he would after all intercept the rebels before they got to London.[38] The duke of Richmond, however, was not so sanguine. "I don't see why they should not be at Northampton as soon as us, as they are certainly at Derby tonight," he wrote on 4 December, while next day he was "apprehensive they may get to London before us".[39] Even Cumberland faced that possibility, advising Newcastle "that if, without alarming the City, the infantry that is about London could be assembled on Finchley common, it would prevent any little part of them who might give me the slip (for I am persuaded the greater part can't) from giving any alarm there."[40]

Nothing could prevent the news that the rebels were at Derby from alarming London. Londoners had become more and more despondent as the rebels approached. "There never was so melancholy a town," Horace Walpole observed on 29 November. "No kind of public place, but the playhouses, and they look as if the rebels had just driven away their company."[41] "Coffee houses in Town are now like Quakers' meeting houses," commented another resident about the same time.[42] "This profound silence cannot proceed but from the two great passions, Hope and Fear, which may be read in every man's face." The reaction to the report that the rebels were a day's march nearer to them than Cumberland's army, when everybody had expected the duke to stave off their approach, revealed that the vast majority lived in fear rather than hope.[43] The simultaneous rumour that the French were launching an invasion added to the alarm. These threw the capital into a state of panic and even terror. "We have been in a monstrous fright here" Lady Malton admitted to her husband when it was all over.[44] Those who had been fed on stories of rebel atrocities by government supporters would be particularly terrified. According to O'Sullivan, the Young Pretender's companion in arms, the government "sent emissarys all over England and spread the most abominable things of the highlanders that could be imagined, that they murdered, ravished, burnt, and destroyed all that came in their way."[45] John Tucker, a whig MP who was taken in by such stories of atrocities committed by the rebels, wrote to his brother that they[46]

> commit all manner of disorders and violence wherever they go. A burger of Carlisle writes to a correspondent not to forward a parcel of goods he had ordered for as he expects to have it plundered from him, his whole house having been lately strip'd by the highlanders and his daughter ravished by two of them before his face. This kind of behaviour must exasperate the country prodigiously against them, and when they come to be dispersed... they must expect to be massacred wherever they are found.

In fact the rebel army committed no outrages on its way through England, and even the *London Gazette* grudgingly admitted later, when their retreat had begun, that "the rebels behaved tolerably well in their march southwards".[47] This did not stop Henry Fielding contributing a nightmarish vision to *The True Patriot* on 19 November in which he imagined what would happen if London were to be occupied by the Highland host. He predicted that his own fate for writing such loyal essays would be to have a rebel, clad in tartan, drag him from his home and family through streets full of bodies and rubble to Smithfield, scene of Mary Tudor's execution of Protestants. He would be tried by a judge who spoke broken English, and sentenced to death with hosts of others. If Londoners had reacted to horror stories of this kind by being petrified into surrender, then the government propagandists would have been hoist on their own petard.

Yet too much can be made of the scare which led Horace Walpole to call 6 December 'Black Friday'. Certainly too much was made by the Jacobite Chevalier de Johnstone, who claimed that "King George ordered his yachts, in which he had embarked all his most precious effects, to remain at the Tower Quay, in readiness to sail at a moment's warning. I was assured on good authority, when I was in London some time after our unfortunate defeat," he confidently continued "that the Duke of Newcastle then Secretary of State for the War-department, remained inaccessible in his own house the whole of the 6th of December, weighing in his mind the part which it would be most prudent for him to take, and even uncertain whether he should not instantly declare himself for the Pretender."[48] This tells us more about the Jacobite capacity for self-delusion than it does of the government's reaction, for the story is the purest fantasy. Newcastle in fact spent the day in his office, executing the king's instructions for the defence of the City. He wrote to the lord mayor to augment the city guard, and to ensure that the trained bands were constantly marshalled to preserve order. He also informed Cumberland that "a camp had been marked out between Highgate and Whetstone" to accommodate regiments sent to Finchley to defend the northern approaches to the capital.[49] Meanwhile the king, far from packing to leave, announced his intention of going on the 9th to Finchley to raise his standard at the head of the troops. This decision was so public that "the weavers not only offered him a thousand men, but the whole body of the law formed themselves into a little army under the command of Lord Justice Willes, and were to have done duty at St. James, to guard the royal family in the king's absence."[50] These preparations invalidate even O'Sullivan's rather more restrained version of royal intentions, to wit "that the Duke of Hanover had given orders to have everything ready for the departure of his family". On the other hand O'Sullivan's account of the king's reply to those who wished him to leave the country rings true, especially coming from a Jacobite: "he intended to remain and die King of England."[51]

"But the greatest demonstration of loyalty," observed Horace Walpole, having noted the response of the weavers and the lawyers, "appeared on the prisoners being brought to town from the *Soleil*", a French ship taken by the navy on its way to Scotland.[52] One of them was thought to be the Pretender's younger son, though in fact his father was Lord Derwentwater. The mob gave him a rough reception even though his reputed brother was reported to be almost at the City gates. He was "so frightened" that he told his guard "he had heard much of an English mob, and now he saw 'em, he heartily wished he was in the Tower. When they came near the Tower the mob swore...the Dogs of Invaders should be tore to pieces before the gate was open."[53] One who lived through 'Black Friday' in London claimed only four weeks later that the Young Pretender's army "might have been eaten up here, where nine men in ten were resolved to expose themselves to all hazards in opposition to him."[54]

In the event the hastily contrived panic measure depicted by Hogarth in his *March to Finchley* proved to be an unnecessary precaution, for the rebels decided on 6 December to retreat from Derby back to Scotland. There were two basic reasons behind this decision: the lack of support which they had received since entering England; and the formidable strength of the forces arrayed against them.

"There have been many reasons assigned for their making this sudden retreat," wrote James Ray, a contemporary chronicler of the rebellion.[55] "I take to be the true cause, the disappointment they had met with in the augmentation of their forces; for they flattered themselves with a great insurrection in England in their favour." Without assurances of a rising in their favour, agreed Lord Fitzwilliam, "their march south of Tweed is the rashest project that was ever put in execution, and what none but madmen or fools would have ever thought of."[56] In the event, however, very few men actually joined the rebel army as it made its way down from Carlisle to Derby. According to Horace Walpole they "got no recruits since their first entry into England, except one gentleman in Lancashire, one hundred and fifty common men, and two parsons at Manchester, and a physician from York."[57] There were various estimates of how many men were recruited in Manchester. Lord Malton's was lower than Walpole's "viz. about 100 mob and 4 or 5 half gentry".[58] The Jacobites of course boasted several hundreds. Probably about 200 joined them there, which hardly made up for the garrison left behind in Carlisle.

It has been claimed that mere numbers were no guide to the true extent of support for the Young Pretender, and that had he been manifestly supported by France, which only a French invasion on his behalf could have demonstrated, then thousands would have flocked to him. The fact that there was no invasion makes it hard to test this claim, but it is significant that those who urged a retreat from Derby did not just argue that few had joined them. As Lord George Murray pointed out to Charles Edward, "if there was any party in England for him, it was very odd that they had never so much as either sent him money or intelligence or the least advice what to do."[59] The Young Pretender had tried to get in touch with his alleged supporters in England, even if they had not contacted him. He sent a message to Lord Barrymore, informing him "we are now coming on and I hope our friends will joyne us as we find nobody opposes: Now is the time or never or Adieu to all."[60] The fate of this message speaks for the true extent of Jacobitism in England more than all the volumes of the Pretender's papers. Barrymore was in fact in London, attending what Charles Edward condemned as a "pretended parliament", despite his proclamation against such attendance. His son Lord Buttevant was at the family seat in Shropshire when the message arrived. He immediately threw it into the fire, and proceeded to hand over the messenger to the law. The answer of the English Jacobites to the Young Pretender's appeal was plainly "never". As James Ray said of them, "no people in the universe know better the difference between drinking and fighting."[61]

On the military side numbers did count. The rebels had at most 5,000 men in arms at Derby on 6 December. Against this Cumberland had at least 9,000 in his army, of which the artillery, cavalry and two foot regiments were already at Coventry, while the rest of the infantry were nearby on Meriden common that day. He had got them there by dint of marching them twenty miles a day, despite terrain so difficult that the duke of Richmond tartly commented "I dare swear thousands in London now sit upon their arses, and say, why does not the duke march up to them? And if it was all Hounslow heath between us, it would be a shame if he did not. But it (is) not to be conceived what a cursed country this is for marching."[62] Cumberland was confident that "by this movement we have gained a march on the rebels, and had it in our power to be between them and London."[63] His opinion was shared by General Cuthbert Ellison, who wrote from Coventry on 7 December that "the long and forced marches we made from Stafford to this town with our cavalry and followed close by our infantry had rendered that design of theirs [the rebels] abortive", i.e. to slip between the duke and London.[64] Even if they could still have done it, there were over 4,000 regular troops either at or approaching Finchley, while behind them there were the city trained bands, several thousands strong. Wade's army had 779 cavalry and 5425 infantry "fit for duty".[65] "Had it been possible for him to have marched in six days what we have in three," protested Sir John Ligonier "I think there would not be such a thing as a rebel army existing at this hour."[66] Fortunately for the rebels Wade was no nearer than Wetherby. But for them to have gone on further towards London would have been suicidal. As Lord Malton put it "they are now so near two much superior armies that their destruction seems inevitable."[67]

If they could get back to Scotland, however, there was at least a fair prospect of keeping the rebellion alive. Although the government had reasserted its authority in Edinburgh since they left, the arrival of reinforcements from France at Montrose had revived their cause elsewhere.

Even before the rebel army left Scotland there had been some consolidation of the government's position there. The garrisons of Edinburgh and Stirling castles held out against all attempts to overcome them, while the earl of Loudoun and Lord President Forbes had established a strategic base in Inverness. By the end of November they had taken 1,500 Highlanders into pay, and planned to use them to regain control of the Great Glen, and to obstruct recruitment for the rebels in the Highlands. Other parts of Scotland remote from the capital also raised men for the king. By the time the Young Pretender marched south there were three companies in Argyllshire under Major General John Campbell, and two on the Isle of Skye under Sir Alexander MacDonald. As soon as Marshal Wade learned that the rebels had left Edinburgh, he arranged to send General Handasyde there with two infantry and two cavalry regiments to protect the civil authorities, who returned to the Scottish capital within days of the Young Pretender's departure. Handasyde set out from Berwick on 12 November and arrived in Edinburgh on the 14th, despite the severe weather, which killed several men on the march. Newcastle hoped that all these forces would be sufficient to suppress any fresh levies that were being raised for the Pretender in Scotland.[68]

Then on 1 December Handasyde wrote to inform him that 800 men had landed at Montrose, Stonehaven and Peterhead. He estimated that these reinforcements made the rebels left behind in Scotland about 3,000 strong.[69] They had in fact arrived from France under the command of Lord John Drummond on 22 November, and had even taken a royal sloop, the *Hazard*, in Montrose harbour. It was the news of their arrival, and exaggerated reports that they numbered 4,000, which persuaded their colleagues in Derby that the game was far from lost if they went back to Scotland.[70]

As soon as he knew that the rebel army was retreating Cumberland sent an express to Wade to march across to Lancashire in order to block their retreat, stressing that if he could not get there before them "these villains may escape back unpunished to our eternal shame".[71] Wade got the message on 8 December, when he was at Doncaster with his cavalry, while his infantry were at Ferrybridge. He replied that he would march west to Rochdale or to Manchester to intercept the enemy, but gave the duke little hope of his being able to prevent their retreat to Scotland. By 10 December he had got no further than Wakefield, where he held a Council of War which concluded that, since the rebels were reported to have been at Manchester the day before, there was no way in which they could catch up with them. It was therefore decided to march the main body of the army back to Newcastle, though a detachment of about 500 cavalry was sent across the Pennines under General Oglethorpe, to follow and harass the enemy.[72]

Meanwhile the duke of Cumberland set out in hot pursuit with all his cavalry, and 1,000 volunteers who were provided with horses by local people. "Our foot soldiers not being accustomed to riding," observed James Ray, who went with the duke, "I thought they looked odd on horseback with their muskets and knapsacks flung over their shoulders, but their desire to come up with the rebels was visible in every one of their countenances with so much pleasure they rode along, and the countrymen with fresh horses, coming to remount our soldiers, running themselves on foot very cheerfully, that it really afforded a most pleasing prospect."[73] By 9 December they were at Lichfield, having covered thirty miles that day. Even so the rebels were retreating at such a rate that Cumberland despaired of catching up with them, though he was determined "to pursue with this flying corps till I shall lose every glimpse of hopes of a possibility of overtaking them".[74]

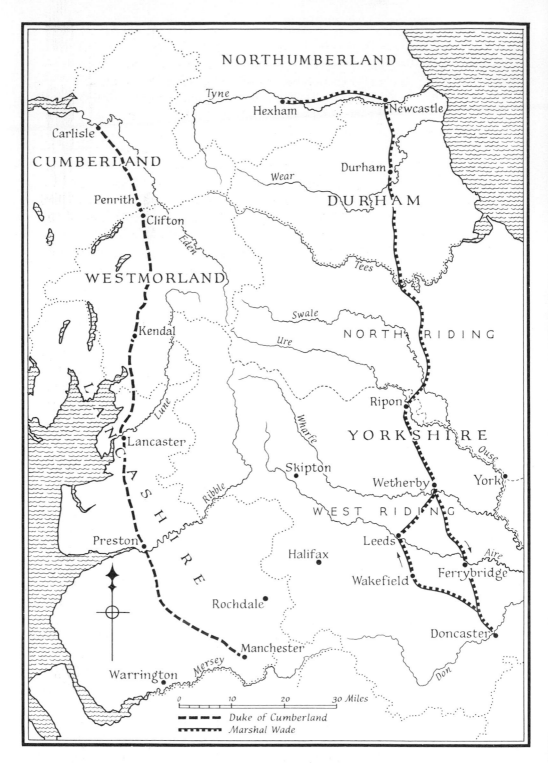

Routes of the royal armies in northern England, November to December 1745

94

Sir John Ligonier was left in charge of the infantry, which returned to camp at Coleshill and Meriden common. They were so worn out by their marches and counter-marches in the dead of winter that, although they displayed "a most surprising cheerfulness and health", Cumberland was concerned that they could not hold out much longer without rest and recuperation. He also thought they needed fresh shoes and stockings, which he asked the king to supply.[75] In fact the men were about to be equipped with considerably more than new footwear. A body of citizens started a subscription at the Guildhall which raised £10,000 by 10 December and ultimately reached £18,910.[76] The Prince of Wales subscribed £500, and the actor John Rich gave his £600 benefit for acting in *The Beggar's Opera* for three nights. The fund was specifically to provide comforts for the soldiers. The subscribers appointed a committee under the Lord Mayor to administer it, and by 3 December this had contracted for 4,500 pailliasses, 810 watch coats, and 1,200 pairs of blankets.[77] Samuel Smith, one of the committee, wrote to Sir Everard Fawkener to inform him that they were also arranging to send shoes, stockings and gloves, and to ask him if spirituous liquors or woollen caps would be acceptable to the men. Sir Everard replied that "they meet good malt drink here which is better than spirituous liquors".[78] The committee, therefore, contracted for 10,000 woollen caps instead, as well as 16,500 pairs of woollen gloves and 9,000 pairs of woollen ankle spatterdashes. They did not order any shoes after all since the king had agreed to Cumberland's request for these.

By 11 December the duke himself was at Macclesfield with the cavalry, "having marched from Lichfield hither in two days which is fifty measured miles and over a most dreadful country."[79] The rebels, for whom nobody was knitting caps or gloves, were finding the going hard too. It was said that many of them were in such "bad condition that they may be followed by their blood".[80] Those unable to keep up with the main body, and who fell into Cumberland's hands, were sent to jail, because, as he explained to Newcastle, "as they have so many of our prisoners in their hands I did not care to put them to death. But," he continued grimly, "I have encouraged the country people to do it as they may fall into their way."[81] Those brutal words ominously portend his reputation as a butcher. It is significant that he apparently felt no qualms about communicating them to the secretary of state. The pursuit of the rebel army seems to have brought out the worst in those who directed it, as though the dread of their earlier successes was transformed into hatred of them. Even the mild Henry Pelham could think of no better word to describe the rebels than "animals".[82] A tough-minded soldier such as the duke of Richmond could talk of the pursuers as clearing the kingdom of "vermin" and thought "it would have been much better to have destroyed them".[83]

These sentiments seem to have become commonplace. When a body of Yorkshire foxhunters formed a company called "the royal Hunters" it inspired a crude verse which epitomised a widespread view of the rebellion.[84]

> Let us unite
> And put to flight
> Those Monsters of our Isle
> The Fox and Hare
> Awhile we'll spare
> To seek a worthier prey...
> Who would not strive
> Away to drive
> These vermin from the Land?

The conceit of the chase could be all too readily applied to the pursuit of the rebels from Derby. Even Philip Doddridge, a dissenting minister celebrated for his piety, could assert that the nation would "be much discouraged if these few sons of rapine be not strenuously hunted down".[85] They became dehumanised, "animals", "monsters", "beasts in confusion", "vermin", fit only to be "hunted down" and destroyed. Just how far this process could be taken is illustrated by the report that, when a rebel who had been overtaken was hanged at Cheadle, an apothecary surgeon in Macclesfield bought his body for 4s. 6d. "to have had leather of the skin (worth his money) which he accordingly gave to a tanner to dress."[86] For some reason the tanning did not succeed, which led Jacobites to claim that the skin had magical properties, and its purchaser to bury it. Neither superstition nor revulsion restrained one Murrall "who had a highlander flead to make himself a pair of breech of the skin and sent it to three tanners to have it dressed." The reporter of this macabre tale confessed "for my part I do not desire any part of them so near me".[87]

Even those who were not prepared to degrade the rebels from the human race accepted a stereotype of them as uncouth barbarians from the remote fastnesses of the Highlands, who were beyond the pale of normal civilised behaviour. Stories of their allegedly disgusting habits in the places where they stayed were widely circulated to reinforce this notion. "Whereever they rested they had let fall their odour all over the towns, and at people's doors, so caused the towns to stink intolerably; many of them also fouled their beds, and commonly the rooms."[88] An epigram "on their filthy behaviour during their flight" appeared in the provincial press with the lines[89]

Such filthy farting, pissing, shiting
(From Nature be't or Fear of fighting)
Gives a shrewd proof, to make an end on't
Charles is a warming pan descendant
When thus he leads, from kindred clans
An Army of Scotch warming pans

"If the duke drives them into their native barren villanous mountains," asserted Sir John Ligonier, "he does his country infinite service, and inflicts pretty strong punishment on those brutes that have now seen a better climate."[90]

Cumberland was actually going to give up the chase at Macclesfield, since he received instructions there from the Cabinet to station the army at Coventry, and not to advance unless he felt it absolutely necessary, but to hold himself in readiness to deal with an apparently imminent French invasion. Yet upon hearing that panic had struck the rebels, and that they were throwing away their arms, he thought it would be unpardonable if he did not profit from this by pressing on after them. He also sent instructions to the lords lieutenants of Lancashire, Westmorland and Cumberland to retard their flight by breaking up roads, felling trees and dismantling bridges. At Preston on 13 December he was joined by General Oglethorpe, who led the cavalry detachment sent by Wade, which appropriately included his own Royal Hunters. The rebels, however, were already at Lancaster, so they escaped being caught between the two forces. Cumberland sent Oglethorpe ahead to within three miles of them, and was quite convinced that a battle was inevitable. Even the Young Pretender looked around for a likely battlefield near Lancaster.[91]

Then on 15 December orders reached the duke from his father to return immediately to London.[92] They had been despatched on the 12th, when "the duke of Newcastle received an express from Hastings...at 3 o'clock [in the] morning with an account that 12,000 French were landed, upon which he got out of bed immediately and went directly to the king, and a Cabinet Council was called."[93] Although it proved to be a false alarm, orders were sent both to Cumberland and to Sir John Ligonier to bring the army back. Those sent to Sir John were accompanied by a private letter from Newcastle informing him that "we are now under the greatest alarm of an immediate invasion from Dunkirk and perhaps some other ports." The Secretary of State was clearly apprehensive about Cumberland's reaction, hoping that

as his Royal Highness's pursuit seemed to be at an end...he will not dislike coming here with his troops...I am sure, if he knew the real apprehensions people are here under, of an invasion from

France, and how much the king desires to have him with him, in times of action and danger, H.R.H. would fly faster and more cheerfully hither, than ever he did to meet the rebels. I must beg your good offices to make my peace with H.R.H. I doubt he is angry with me; but I am his most dutiful slave.[94]

Ligonier did his best to soften the blow. "The alarm is so great that nothing less than your presence will satisfy the king or the people," he wrote to Cumberland. "I fear this snatches the rebels out of your Royal Highness's hands, but if their fears are well grounded I don't know how to blame them."[95]

Newcastle's apprehensions were justified, for Cumberland was mortified to be robbed of a prize which deemed to be dangling tantalisingly within reach. "It was the greatest disappointment that ever befel me," he wrote to the secretary. Next day, however, he received an express that the orders had been countermanded to allow him to renew the pursuit. "A gentleman ...who was in the room when the Duke received it, and heard it read," reported that Cumberland "jumped around the room for joy and declared that he would follow them to the furthest part of Scotland."[96] He was nonetheless convinced that the twenty-four hour delay had cost him a real opportunity of defeating the rebels in England.[97]

And yet despite it he caught up with the rebel rearguard at Clifton, just south of Penrith, on 18 December.[98] The activities of the local people had helped to slow down their flight.[99] One rebel recorded how "the road from Kendal to Penrith was so broke that no carriage cou'd pass ...so that the Prince...was obliged to take the mountain road, where he had all the peines in the world to passe his cannon."[100] This was also one of the most loyal areas in the whole country. The men of Penrith had formed themselves into a company late in October, declaring their support for George II.[101] Although they prudently laid low when the rebel army marched through their town on its way south, they had successfully beaten off a party of marauders from the garrison at Carlisle which had attempted to ransack Lowther Hall. They also stopped the duke of Perth, who had been sent ahead by the Young Pretender to make contact with his supporters in Scotland. Rumours that the duke of Cumberland had beaten the rebel army in battle at Lancaster, and that Perth's men were the fleeing remnants, no doubt emboldened the men of Westmorland as well as Cumberland to attack them.[102] They were given a warm reception at Kendal, where "the Kendalians demolished two or three of them", but managed to get through.[103] At Langwathby, however, they were intercepted by the Penrith men, and chased back for five hours through Milburn, Kirkby Thore, Bolton, Morland and Newby down to Orton, where the pursuit was dropped. Perth lodged that night in an alehouse, while his men rejoined the rebel army at Kendal. Recounting the chase, or the "Sunday hunting" as it was significantly called, Will Monkhouse extolled the zeal of his neighbours around Penrith: "the hopes of plunder is so prevailing upon the mob to attack the rebels that I am fully persuaded had the king issued a proclamation giving five pounds for every rebel dead or alive that should have been taken, that never a rebel would have been left when they got to Manchester."[104]

When the duke's cavalry came up to the rebels at Clifton there occurred the last engagement between the two armies on English soil, though it is usually dismissed as a skirmish rather than being described as a battle. Some cavalrymen were dismounted to fight about 1,000 rebels commanded by Lord George Murray, who had lined the hedges leading to the village in order to cover their army's retreat. The ensuing encounter took place at five o'clock in the afternoon, in darkness occasionally dispelled by moonlight. There was a brisk exchange of fire, and then some rebels charged across the hedges broadswords in hand, inflicting several casualties on some of the dismounted dragoons, even though they wore skull caps to protect their heads. These dragoons broke ranks and withdrew, "it being dark, and our men having boots on, and amongst ditches and soft watery ground, made it the worse for them."[105] The rebels claimed that "their dead bodies lying in the ditch" made it easier to charge.[106] As they retired they were fired on by men lined up behind another hedge alongside the road. In his official despatch on the incident the duke of Cumberland insisted that when some of his officers were wounded "the rebels cried 'No quarter, murder them', and they received several wounds after they were knocked down."[107] Their comrades, however, drove the rebels back and out of the village, though they did not pursue them to Penrith. Both sides subsequently claimed a victory, and each with justice. Lord George Murray had held off the hot pursuit. On the other hand the duke of Cumberland had flushed the rebels out of Clifton, which he described as "one of the strongest posts I ever saw", and had spent the night there.[108]

The duke stayed at the house of a local Quaker. There could hardly have been a more incongruous host and guest than Cumberland, a military man through every inch of his stout frame, and the pacific Friend. Yet they apparently got on very well, for the Quaker wrote to another Friend "and pleasant agreeable company he was — a man of parts, very friendly, and no pride in him."[109] Next day the duke went to Penrith where he waited until all his forces came up on 20 December. By then the rebels had passed through Carlisle, where they left a garrison of about 400 men, and were making their way into Scotland. Cumberland reached Carlisle on 21 December, and is said to have boasted that the castle was "an old hen coop, which he would speedily bring down about their ears when he should have got artillery".[110] It was however, to take him ten days to reduce the garrison to surrender.

In the south of England people were more concerned about French invasion plans than with the second siege of Carlisle. Sir John Ligonier sent a march route to Newcastle on 14 December indicating that his army would reach London between the 22nd and 25th.[111] The secretary replied immediately to urge a more expeditious march, since there was reason to believe that the transports at Dunkirk were about to put to sea. The king had suggested the provision of horses and waggons to bring the men up to town more speedily, and Newcastle had actually written to magistrates along the route to requisition them.[112] As Ligonier patiently pointed out to him, however, "all my Lord that can be done to make the troops arrive at London one day sooner is to make them march without halting, and I am dispatching orders to the several battallions accordingly. For my Lord the roads are so extremely bad that men march faster than wagons can go."[113] Sir John reached the capital on 23 December.

Besides ordering the regular army to London, Newcastle directed the lords lieutenant of the coastal counties from Dorset to Norfolk "to employ a sufficient number of persons to keep a constant watch all along the shore, and upon the first appearance of any which there may be reason to suspect are either French or Spanish to send an immediate account of it, to me, by express, for his Majesty's information."[114] Upon the first appearance of the enemy, all horses and other draught animals were to be moved twenty miles inland. Newcastle also got the Lord Mayor of London and Master of the Ordnance to set up alarm posts and arrange for signals to give warning of any uprising within the city.[115] When it was feared that the French were about to land in Sussex, the king sent orders to the lord lieutenant on 17 December to post the companies raised by the county Association along the coast "to prevent or obstruct their landing".[116] How they were to do this when they had not then received any arms from the Tower was not explained. Nevertheless the response in Sussex to the threat of an invasion was remarkable. On 11 December there was a rumour that the French were actually landing in Pevensey bay, which put the inhabitants of Chichester into "the utmost consternation and distress but withall determined to oppose the enemys of the Government". An eye witness "was very glad to find the glorious spirit of loyalty that appear'd through the whole country on the occasion, almost every farmer leaving his plow to make all the preparation in his power to act as occasion should require for the common good."[117] The scare blew over when it was discovered that people had mistaken armed smugglers for invading Frenchmen, and "at the same time Admiral Vernon with his fleet hovering over our coast, was at a distance interpreted to be a French squadron to cover their troops as they landed." The coastline in fact was swarming with shipping at this time. There were "six and twenty line of battle ships between Plymouth and the Nore, and great numbers of small ships, sloops, cutters, yachts, etc. continually on the French coast; the Admirals Vernon, Martin and Mayne in the Downs; Captain Knowles on the coast of France; Captain Thomas Smith in the Swin; Captain Boscawen at the Nore; and Admiral Byng on the coast of Scotland."[118]

In Kent too the threatened invasion provoked an impressive display of loyalty. The lord lieutenant had recently died and the deputy lieutenants had to organise resistance. There had been a county Association, but it had not been followed up with a subscription, so that the only force available was the militia. One of the deputy lieutenants, Sir George Oxenden, thought it would take two months to muster it; "if the French come in March," he wrote "we shall be ready with our militia."[119] Since according to a letter from Admiral Vernon to Sir John Norris they were on their way and expected in Dungeness at any time, something else had to be done quickly. Oxenden therefore printed Vernon's letter in the Canterbury newspaper, with an invitation for volunteers to come armed on 22 December to Borham Downs. At least 1,500 men turned up that day, and 600 more the next. A second meeting was held on the 31st, when on Sir George's conservative estimation about 4,000 came on horseback and 1,000 on foot, while some claimed that as many as 8,000 attended. "If this can be done without one peer being in the county," Oxenden enthused in a letter to Newcastle, "without any Lord Lieutenent and against the grain of many gentlemen who I call in the old plain style Jacobites, what may not be expected now that the spirit is lighted up, and the hearts of the country people inflamed with a desire to defend their country and particularly against the French?"[120] By then the scare had diminished so they agreed not to assemble again until they learned of an actual landing.

The only spark of rebellion left in England was extinguished at the end of December. Cumberland obtained the artillery he needed for the siege of Carlisle from Whitehaven, though it took three days to take six pieces, pulled by Sir James Lowther's horses, from one place to the other. He also sent away to Newcastle upon Tyne for gunners, powder and other requisites. Marshal Wade responded on Christmas Day by sending 200 barrels of powder and all the gunners he could get, Dutch as well as English, under Major Belford. On 28 December they began to batter the walls with six eighteen-pounders, which led the defenders next day to offer to capitulate if they were allowed the privileges of prisoners of war. They also sent a letter to the commander of the Dutch troops among the besiegers, desiring them to withdraw on the grounds that they had agreed not to fight the forces of the king of France, some of whom were in the castle. Cumberland ignored both letters, since he was not prepared to negotiate with rebels, though he did order back to Newcastle the nine Dutch gunners sent by Wade.[121] (See p. 104 for a plan of the siege.)

On the morning of 30 December the rebels hung out a white flag, at which the duke stopped firing and sent Colonel Conway and Lord Bury with two messages: one asked what the white flag signified; the other informed any French officer who might be with the garrison "that there are no Dutch troops here, but enough of the king's to chastise the rebels, and those who dare to give them any assistance."[122] The rebel governor replied that the flag was "hung on purpose to obtain a cessation of arms" for a capitulation, if Cumberland's terms were acceptable. The duke had earlier been for giving no quarter, and had even had four prisoners hanged in sight of the castle "as a specimen of what the rest may expect".[123] Now he returned for answer "all the terms His Royal Highness will or can grant to the rebel garrison of Carlisle are that they shall not be put to the sword but be reserved for the king's pleasure." The king had in fact indicated to his son earlier that he was prepared to grant the rebels transportation to the West Indies, but Cumberland would have none of this, writing to the duke of Newcastle "they have no claim to the king's mercy and I sincerely hope will meet with none." Yet they clearly thought that some leniency awaited them, for at four o'clock that day they accepted the terms, "recommending themselves to his R. Highness's clemency, and that his R. Highness will be pleased to interpose for them with his Majesty". Thereupon the royal army took possession of the town. That night Cumberland wrote "now we may have the happiness to say that this part of the kingdom is clear of all the rebels."[124]

CHAPTER FIVE

"Go, glorious Youth, belov'd of Britain, go"

Go, glorious Youth, belov'd of Britain, go,
And pour just vengeance on the trait'rous foe;
If millions, lifting hands and eyes to Heaven,
Avail, to thee will victory soon be given.

Verses on the Duke of Cumberland's going to Scotland,
January 1746

After the fall of Carlisle popular interest in the rebellion shifted from England to Scotland. So far as the government was concerned, however, Scotland had been of paramount importance since it first became clear that the Young Pretender was making his way back there.

Even before the retreat from Derby the ministers had given serious thought to the problem of the high command north of the border. The landing of reinforcements at Montrose late in November had rekindled the rebellion in Scotland, so that some force would have to be sent there even if the rebel army were to be defeated in England. Lord Stair proposed that loyal Scottish peers should raise new regiments, as some lords in England had done. The English regiments had caused such trouble, however, that the Pelhams "had a strong battle with M. Stair" over his proposal, and prevailed. "You certainly did right to repulse Stair's Scotch regiments," Lord Chesterfield assured Newcastle. "Upon my word, if you give way to Scotch importunitys and jobs upon this occasion, you will have a rebellion every seven years at least."[1] Instead the Pelhamites urged that an army should be sent to Scotland, and, astonishingly in view of the criticisms now openly being made of Wade, they suggested that the Marshal should be its commander. This might have been a ploy to get the king's approval, for he first offered the command to Wade. The duke of Cumberland was aghast at the idea, and wrote privately to Newcastle

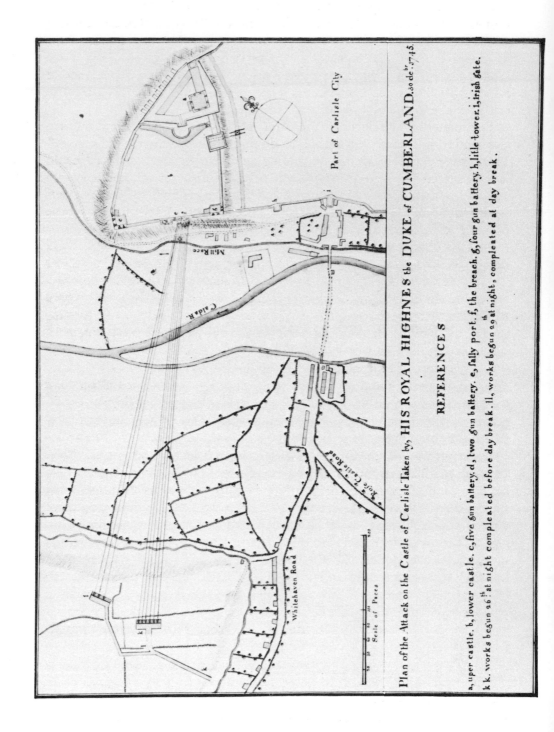

Plan of the Attack on the Castle of Carlisle Taken by, HIS ROYAL HIGHNES the DUKE of CUMBERLAND. 30 de.br 1745.

REFERENCES

a, uper castle. b, lower castle. c, five gun battery. d, two gun battery. e, sally port. f, the breach. g, four gun battery. h, litle tower. i, irish gate. k.k. works begun 26.th at night compleated before day break. ll, works begun 29 at night, compleated at day break.

Part of Carlisle City

Mill Race

Calda R.

Jojé Castle Road

Whitehaven Road

Scale of Paces

104

"experience every day shows us his insufficiency, and it is of infinite consequence that some one more able be sent there."[2] The earl of Chesterfield also questioned the Secretary about the desirability of the appointment: "I depend upon my Marcellus (Cumberland) for exterminating these rascals more than I do upon your Fabius. Why did he stay a month at Newcastle? Why wait for a train of artillery against such fellows? Why not attack 'em with any numbers?"[3]

Fortunately Wade declined the offer, pleading that his age and infirmities made him utterly incapable of discharging the duties of the post.[4] There were some difficulties in finding an alternative. Cumberland could not be spared from the pursuit of the rebels. Lord Stair volunteered to go himself at the head of six hand-picked regiments, but, perhaps not surprisingly, no more was heard of this.[5] John Huske was considered, to be discounted because he was only a Major General. Eventually Huske was made second in command, the position of commander in chief in Scotland being given to Lieutenant General Henry Hawley. The new commander was a veteran of Marlborough's wars with such a fierce reputation as a disciplinarian that he was known as "Hangman Hawley". He was alleged to have asked for the skeleton of a soldier hanged for desertion to hang up in the guardroom after his body had been dissected by a surgeon.[6] "His first exploit" on taking up his command in Scotland was to have gallows erected in Edinburgh and Leith.[7]

When he was appointed Hawley was with Cumberland at Carlisle, and wrote from there on 24 December to accept, though he held out for an increase in his salary and in the number of his aides de camp commensurate with his promotion. "I have no money, for I am in debt," he wrote in his blunt way to Newcastle, "want none as I have no heirs. I only desire to live as others of my rank."[8] He got his way, the king agreeing to augment his allowances.[9] Meanwhile he went to Newcastle upon Tyne to assemble his troops for their march to Scotland. Upon arriving there he complained bitterly about Wade's failure to make adequate provision for his journey north. The Marshal even refused to provide him with a map, saying that the only copy was in the king's possession. Hawley, protesting that he was "going in the dark", not unreasonably pointed out that the map should be "either copied or printed or that his Majesty would please to lend it to me."[10]

It was decided not to take the Dutch troops stationed at Newcastle

(Opposite) Plan of the second siege of Carlisle in 1745. Carlisle fell to the rebels in November, to be retaken in December. The duke of Cumberland was reported to have described the castle there as "an old hen coop, which he would speedily bring down about their ears". In fact it took him ten days to force the rebel garrison to surrender.

to Edinburgh. Lord John Drummond, claiming to be commander in chief of the French king's army in Scotland, had sent a letter to Wade objecting to the use of Dutch forces against him, on the grounds that the States General had agreed not to employ them against France. As we have seen, when the garrison at Carlisle made similar demands the duke of Cumberland thought it best to dispatch the Dutch gunners back to Newcastle. Similarly, although the king instructed Wade to reply that he could not deal with rebels, prudence dictated that the Dutch were not sent into action. The earl of Harrington had acknowledged when sending for the Dutch in the first place that they were "absolutely tied up from bearing arms either against French or Spaniards."[11] Their commanders were uneasy about their situation anyway, while the rank and file had behaved so badly that few were sorry for an excuse to dispense with their services. In December George II sent for 6,000 Hessians, with the requirement that they should sail straight to Scotland to join his army there. These came to be regarded as an equivalent for the Dutch, who were sent home in the same transports which brought the Hessians.

Hawley left Newcastle on 2 January and arrived in Edinburgh on the 6th. The authorities were pleased to see him, as they had been clamouring for help ever since they learned that the rebels were heading back to Scotland to join forces with Drummond. At a Council of War held on Christmas Day they had decided that the 1,200 men then in or near the city were not sufficient to go out and attack the rebels if they approached. Indeed they estimated that they could hold out against an attack for no more than a week, unless more troops were provided.[12] The fact that the two cavalry regiments sent there with Handasyde were those which fled at Prestonpans cannot have done a great deal to reassure them. News that the rebels were converging on Stirling led them to panic and call in the militia. As the first detachments from Newcastle crossed the border they were hurried on their way upon horses provided by civilians. Their arrival calmed the nerves of the City fathers, though Hawley thought that they had panicked unnecessarily, since as he put it in his "rough military stile", "the scrub remains the Duke has drove before him are not capable of undertaking anything."[13] By the middle of January he had at his disposal twelve regiments of foot, five of dragoons, the Edinburgh regiment, the Glasgow and Paisley militia under Lord Home, and the Yorkshire Blues, a company raised by William Thornton at his own expence. There were also 1,000 Argyllshire men under Colonel John Campbell at Dumbarton, whom Hawley ordered up to Stirling to join forces with him there.

It had been hoped that Lord Loudoun would link up with him too, to make a formidable army against the combined forces of the Young Pretender and Lord John Drummond. Loudoun and the Lord President had planned to consolidate their hold on the Great Glen, and then to advance towards the rebels at Perth. They had managed to reinforce Fort Augustus without incident early in December, but were rightly suspicious of the intentions of the Frasers under the slippery Lord Lovat.[14] An attempt to place his Lordship under house arrest culminated in his escape, even though he was so old and incapacitated that he had to be carried on a servant's shoulders. Loudoun could not risk taking too many men from Inverness in case the Frasers rose. Nevertheless troops were sent towards Aberdeen, and initially they made headway against the rebels, but on 23 December they were surprised by Lord Lewis Gordon at Inverurie and forced back across the Spey. This reversal nipped in the bud the expectation that any of Loudoun's 2,000 men would be available for the relief of Stirling, which the rebels took on 8 January.

Hawley's concern now became the castle, which held out under General Blakeney. Before he could march to its assistance he tried to prevent the rebels taking cannon there in order to lay siege to it. A combined naval and military expedition was sent to Alloa to try to stop a rebel brig carrying cannon to Stirling, but unfortunately the affair was bungled, and the rebel artillery got through.[15] Hawley's artillery, on the other hand, was held up in Newcastle, and he had to make do with what Edinburgh castle provided. He also had to do without the services of Major Belford, the engineer who had proved useful to Cumberland at the siege of Carlisle. Belford pleaded illness, but Hawley suspected that his sickness was "only a young wife he wants to be with". Captain Archibald Cunningham, who was in charge of the artillery, Hawley considered to be "such a Sott and so ignorant" that he doubted whether they would agree for long. "Nobody can work without tools," he protested on 13 January "and as to that point my situation is as bad as ever anybody's was."[16]

Hawley had been complaining ever since his arrival in Edinburgh. He objected that he was in dire straits for money. Though Wade had led him to believe that the two Banks would advance him £30,000, there was not a penny to be had in exchange for bills drawn on London. He also grumbled that poor old General Guest doted, having "quite lost his memory", and was of so little use that he had told him "to go away whenever he will".[17] Despite these difficulties he was confident that he had not only secured Edinburgh, but would easily deal with the rebels. The duke of Cumberland shared his confidence, writing to him on 11 January "you and I being of the same opinion with regard to that despicable enemy you have to deal with, I am fully convinced that far from besieging Sitrling they will retire to Perth upon the first appearance of the king's troops."[18] In his reply Hawley told the duke that he proposed "driving the rascally scum out of Stirling," adding "I think as your Royal Highness does that they will go off or else they are mad."[19]

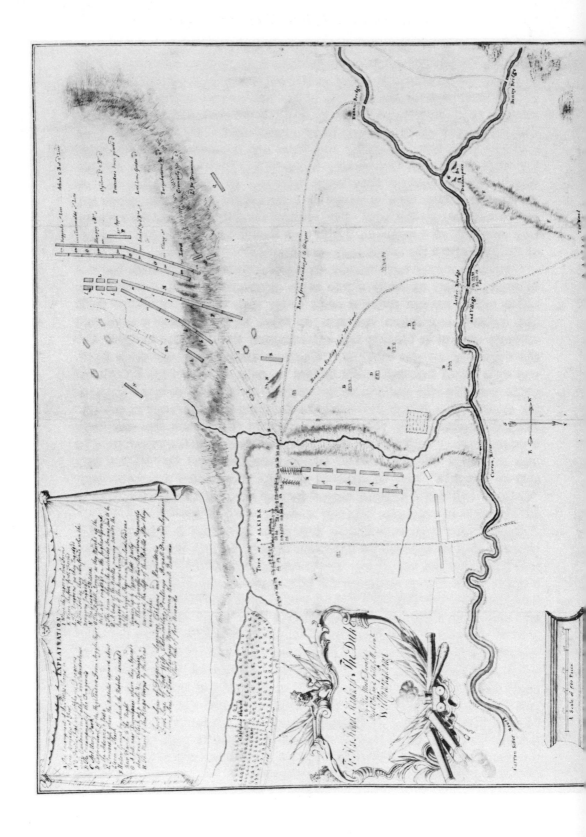

"Go, glorious Youth, belov'd of Britain, go"

Far from going off the rebels actually advanced to meet Hawley at Falkirk. He himself made his way there on 16 January, linking up with Huske who had gone in advance. They were joined by Colonel Campbell from Dumbarton on the morning of the 17th, which brought their total army up to about 8,500 while the rebels had 8,000. For once the royal side accepted that they were superior in numbers.[20] Hawley was so confident that his opponents would not offer to fight that he was enjoying a leisurely lunch when he was told that they were forming up at the top of a hill about a mile south-west of Falkirk. He rushed from the table at 3.00 p.m. to order his men to march in two columns, led by the dragoons, to do battle with them. Brigadier Cholmondley, who thought they should have waited for the rebels to attack, complained that "as we march'd, all the way up hill, and over very uneven ground, our men were greatly blown".[21] Being convinced that the Highlanders would not withstand a cavalry charge, Hawley ordered the dragoons at the head of the army, forming its left wing, to attack the rebel's right wing. One of those who charged later accused him, with pardonable exaggeration in view of what happened, of drawing "only 400 dragoons, sword in hand, up against 10,000 of our enemy, and we had orders not to draw a pistol nor fire a gun; and as soon as he had given these orders to the rest of the officers he rode away from us and we never saw him more till next morning."[22] When the dragoons attacked the result was devastating, not on the rebels but on themeslves, for they rain straight into a volley of "a very sharp, popping kind of a fire," which thinned their ranks so terribly that an onlooker "saw daylight through them in several places".[23] Then they turned tail and fled, some of them into the ranks of the infantry on their immediate right, which plunged them into confusion also. On seeing their flight Cunningham, who had been having difficulties getting the artillery up the hill, abandoned it and ran away too. "Whereupon the horses were unyoked, and the drawers of them fled. Yet 3 of them were brought off, by a brave young man who belonged to the train." The rebels chased after the retreating cavalry. Some of the infantry tried to stop their advance with musket fire, but heavy rain driving straight into their faces had drenched their cartridges, so that few actually fired. They too thereupon ran away. Only the right wing held, rallied by General Huske and Brigadier Cholmondley. Cholmondley "got the men to be quite cool, as cool as ever I saw men, at exercise", and even managed to get some of the dragoons to come to their aid.[24] These "drove everything before them for an hour and

(Opposite) Plan of the battle of Falkirk, fought 17 January 1746. General Hawley ordered his troops to attack the rebels, who were at the top of a hill to the south-west of the town. Deadly fire and driving rain forced "Hangman" Hawley's men back down the hill, leading the Jacobites to claim a victory.

109

did great execution. They kept engaged till their powder was so wet it would not burn…it blew a great storm and rained and hailed so hard that the water came out of our soldiers' shoes."[25] Dusk coming on, and the driving rain continuing, both sides retired from the field, "being sick of one the other"; the rebels went to Falkirk, and the king's forces to Linlithgow that night and Edinburgh the next day.[26]

The fiasco at Falkirk temporarily lulled Hawley's blustering. "Sir, my heart is broke," he confessed to Cumberland, "I can't say we are quite beat today, but our left is beat, and their left is beat…such a scandalous cowardice I never saw before. The whole second line of foot ran away without firing a shot."[27] Others blamed the dragoons more, especially since they were the same regiments who had fled at Prestonpans. Yet others held Hawley himself responsible, Lady Elizabeth Hastings asking her brother "don't you think Hawley deserves hanging?"[28]

Once he regained his confidence, however, which did not take long, Hawley had other ideas about who deserved to be executed. "As I can charge myself with no neglect nor fault," he wrote to Newcastle two days after the battle, "and as I hope nobody else can lay anything to my charge, I am not at all cast down."[29] Instead of offering himself for sacrifice he recommended that those who were guilty of cowardice should be shot. Five officers were court martialled, including the unfortunate Cunningham, who tried to escape his fate by an unsuccessful suicide bid. He recovered, to be drummed out of the army.

Some took longer than the general to regain their composure. Although the lord justice clerk put a report of the battle in the papers giving a most favourable slant to its outcome, he privately regarded it as "this disagreeable news". In Edinburgh the City guards were doubled, while a newly arrived regiment "were not allowed to put off their clothes". Reporting these preparations to resist the rebels, who were expected to follow up their success with an attack on the capital, Fletcher concluded that "the Duke of Cumberland's presence is the only here [sic ?thing] that occurs to me."[30]

It also occurred to the king. After the surrender of Carlisle Cumberland had gone to London, "highly pleased and satisfied with having driven the rebels into their own country,"[31] His presence in the south was felt to be needed in view of continuing fears of a French invasion. These were ebbing, however, when news of the battle of Falkirk arrived. That Hawley should be replaced as commander was immediately agreed, though it was also decided that he should remain as second in command, since he had apparently retrieved the situation when complete defeat seemed inevitable. "I can assure you," wrote Cumberland, "that I think you have done wonders in coming off so after such a panic was struck in the troops."[32] This was by no means a widely held view. Most accounts agree with the conclusion that "the battle appears to have been ill conducted...and would have been utterly lost, if General Huske assisted by Brigadier Cholmondley had not retrieved matters."[33] Nevertheless, when Sir John Ligonier was proposed, the king objected that his appointment might be thought to be superseding Hawley. So Cumberland was chosen instead. He broke the news very gently to Hawley, who claimed to be delighted: "your coming here has given the greatest pleasure to everybody," he assured the duke, "but in the strongest measures to me, and beg to be believed when I solemnly protest that the sincere desire of always serving under you by far outweighs all the vanity that could have crept into my thoughts. I hope I never had much, and that unfortunate day was enough to cure all that I had. 'Twas a rough remedy, but I hope t'will do me good."[34]

Cumberland left London on 25 January and arrived in Edinburgh at four o'clock in the morning of the 30th. He was so determined to get there that he had no time for civic entertainments en route, which disappointed the corporation of Newcastle upon Tyne, where he arrived at 1.00 a.m. and left before seven o'clock. He was, however, able to give attention to one urgent problem as he went through County Durham. On 22 January a group of about 300 Sunderland men, said to be mostly apprentices and sailors, armed with pistols and cutlasses, "and with drums beating and colours flying", went to a Roman Catholic chapel in the town, where a wedding service was in progress. The couple and their guests prudently fled, whereupon the men pulled down the chapel, ransacked the contents and burned them.[35] They then proceeded to visit private houses occupied by Catholics in the neighbourhood, extorting protection money from one, plundering another and demolishing the contents of a third down to its wainscotting. Upon returning to Sunderland they threatened to pay the Catholics in Durham a similar visit. This led the bishop to write to the duke of Newcastle informing him that "no one hath ventured to read the proclamation, and no magistrate hath given any opposition to it. It is suspected if they go on without control the Pit men will join them."[36] He suggested that the Secretary might approach General Wentworth at Newcastle for help. The duke promptly wrote to Wentworth asking him to tell the sheriff of Durham that he had received the king's order to assist him if required. Wentworth replied that he had offered help, but was informed that the rioters had dispersed.[37] "His Royal Highness had in passing through Durham given his directions to the commandant of the Swiss to assist the civil magistrate in suppressing the rioters, who afterwards began to assemble but upon the Swiss beating to arms they separated and have not made the least attempt since." Although the bishop had warned against employing Dutch soldiers on the grounds that they were all "too ready to rob and steal" themselves, Count

Schwartzenberg informed William Maurice of Nassau from "Neukastel" that, having received orders from the Court in London to suppress the Sunderland sailors, he had instructed the Dutch troops billeted in the district to lend a hand to local justices of the peace.[38] Cumberland must have been impressed by the degree of anti-Catholic feeling in the north-east of England, for the night before he went through Newcastle, a chapel and two dwelling houses in Gateshead were badly damaged, and though a reward of £50 was offered the culprits were not apprehended.[39]

Although he had eschewed civic receptions on his way north, after entering Edinburgh Cumberland held Court at Holyrood to the elite of the city. It helped to re-establish the power of the Crown to do so in the very place where the Young Pretender had stayed just three months earlier. Among those presented to the duke was a young lady who attracted attention by wearing a crown over her bosom, bearing the legend "William Duke of Cumberland, Britain's Hero".[40] After paying his respects to the local dignitaries, Cumberland addressed the army he had come to lead:[41]

> The only apology I can make for troubling you with this short address is the hearty and sincere zeal I have for the noble cause we are now engaged in. Many of you, after severe campaigns abroad, in defence of the liberties of Europe, wherein you have gained immortal reputation, are now called home to confirm it in defence of your king, your religion and the liberty of your country...after what you have already done, you'll find it an easy matter...to crush the insolence of a set of thieves and plunderers, who have learned from their fathers to disturb every government they have lived under...remember you are the free soldiers of a free people...go forth, show yourselves like men, and your enemies will as snow in the sun melt before you...

The duke then announced his intention of progressing immediately to Stirling, where Governor Blakeney estimated that he could only hold out for another ten days. On 31 January, therefore, "at 9 in the morning his Highness set out. He rode thro' the City in the Earl of Hopeton's coach; and when he had got without the suburbs, he mounted his horse, the populace loading him with blessings, to whom he returned thanks in a most obliging manner. Then turning to the Nobility and Gentry about him, said, Shall not we have one song; At which he stretched out his hand, and springing his horse into a gallop, went off with — Wilt thou play me fair, Highland laddie, Highland laddie."[42] He took with him enough troops "to drive them off the face of the earth, if they will do their duty, which we must expect".[43] The troops were eager to do battle, too, for although they were "in raptures at the Duke's coming", yet "they were asham'd to look him in the face till they had been try'd again."[44]

Upon arriving at Falkirk, however, they discovered that the rebel army had abandoned the siege of Stirling and was heading to the north away from the duke. They had in fact agreed to make for Inverness, the Young Pretender taking the Highlanders directly there, while Lord George Murray went with the Lowlanders and the cavalry by the coastal route. The duke moved to Stirling, determined to follow them. On 3 February he wrote to the earl of Loudoun to tell him of the precipitate retreat made by the rebels, and to order him to do all he could to harass them from Inverness, while he pursued them to Perth.[45]

Cumberland was bitterly disappointed that they had not been tempted to stay and fight another battle. He was confident that he could have beaten them especially since his arrival had boosted the morale of the troops after their humiliation at Falkirk. "The good spirit I found the king's troops in," he wrote, "made me wish the rebels would have ventured an action, and I doubt not but then I should have shared in their glory of giving them a total defeat and crushing at once this band of robbers."[46] Now their retreat raised the prospect that the rebellion would no longer be finished by the one decisive action he so ardently desired. Instead he thought that they would scatter and disperse through the Highlands where it would be impossible to follow them with the body of his army. The only policy he could devise to deal with this situation was to go up the coast, in order to send small parties into the Highlands "to burn and destroy that nest of robbers. And orders shall be given to kill all that have arms in their houses as that will be the only trace of treason left...I shan't be surprised to hear it affirmed that there never was a rebellion."[47] The policy of fire and sword thus began almost immediately after Cumberland arrived in Scotland. As his aide de camp Joseph Yorke put it in a letter to his father the earl of Hardwicke, "I hope...we shall be able to...extirpate the Race if we are not stopt by lenity...I don't doubt soon but we shall have shut 'em up within the Lochs where it will be at least a summer's work to clear those parts of 'em and to destroy their clannism, but it must be gone thro' with."[48] On their way from Stirling to Crieff they passed through "some of the Drummond, Strathellan and other disaffected persons estates", where Cumberland "thought fit to let the soldiers a little loose, with proper precautions, that they might have some sweets with all their fatigues."[49] The duke himself threatened the duchess of Perth that he would burn down her castle if her husband did not release the prisoners he had taken. Her Grace and Lady Strathallan were sent to Edinburgh castle for their part in the rebellion. He was annoyed when some of the Highlanders in his own ranks "absolutely refused to plunder any of the rebels' houses, which is the only way we have to punish them and bring them back."[50]

Informing the duke of Newcastle of these developments on 5 February, Cumberland concluded that "the rebellion is now crushed, and nothing left but the punishment due to their crimes."[51] This was just the news which the Pelhams had been waiting for, as it enabled them to bring to a head their dispute with Lord Granville.

After the king had come round to their way of thinking about the best way to handle the rebellion, relations between him and the Pelhams had improved considerably. Towards the end of September George had informed Thomas Winnington that he could not endure Lord Stair, and as for Tweeddale "if they have a mind to push him in parliament," he had said "I shall not oppose it."[52] Stair's proposals for subduing Scotland had not found favour with him in December, while on 4 January Tweeddale resigned as Secretary of State for Scotland, and shortly afterwards his protegé Robert Dundas stood down as Scottish Solicitor General.

The Pelhams had also staved off attacks upon their policy in parliament. Pitt had continued to dispute it, but without success. When he tried to raise the question of augmenting the navy on 21 November, Henry Pelham persuaded the House that it was inappropriate to discuss naval matters while the rebellion was raging. Another proposal by Pitt on 10 December, to address the king about the recall of the cavalry, was quashed by 138 votes to forty-one. "Mr Pelham assur'd the House they were order'd over above 3 weeks ago, but have been prevented by contrary winds ever since," Lord Fitzwilliam informed the earl of Malton, "but that did not seem to satisfie his patriotical virtue."[53] Upon the news that the Hessians had been invited over being announced to the Commons on 19 December, Pitt was outspoken against the need for foreign mercenaries, and supported the resolution not to thank the king for obtaining their support, only to find himself beaten by 190 to forty-four. During the Christmas recess Pitt did a deal with the ministry, his political patron Lord Cobham acting as broker. His unsuccessful opposition in the Commons led them to lower the conditions they had previously laid down before he took office. In October they had insisted on a Place Act excluding all army officers under the rank of lieutenant colonel, and all naval officers under that of captain, from parliament; on a thorough purge of Granvillites; and on a change in foreign policy, so that Britain acted as an auxiliary rather than as a principal on the continent, and devoted her main effort to the sea. Now all that they demanded was that Pitt should be made secretary at war, and that preferment should be given to two other members of Cobham's connection. The Pelhams agreed to put these before the king, who initially at least was prepared to listen to them, and only objected to Pitt's insistence on being secretary at war, though he would be willing to give him another post.[54]

This deal took any pressure off the Pelhams in parliament. The only aspect of their handling of the rebellion which was seriously criticised, after the recess, was a proposal to extend the time granted for the establishment of the fifteen new regiments beyond the original four months, which would elapse at the end of February. Henry Pelham suggested an extension of eight months for all of them. Henry Fox tried to confine it to those which had actually been raised in full, and moved that muster lists should first be examined. He was opposed on the ground, as he put it, "that delay was opposition, and no opposition to the name of a soldier in time of rebellion was to be borne".[55] His proposal was defeated by 170 to eighty-nine. There then ensued a debate between those who supported an eight months' extension and those who preferred two, which ended with the compromise of four.

Unfortunately for the Pelhams this unusually happy state of affairs in both Closet and Commons came to an end when the king felt that the rebels no longer posed a threat. Once he was free from fear of them, he seems to have become anxious to release himself from dependence upon his ministers. "During the heat of the rebellion," Newcastle confided in Chesterfield on 6 January, "I was most graciously received. But whether from the danger being more remote; or from whatever other cause I know not, during the last week, there was a visible alteration."[56] Lord Bath had got to work on the king, raising objections to "the behaviour of his ministers in forcing him in such a manner to take a disagreeable man into a particular office and thereby dishonouring him both at home and abroad, and encouraging the king to resist it by offering him...the support of his friends in so doing."[57] When on 6 February Henry Pelham waited on his Majesty to insist that Pitt was made secretary at war, George exploded, refusing "with great indignation to bring a man into his presence whom he did not know by sight, only by hearing of his insolence and impudence, and rather than to submit to it he would publish how he was used in every market town in England and his people would stand by him "[58]

This provided the immediate pretext for the showdown which the duke of Cumberland's letter persuaded the Pelhams they could now bring about without being accused of endangering the kingdom by resigning in the midst of a rebellion. But a more substantial issue was touched on when the duke pointed out in his letter than the crushing of the rebels freed the king's hands "to take what share he may think proper in the affairs of Europe". George II thought he should take a bigger share than did the Pelhams, let alone Pitt, and his thinking was shared by Granville and his associates. This fundamental dispute about Britain's European role once again surfaced after being submerged by the rebellion. When the Pelhamites forced the king to choose between them and the Granvillites by resigning en masse on 10 and 11 February, a well-informed onlooker observed[59]

The generality of mankind, who see only the outside of things, ascribe all this to the refusal of Mr Pitt to be Secretary at War, but that point has been given up these ten days. The true source is the countenance given to Granville and Bath, who have generally opposed whatever had been proposed by the other party and obstructed all their measures. But the affair which immediately contributed to this resolution was a proposition in Council to carry on the war with the utmost vigour on the continent even though the Dutch should not declare war which was opposed with one voice by the Pelhamites, who finding the interest in the Closet to increase against them resolved at last...to make this stand for their country.

Harrington and Newcastle, the two secretaries of state, resigned on the 10th and Henry Pelham and four other ministers on the 11th, while nearly forty more promised to go out too, including the lord chancellor Hardwicke. The duke of Richmond wrote a typically pithy letter to the duke of Newcastle on the 11th explaining why he would resign:[60]

I certainly can serve...no longer for two reasons; the first because the only honest set of men I know are out, and secondly because I know a set of thorough paced rogues will come in. But I am determined as long as I have a tongue to vote and an arm to fight with to keep him and his family, such as it is, upon the throne. My Lord Granville must have a new parliament, and that I fear will be a Jacobite one.

The king tried to form a ministry headed by Bath, who became first lord of the treasury, and Granville, who took over both secretaryships of state. They found it almost impossible to get colleagues to work with them, however, until it became a joke that "it was not safe to walk the streets at night for fear of being pressed for a Cabinet counsellor". They also lacked completely the confidence either of parliament or of the City. The king was warned that his new ministers would not be able to depend upon more than thirty-one Lords and eighty Commoners, while the City withdrew an offer of a loan of £3,000,000 negotiated with the outgoing prime minister, observing "No Pelham, no money". After only two days Granville gave up his attempt to take over from the Pelhams. "This was absolutely the worst period he could have selected," thought Horace Walpole, "when the fears of men had made them throw themselves absolutely into all measures of government to secure the government itself."[61] The Pelhams were reinstated by George II, having won the fight to make him show the world that he approved of them. This mattered more than the details of who served where. Pitt, for instance, did not become secretary at war, but settled instead for the post of joint vice-treasurer of Ireland.

When the news of the resignations reached the duke of Cumberland he felt the greatest consternation, even though Henry Pelham justified their timing by writing "we look upon the rebellion as near extinguished, and what gives the next pleasure to me extinguished by the Duke's single hand."[62] The duke could not accept this excuse. "I don't doubt but that you had all your reasons for resigning," he wrote in a private letter to the duke of Newcastle on 16 February,[63] "yet I think it's at a most fatal juncture, and that the enemies of the king and his family will profit of these inward confusions." The letter contained a rare profession of his own political creed: "I tremble for the Old Whig cause that fixed us here, and that must support us here." The duke's first political patron had been Sir Robert Walpole,[64] and he considered himself to be almost a member of the Old Corps, as the close of the letter implies: "For my part I shall always remember the many kind and obliging offices done to me by those out of power, but particularly by you, and let whatever public changes happen, I shall remain your sincere friend." Then on 13 February Stephen Poyntz wrote to Sir Everard Fawkener to report that the Pelhams were to come back into office: "Lord Granville had the seals for 24 or 48 hours. Yesterday or this morning he quitted them again. And the word to the old ones is *to the right about as you were.* Are we not a pleasant facetious people? But by good luck the Easterly wind has helped a little to conceal our folly from foreign parts, so that I hope our sins and our repentance will be wafted over...in the same pacquet boat."[65] Cumberland was overjoyed, writing to congratulate Newcastle on his reinstatement, and hoping that there would be "no more of these dangerous shakes of Government".[66] At his dinner table on the 17th, according to his aide de camp, Joseph Yorke "he made us all drink a bumper to our old friends and no more changes".[67]

The notion that the rebels had scattered to the four winds and that, apart from a protracted process of rooting them out of their fastnesses, the rebellion was virtually over, completely misjudged them. Their army progressed by different routes towards Inverness despite appalling weather conditions. By 15 February the Young Pretender was at Strathnairn, only eight miles from his destination. Upon learning of his approach Lord Loudoun took 1,500 men on the night of 16 February, to make what he hoped would be a surprise attack upon the rebel headquarters at Moy. Unfortunately his detachment opened fire when they thought they saw some rebels approaching. There were in fact only five men, a blacksmith and four servants of Lady Mackintosh, Charles Edward's hostess, sent out by her to reconnoitre. When they saw Loudoun's party, with great

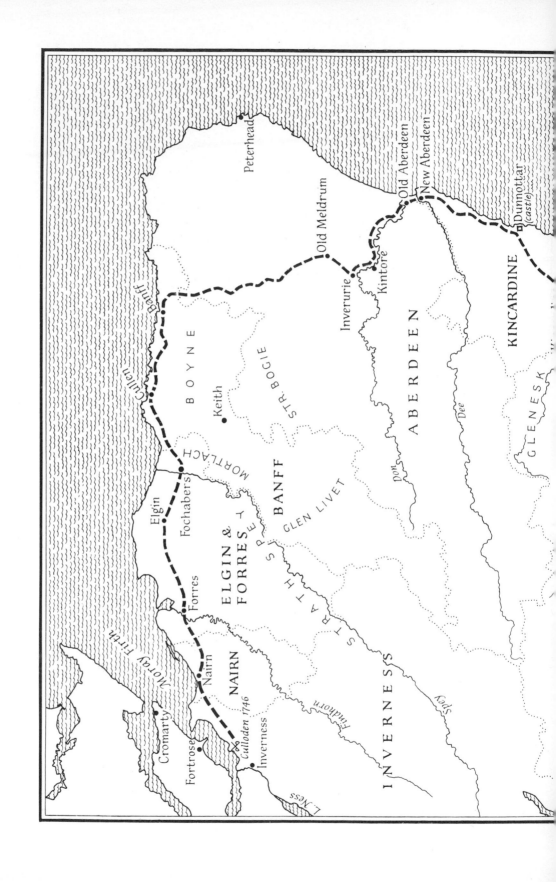

Peterhead

Old Meldrum

Old Aberdeen
New Aberdeen

Dunnottar
(castle)

Inverurie

Kintore

KINCARDINE

Banff

B O Y N E

STR·BOGIE

A B E R D E E N

G L E N E S K

Cullen

Keith

MORTLACH

BANFF

GLEN LIVET

Don

Dee

Elgin

Fochabers

ELGIN &
FORRES

SPEY

STRATH

Forres

Morray Firth

Cromarty

Fortrose

Nairn

NAIRN

Culloden 1746

Inverness

I N V E R N E S S

Findhorn

Spey

L. Ness

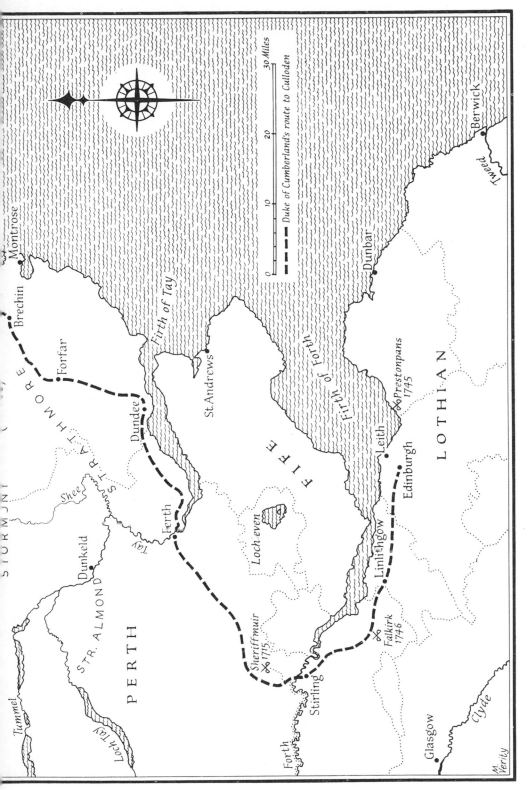

Cumberland's route from Edinburgh to Culloden, February to April 1746

presence of mind they shouted as though calling up the whole army. This induced a panic among the government forces in the darkness, and despite all Loudoun could do they ran back to Inverness. The "Rout of Moy" as the incident became known, is rightly celebrated in Jacobite folklore as a fiasco for their opponents. That five men could turn back 1,500 is indeed extraordinary. The only plausible explanation is that Loudoun's troops were riddled with disaffection. Many who later deserted to the rebels marched with the greatest reluctance that night, so that the rest could not trust them to fight for the king if they did do battle with the Young Pretender. Thus the incredible confusion which undoubtedly ensued in the "rout" was induced by the psychological state of men who feared, not only the broadswords of the rebels, but the bayonets of many in their own ranks.

Loudoun, not surprisingly, was mortified. "If it had pleased God that the accident had not happened in the march I flatter myself that I should have had the happiness at one blow to have broke the neck of the present rebellion", he lamented.[68] Instead of having the glory of ending the rebellion he had the further shame of losing Inverness to the rebels. On 17 February he lost hundreds of men by desertion, and found himself unable to defend the town. At a Council of War attended by the lord president and his most trusted officers, it was agreed to abandon it. He therefore left some men in the castle, and led the remaining 1,700 or so over the Tain into Sutherland. As he went out of Inverness at one end, the rebels entered at the other.[69]

Cumberland's appraisal of the situation was to be much shaken when news of the fall of Inverness reached him. Meanwhile he remained convinced that the major task of suppressing the rebels was behind him, and that a long and tedious guerilla warfare lay ahead. When the Hessians arrived at Leith on 8 February he seriously thought of sending them back, since they could "be of no manner of service", as he had "already as many troops here as are more than sufficient to finish this affair."[70]

The Hessians also strained Cumberland's already hard pressed resources. Both money and bread were in such short supply that he felt he had to go in person to Edinburgh to sort out the situation with those responsible. Andrew Sawyer, the deputy paymaster, was in charge of remitting money from the treasury to the army. In discussion with him, and in correspondence with the ministers in London, the duke arranged for public money in the hands of collectors in the north of England to be sent directly to Edinburgh, rather than being remitted via Whitehall. This system was difficult to organise, since the collectors profited from the one they were used to, any interest accumulating from money they held accruing to themselves rather than to the public. Delay was therefore in their interests, though manifestly against the army's. Once it was eliminated, however, the duke did not run into the serious financial difficulties which had hindered both Wade and Hawley before him. On the contrary, Sawyer efficiently sent him a month's supply of money in advance for the rest of the campaign.[71]

The main contractor for bread in Edinburgh was one Gomes Serra, a Portuguese Jew. Serra's initial inability to supply more than four days' allowance kept the army at Perth longer than Cumberland desired. The arrival of 5,000 extra mouths to feed, in the duke's own words, "puts the finishing stroke to the confusion we are in about bread". He therefore decided to keep the Hessians in Edinburgh until they could be shipped back to Flanders, since "whilst they remain here they only eat up our provisions".[72]

On his visit to see Serra Cumberland managed to obtain two weeks' supply of flour, which enabled him to move his army from Perth to Aberdeen, and to place garrisons in Blair Castle and Castle Menzies. When he reached Montrose Cumberland decided that the Hessians could be useful to him after all, if only to protect places he had left behind. He therefore asked their commander, Prince Frederick, to station four battallions in Perth and two in Stirling, which together with the cavalry would give him a sufficient force "to destroy the rebels should they either attempt to avoid me by rashly getting South, or dare to attack our posts at Blair, Castle Menzies etc." Even so this was merely intended to keep them occupied until they could be sent back. This could not be done immediately, as the shipping which had been used to bring them over was first used to take the Dutch home from Newcastle.[73]

Convinced that the rebels had gone to ground, Cumberland issued a Proclamation at Montrose commanding those of them who were "ordinary common people", as distinct from gentlemen, to surrender their arms and submit to the king's mercy: otherwise they would be "pursued with the utmost severity as rebels and traitors". (Originally this merely concluded with the words "by military execution", but before it was printed somebody prudently added the words "due process of law".[74] As we shall see, that somebody was hardly likely to have been Cumberland himself.) The nobility and gentry were not given the benefit of this Proclamation, and indeed the ordinary common people were favoured largely because the jails were already full to bursting with their betters. To establish who had been in arms, ministers of the Church of Scotland were asked to compile lists of their parishioners who had been 'out' in the rebellion.

The fall of Inverness transformed the situation. "As the rebels are possessed of...the capital in some sort of their own country," observed the lord justice clerk, "it is to be feared that their numbers may increase beyond whatever they had in Scotland, at least of Highlanders."[75] The further north he went, too, the more Cumberland became aware of the strength of Jacobitism, until he realised that he was effectively in enemy country. Not surprisingly, therefore, he changed his mind about sending the Hessians back to Flanders. He now had a war on his hands again, and needed all the troops that were available.

Cumberland also had a concrete objective, Inverness. Before he could go there, however, he had to assemble "such a force together as should be fully sufficient to oppose the rebels".[76] For this purpose he established his headquarters at Aberdeen, where he remained from his arrival on 27 February to 8 April. Even getting the army there was a cumbersome process, as the duke admitted half apologetically to Newcastle: "I persuade myself the king will not think me dilatory in not marching forward faster than we do, but as I am forced to carry magazeens of all sorts of provisions with me it incumbers and retards us so that we can move but very slowly."[77] There were still difficulties about bread supplies. Lord Albemarle complained that a consignment from Serra was so inedible that his men could not even cut it.[78] Another hindrance was the severe weather, which persuaded Cumberland that his troops must be kept under cover "unless we would risk to have them half in the hospitals from one or two bad encampments".[79] It also rendered virtually impassable the River Spey which his army would have to cross as it moved towards Inverness. On 17 March it was reported to be "so swelled with snow melting down from the hills that it will not be fordable without going a great way up the country, until either most of the snow is gone by a thaw, or there is a frost of several days' continuance."[80] The Lord Justice Clerk sent the duke a map of the river which had been drawn up for a law suit, but pointed out that it was not necessarily reliable, since the Spey "by its rapidity alters its course so often that there is no depending intirely on this map, for before the law suit was quite finished, by an alteration of the channel made by the floods the very subject of the controversy was swept away."[81] At the very end of March Cumberland informed the duke of Newcastle that the "continued ill weather which we have had here for this month has raised the waters of Spey so high that I fear it will retard me still a week longer, tho' I propose now to march to Inverness without halting as soon as ever the waters will allow us."[82]

While the royal forces were held up in Aberdeen, the rebels were consolidating their position in the Highlands. In the weeks between their flight from Falkirk and the battle of Culloden they are often depicted as wandering aimlessly about the hills until Nemesis finally overtook them. Nothing could be further from the truth. As an admirer of the Young Pretender, James Maxwell of Kirkconnell, put it: "This is without dispute the finest part of the Prince's expedition, and what best deserves the attention of judicious readers. The vulgar may be dazzled with a victory, but in the eyes of a connoisseur, the Prince will appear greater about this time at Inverness than either at Gladsmuir [Prestonpans] or at Falkirk. It's certain an army of eight thousand men could not be more extensively and more usefully employed."[83] Nor was this the benefit of hindsight, for as the rebels moved north from Stirling in February, their chief officers gave out that[84]

> their place of general rendezvous is to be about Inverness, where they are to be joined by the clans who left 'em at Stirling…They are to unite all the clans in the North and West among 'emselves and to their party, and to compel all the North by fire and sword to join 'em and then give battle to the Duke of Cumberland… Indeed they are talking very confidently that, let the Duke of Cumberland hasten his march northward as fast as he pleases, they'll be masters of Inverness and of all the other forts in the North before he can bring his army to that country.

When they took Inverness they used it as a base from which they attempted to get possession of the forts in the Great Glen from St George to Fort William, and even attacked government troops in other outposts away from the headquarters at Aberdeen.

They gained control of Fort St George two days after taking Inverness. The old barracks at Fort Augustus fell to them on 28 February and the rest of the garrison on 5 March. On 7 March they laid seige to Fort William. If they could take this it would give them a vital outlet to the sea on the west coast through which France could supply them, since the royal navy's patrols on the east coast (where it had three men of war in the Moray Firth alone) cut off Inverness from French aid. Anticipating this last move Cumberland sent Captain Caroline Scott to take command of its defences. "As I look upon Fort William to be the only Fort in the Highlands that is of any consequence," he wrote to General Campbell there, "I have taken all possible measures for the security of it."[85] He arranged for provisions to be shipped there from Liverpool, and arms and ammunition from Dublin, while troops were also ordered to march from Edinburgh to Glasgow to be conveyed from there to the fort.

In the middle of March Lord George Murray took some troops into his native Athol country and on the 17th laid seige to his ancestral home of Blair Castle. As soon as he received intelligence of this, and that the rebels had also taken a small fort at Rannoch the same morning, the earl of Crawford and Prince Frederick held a Council of War in Perth, and made the surprising decision to retreat to Stirling. At least it surprised the duke of Cumberland, who sent an express to Crawford roundly condemning it. Indeed he criticised him so severely that the unfortunate General requested a transfer of his post to another, anywhere so long as it was out of Scotland. The duke thought that, instead of retreating to Stirling, "it was absolutely necessary for his Majesty's service that the castle of Blair should be immediately relieved." Although Crawford and the Hessians went to its relief, Cumberland was not without apprehensions that they would be too late, writing to Newcastle on 31 March that the garrison had only five days' provisions left, "and I am afraid in the manner the Hessians go on they will loyter away the time."[86]

Meanwhile Lord Loudoun had been chased off the mainland by the duke of Perth onto the Isle of Skye. Immediately after his retreat from Inverness Loudoun had become optimistic about the prospects of rallying forces, especially when the earl of Sutherland provided over 300 men, which partly offset his losses through desertion. He even offered to take his men from Ross to link up with Cumberland's army. The duke at first accepted, and arranged a rendezvous at Banff for 10 March. Loudoun, however, found that his forces were reluctant to go. Many of Sutherland's men were farmers who refused to leave their farms, while others were still inclined to desert. He and the lord president consequently decided that the best policy after all was to stay put. Cumberland reached the same decision independently, once he realised that he was in for a long stay at Aberdeen and could not keep his date at Banff. When the Captain of the *Shark* sailed into Cromarty Bay on 19 March and offered to transport them to Aberdeen, therefore, they declined. Although he warned them that they were vulnerable to a rebel attack from Inverness, they considered their headquarters in Sutherland's house at Dunrobin Castle to be remote enough to be out of danger, especially if the *Shark* prevented the rebels from getting across. That very night, however, a party of rebels took advantage of thick fog to cross over and surprise Loudoun and President Forbes, who retreated into Caithness. There they divided, Sutherland's men being sent north "with orders to defend themselves as well as they can against the rebels", while the rest withdrew to the Isle of Skye, arriving there on 26 March.[87]

The government was disgruntled at "the very little advantage that has been had from the troops under Loudoun, tho' raised at great expence and upon the prospect of their being useful", while the king had expressed "hopes that the force under Lord Loudoun would still have been able to have kept possession of Inverness."[88] Yet his achievement was underestimated. A Jacobite appreciated that Loudoun's regiment "was of vast service to the established government. While it was at Inverness it was impossible for those that lived beyond that town to rise; they must be crushed before they could assemble and be in a position of defence." What is more, he claimed that Loudoun and the lord president "behaved all along like men of honour, and their attachment to their cause never made them forget the duty of humanity."[89]

A rebel force also surprised an advanced detachment from Cumberland's main force at Keith on 20 March. The duke had sent General Bland forward from Aberdeen to clear the way to the Spey, and by 18 March he was established at Strathbogie, having driven out a band of rebels under Colonel Roy Stewart, who "were struck with such a panic that they did not halt at Keith but pursued their march thro' that town in the night to Fochabers." "In order to keep up the terror amongst the rebels and the Jacobites of this country, of which cattle it too much abounds," Bland reported back, "I have sent a written order to the Justices or chief magistrates of Keith to prepare, on pain of military execution, quarters for 2500 foot and 500 horse and dragoons on that town, together with hay, oats, straw and all other provisions for that body of troops, being only the vanguard (under my command) of H.R.H's army."[90] On 23 March he wrote that the was impatient for orders to move forward "that we may drive this Highland banditti to their Ne Plus Ultra, that is to the Devil."[91] Instead Cumberland sent the earl of Albermarle to take over the command at Strathbogie, in order to consolidate the position before the main army left Aberdeen for it. A party of about 900 men under Alexander Campbell was also sent to Keith to reconnoitre. There Campbell was attacked by a superior force, which killed several of his men and took the rest prisoners, he himself losing an arm. The rebels claimed this as a major setback for the duke's forces, though he rather dismissed it as the consequences of Campbell's "obstinacy and negligence", and was only concerned for the loss of about thirty of the duke of Kingston's light horse, since he "could not sufficiently commend the behaviour of that regiment upon all occasions."[92]

The successes of the rebels in the Highlands encouraged their supporters along the coast to defy the duke's army even though it was in their midst. "I am extremely concerned that every dispatch of mine must be filled with repeated complaints of the disaffection of this part of his Majesty's dominions," Cumberland wrote on 9 March, "but so it is, that tho' his Majesty has a considerable army in the heart of their country, yet they cannot help giving impotent marks of their ill will by making efforts to raise men and to set prisoners at liberty in the places we have passed through." He instanced Forfar, where rebel officers had been concealed while his troops stayed overnight. "The magistrates of that town are remarkable for being good politicians," he remarked wrily, "for when they were chosen in the midst of these troubles, they made a minute in their Council book that they would not take the oaths till they should see which side was like to be uppermost."[93]

To deal with the blatant disaffection in the area Cumberland drafted a Proclamation in Aberdeen, which was sent to the lord justice clerk for his observations. A comparison of the draft with the final version illustrates not only the difference between plain English and the language of the law, but also the contrast between Cumberland's military approach to the problem and the legal training of Andrew Fletcher.[94] For instance, the duke claimed that designs had been formed to break open prisons in which "rebels and disaffected persons" had been confined, while the lord justice clerk preferred that those held should be described as "prisoners for treason or upon suspicion of treason". But it was in their stipulation of penalties for recruiting for the Young Pretender, and other treasonable activities, that the two documents most differed. Cumberland's version threatened "military execution" on the persons and houses of those engaged in them; Fletcher's changed this to "the utmost rigour of the law". As he explained in a covering letter:[95]

> The reason why I presumed to leave out the words military execution, and which I most humbly submit to his Royal Highness's consideration is that, though in a war with a foreign enemy every man may take what he can of the enemy's goods, and thereby the goods become the property of his captor, yet in a rebellion or civil war that matter appears in a different light. Every subject retains the property of his own goods until that property is either forfeited for his crimes or transferred by his consent. And tho' every person convicted of treason forfeits not only his goods and chattels but his lands and all other estate, yet that forfeiture is not to every soldier or other person who shall take them, but it is to the king only, and such as shall have right from him; and even his Majesty's right is subject to the payment of the rebels' just and lawful debts, which very often exceed the value of the goods or estate forfeited. So that the taking away those goods is really in the issue doing injustice to such of his Majesty's lawful subjects as happen to be creditors. But neither is that all the difficulty. Until the rebels are attainted or convicted there can be no forfeiture...

This elementary lesson in the law was not one the commander relished. Fletcher excused it on the grounds that he had "a greater love and regard for our Constitution" than for himself. It was important to remind the duke that one of the major issues in the rebellion, at least as the king's supporters saw it, was the defence of a Constitution which upheld the right to life, liberty and property by due process of law, against a dynasty which was more inclined to ride roughshod over them, using methods not unlike "military execution".

The lesson was lost on Cumberland, who felt that legal niceties treated rebels too leniently, and that "nothing will cure this but some stroke of military authority and severity".[96] He was convinced that overscrupulous-

ness in dealing with the Fifteen was the reason why Jacobitism had
survived, to break out in a fresh rebellion now. The sword and not the
law was the only way to ensure that it would never break out again. His
aide de camp, Joseph Yorke, though the son of the Lord Chancellor,
agreed with him, writing to his father to excuse "violent measures,"
since "lenity is construed cowardice, and that's a fault soldiers ought
never to bear the reproach of."[97] Yet the duke was sufficiently disturbed
by Fletcher's advice to write to Newcastle a few days after receiving it,
to ask for some guidance from the king on the matter: "for there must be
some rule and that must (be) closely stuck to and I should know what
that is to be."[98] Meanwhile he disregarded the justice clerk by ordering
that it should be "observed as a rule that all provisions, cattle, forage or
arms which shall be taken from rebels shall be given to the people." He
also desired "all methods" to be "used for disarming the disaffected
people in the hills, and even that they should be destroyed if they
resist."[99]

On 21 March Newcastle sent an official reply to the duke's request for
a general rule: "as General of His Majesty's army, your Royal Highness
has authority to do whatever is necessary for suppressing this unnatural
rebellion, and preventing the further progress and encrease of it...His
Majesty apprehends no general rule can be given for your Royal Highness's
conduct in this respect as that must depend upon the circumstances that
attend the particular cases."[100] The same day the Secretary wrote another
letter, "most private. To be open'd by H.R.H." Apprehending that the
duke would not find the official reply satisfactory, he explained that
"upon the most mature deliberation it has been found impracticable to
give any more particular direction than is there contained. Your Royal
Highness knows how delicate the point is, and consequently how difficult
it is to give any general order upon it." On the one hand he was expected
to do everything that might be necessary to put a speedy end to the
rebellion. On the other he was depended upon not to "give any just cause
of complaint to a country so ill disposed to the king, and so willing to find
fault with everything that is done for His Majesty's service." Newcastle
was so worried about sending this letter that he wrote it in his "own illeg-
ible hand for the greater secrecy" and hoped Cumberland would burn it.[101]
Cumberland thanked the Secretary for his concern, and admitted that he
"could have wished the king's order had been fuller. Yet I'll take the hint,
and will do all in my power to put an end to this unhappy rebellion." In
a postscript he added "don't imagine that threatening military execution
and many other such things are pleasing to do me. But nothing will go
down without in this part of the world."[102]

The conflict between what the Generals considered to be militarily
necessary, and what the civil authorities regarded as legally proscribed,

127

was to continue for the rest of the rebellion, and long after. One who felt it acutely at this time was none other than "Hangman" Hawley. He was chagrined to discover that he was being prosecuted in the courts of law for hanging a spy at Stirling, and also for pillaging Callendar house. When he sought the lord justice clerk's advice on these matters, Fletcher considered that "the great law of military necessity will probably justify what was done" with the spy; but that "there can hardly be as much said for the affair at Callendar, and therefore I really wish it had not happened, for it occasions a great clamour, and I doubt if it can be well justified at law."[103]

Another who had scruples about where to draw the line was General Bland. He could quite cheerfully order billets for his troops at Keith under threat of military execution, and even confiscate livestock belonging to the wife of a rebel. When he sent some Campbells to get the latter he did warn them not to touch anything else, but was unconcerned at the thought that they almost certainly did, since "all highlanders are naturally thieves...but as it is done by their own country men, it is only diamond cut diamond".[104] He had qualms, however, about trying a nonjuring minister for spying in a court consisting only of officers, since there was no justice of the peace available. He claimed that Oliver Cromwell had tried civilians by such bodies, but admitted that "as these military committees were not even relished in Oliver's time, I am sure they will be much less so now". He drew the conclusion that he "would have us soldiers only imitate the Great Rebel's military exploits, and leave the civil criminals to the civil powers, being sensible that few of us have so extensive a Genius as to arrive at a tolerable knowledge in both professions."[105]

This was a sensible distinction, but not one which Cumberland was prepared to admit. He sent a detachment to Glenesk towards the end of March "to destroy all them...in arms and to burn the habitations of all those who have left them and are with the rebels."[106] The Major in charge boasted that he made use of "penitent rebels to carry my orders to them upon pain of military execution, which word I use as freely as Lord Elcho did in England." The journal of his progress shows that he was as good as his word. He burned a nonjuring meeting house, plundered the provisions of a man merely "suspected of harbouring and holding intelligence with the rebels", and set fire to a house, only to extinguish it when he was satisfied that its occupant was "a good and loyal woman".[107]

Yet Cumberland thought that the expedition was necessary, since Glenesk had showed signs of a serious uprising in his rear. He hoped that the detachment had "quieted all behind us" before his army advanced towards the Spey.[108]

On the eve of Cumberland's departure from Aberdeen, the spectacular run of successes which the rebels had enjoyed while he remained there came to an abrupt end. On 2 April the siege of Blair was raised. Lord George Murray withdrawing from it "in a great hurry and confusion" just before the earl of Crawford and the Hessians arrived.[109] Next day the siege of Fort William was also called off, the besiegers accepting that they could not take it.[110] But the biggest blow of all was the recapture of the sloop *Hazard*, which the rebels had renamed the *Prince Charles*. Commodore Smith, who was the officer in charge of naval patrols along the Scottish coast, had been criticised by Cumberland for not keeping him informed of his movements, which had earned him a rebuke from the first lord of the admiralty; though the duke was prepared to put it down to "a sea education" and not to "want of attention".[111] Certainly the Commodore's patrols were extremely vigilant, for the Captain of the *Sheerness* man of war spotted the *Hazard* hugging the northern coast of Sutherland on 25 March. He chased it for five hours, until it ran aground trying to avoid him in the shallow waters near Tongue. As those on board went ashore they were picked up by a detachment of the troops which Lord Loudoun had sent north a few days earlier. Not only did arms and men fall into the government's hands, but so did £13,600 sent from France which Charles Edward desperately needed to pay his troops. Even before this disaster he had been reduced to paying them in meal, which had led to desertions. Now there was little prospect of ever having enough cash for their wages. As the lord justice clerk commented "the taking the Hazard sloop is taking the Pretender's whole fleet, and catching the money while the rebels are in great want of that commodity will I hope produce good effects. Discontents, Diversions, Desertions, etc., etc."[112]

By contrast with the rebel army Cumberland's troops were well provided. Andrew Sawyer continued to remit money from Edinburgh regularly, and shortly after the duke left Aberdeen despatched another £20,000.[113] Moreover the army was still benefiting from the Guildhall subscription. On 26 March a consignment of 9,000 pairs of gloves, stockings and other garments arrived in Scotland.[114] Far from losing deserters Cumberland was gaining recruits. Bligh's regiment arrived in Aberdeen on the 25th, while in May Joseph Yorke was to claim that over 2,000 men had been recruited since the army left Edinburgh.[115]

The duke, not surprisingly, was in good spirits. "His Royal Highness is in good health and all degrees of people are charmed with his deportment," reported a letter from Aberdeen during his stay. "Even the disaffected cannot help saying that his presence alone is equal to an army; and our friends when they see him equally attentive to business and diversion and as solicitous to please, as to execute his office, ask whether the Duke was sent down to civilise or to subdue the North?"[116] "While at Aberdeen his Highness acted in so princely and amiable a manner," claimed his biographer Andrew Henderson, "that friends and enemies were obliged to confess the superiority of his genius, and the most distinguishing abilities. He daily rose at four, reviewed his troops, appeared at entertainments, walked the streets with his officers, and established hospitals for the sick."[117] He also prepared the infantry, at least psychologically, to deal with the rebels' tactics, which had struck such panic and terror into the king's troops at Prestonpans and Falkirk. They were trained to cope with the dreaded broadsword by pointing their bayonets, not at the enemy immediately in front of them, but at the man to his left. The theory was that the highland shield, or target, could only protect the left side of the body, the right side being unguarded and vulnerable to the bayonet, especially while the broadsword was being wielded to strike a blow. The men therefore practised stabbing to their right instead of straight ahead.

Although his long stay in Aberdeen made him impatient to be moving against the rebels, Cumberland was determined to wait until the moment was right. It came on 4 April. On that day two officers went to reconnoitre the river Spey and found it "low and fordable in so many places". By the 6th the duke could inform Newcastle "we are at last getting into motion".[118] After a tedious six weeks of waiting, events were now to move very quickly, for ten days later he met the Young Pretender at Culloden.

CHAPTER SIX

"So many butchers"

The moor was covered with blood; and our men, what with killing the enemy, dabbling their feet in the blood, and splashing one another, looked like so many butchers.

The History of the Rebellion…extracted from the Scots Magazine

On 8 April the duke of Cumberland's army at last marched out of Aberdeen, and proceeded by way of Old Meldrum and Banff to Cullen, where it was joined by the earl of Albermarle's forces from Strathbogie. They then advanced to the Spey, arriving there on the 12th. Crossing the river was something of an anti-climax after the expectation of physical and military obstacles which had been building up during the previous weeks. With winter gone, and "the finest weather that could be wished", the waters were low enough to ford. Even though they "came up to their middles" the men waded over "with great cheerfulness". Five people were nevertheless drowned in the crossing, a dragoon and his wife who fell off their horse "lovingly together", and three other women. The so-called "Army of the Spey", with which the duke of Perth and his brother Lord John Drummond had boasted that they would prevent the royal forces getting over the river, proved even less of an impediment to their progress. As the cavalry advanced at the head of his troops led by Cumberland himself, they saw that "the rebel army were assembled with their white flags displayed, making a formidable appearance". After they had fired a few shots, however, they "burnt their barracks and magazines and run off precipitately for Elgin".[1] "It is a very lucky thing we had to deal with such an enemy," Cumberland concluded, "for it would be a most difficult undertaking to pass the river before an enemy who should know how to take all advantages of the situation." Each soldier received some rum and a biscuit when he got across, and the army camped that night on the river bank.[2]

Next day they marched through Elgin to Alves. As they went through

Elgin, people, "crowded about the Duke with uncommon alacrity and gladness, pouring out their blessings upon him, and even reckoned themselves happy if they could but kiss his boot", or so we are told by Andrew Henderson, whose biography metaphorically does so too.[3]

On 14 April the army marched from Alves to Nairn. While on their way towards it a large party of rebels tried to cut off an advance guard which had gone ahead to mark out a camp site. Cumberland therefore sent General Bland forward with the cavalry, at which the rebels withdrew to Nairn. The duke ordered 100 cavalrymen to pursue them, and these drove the rebel rearguard up to their main body. The rest of the cavalry then cleared them all out of Nairn and chased them for five miles. Since the foot had still over five miles to march Cumberland called off the pursuit, and the enemy encamped at Balblair, about a mile south west of Nairn, "after four hard days' marching".[4]

The army went round the coast from Banff to Nairn in order to have the advantage of an accompanying fleet under Commodore Smith, which kept them supplied with victuals and could report back on rebel movements. It even "fired incessantly on the rebel runaways, who took the sea side".[5] As he lay off Nairn on the 14th, the Commodore passed on to the duke's secretary intelligence he had received that the rebels at Inverness were fourteen or fifteen thousand strong, "and design to give his Highness battle". Cumberland found the numbers hard to credit, for as he wrote on the 15th to Newcastle "all accounts agree they cannot assemble all their clans". The news that they had burned down Fort Augustus, however, convinced him that they were prepared to fight a pitched battle, though even if they could get all their forces together he was confident that "the affair would not be very long".[6]

In fact the rebel army had drawn up alongside Culloden house some twelve miles away that very morning, expecting the royal force to march towards them. Cumberland was right to think that all their clans had not assembled, for their numbers had diminished considerably since Falkirk. Knowing that they were at a serious disadvantage, they determined to try to offset it by making a night attack on the duke's camp at Balblair. The 15th was actually his twenty-fifth birthday, and they expected that his soldiers would celebrate it until their guard was seriously relaxed. "We have another advantage that people do not think of," Lord George

(Opposite) The duke of Cumberland leading his army across the river Spey on 12 April 1746. The Jacobite "army of the Spey", which had threatened to prevent their crossing, in fact retreated after firing a few shots. "It is a lucky thing we had to deal with such an enemy," Cumberland observed, "for it would be a most difficult undertaking to pass the river before an enemy who should know how to take all advantages of the situation."

133

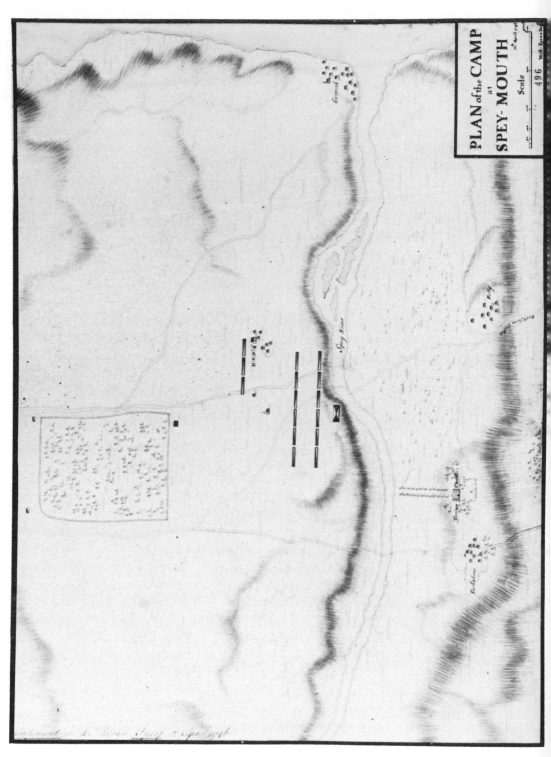

PLAN of the CAMP at SPEY-MOUTH

Scale

496

134

Murray is reported to have said. "This is Cumberland's birthday, they'll all be as drunk as beggars."[7] The plan was to cross the moor between Culloden house and Balblair rather than to go by the Inverness to Nairn road, in order to keep their movement secret. They set out at eight o'clock that evening in two columns, one led by Murray, the other by Perth and Drummond, while Charles Edward followed behind with the French troops. The going was hard in the pitch dark over the marshy moor, and even the first column took an hour longer than they had expected to get near Cumberland's camp. At three o'clock in the morning Lord George Murray's party could hear the sentries at Balblair, about two miles away, exchanging calls: "Is all well?" "Yes all's well." By that time, however, the other column had fallen hopelessly far behind, largely due to the Young Pretender's constantly sending ahead to it to slow down, and wait for the heavily accoutred French to catch up with them. As dawn began to break the element of surprise was lost, so Lord George called off the attack, much to Charles Edward's dismay.

In any event it could not have surprised the duke's forces. They did not become blind drunk, but celebrated his birthday, by eighteenth-century standards at any rate, relatively abstemiously, on half a pint of brandy and a biscuit which he had allowed each man. Cumberland had insisted on the most vigilant guards, and had kept his men ready for battle. "My brave boys, we have one march more," he said to them, "and all our labour is at an end; sit down at your tent doors and be alert to take your arms." He himself slept in his boots, and was actually rising at the time Lord George Murray heard the sentries. Between four and five o'clock his whole army was mobilised and on the march for Inverness.[8] "It was a very cold rainy morning," Private Alexander Taylor wrote to his wife, "and nothing to buy to comfort us...not a dram of brandy or spirits, had you given a crown for a gill, nor nothing but a loaf and water."[9]

The army advanced in four columns, with the cavalry on the left, and the artillery and baggage on the right bringing up the rear of the third infantry column. At first progress was not difficult, with the cavalry crossing fields while the artillery rumbled along the road to Inverness. But after two or three miles they turned off the road to the south west, to make for the rebels across the moor, more or less taking the same route as their enemies had done in the abortive night attack, by way of the Loch of the Clans and Loch Flemington. They marched up to Drummossie Moor, a slightly convex plateau some 500 feet above sea level, between the Moray Firth and the river Nairn. Now the going became

(Opposite) Plan of the camp formed by Cumberland's army after it had crossed the Spey.

hard, through bogs in which men sank to their knees and the artillery to its axles. A bleak easterly wind, which had been blustering since they set out, began to shower hail onto their backs, reminding some of the fateful role played by the weather at Falkirk. Progress over this terrain could only be painfully slow, and it was half past eleven before they had gone eight miles from Balblair. At this point the advance guard brought back intelligence that the rebels were lined up in battle formation ahead, and seemed about to march towards them. Cumberland ordered his own troops to fall into line for battle, and the four columns deftly wheeled into three lines, with Lord Albermarle commanding the first, Major General Huske the second, and Brigadier General Mordaunt the third. They marched in that formation for about two miles, bayonets fixed, which private Taylor considered to be "a very uneasy way of marching".[10]

When it was realised that the rebels were not coming to meet them, but stayed in their position between Culloden park and the river Nairn, the duke commanded his army to fall back into columns again and advance, which they proudly did with clockwork precision. They advanced until they came within a mile of the rebel army, and then performed the manoeuvre of falling into lines, again with parade ground efficiency. As they moved further forward, however, a morass which had been protecting their right came to an abrupt end, obliging the duke to order some of Cobham's dragoons and Kingston's horse to protect the now exposed flank. Cumberland then addressed his men, riding along the lines, so that only some of his words were picked up through the wind and sleet. One man heard him say as he rode by "Depend my lads on your bayonets: let them mingle with you; let them know the men they have to deal with." The gist of the full address was reported to be "My brave boys, your toil will soon be at an end; stand your ground against the broad sword and target; parry the enemy in the manner you have been directed, be assured of immediate assistance, and I promise you that I shall not fail to make a report of your behaviour to the king; and in the meantime, if any are unwilling to engage, pray let them speak freely, and with pleasure they shall have their discharge."[11] Various versions of this speech found their way into print, some more for the consumption of English whigs sitting at home, than for an army drawn up on a bleak Scottish upland within sight of an enemy they had pursued for many weary months. All variants agree, however, that the duke offered a free pardon to any soldier who quit before the fight. One claimed that he had said "I had much rather be at the head of one thousand brave and resolute men, than ten thousand amongst whom there are some who, by cowardice or misbehaviour, may dispirit or disorder the troops, and so bring dishonour and disgrace on an army under my command."[12] If he did use such moral blackmail, it worked, for not one of the men assembled fell out of line.

Opposite them, no more than 500 yards ahead, were the rebels, drawn up in two lines, their left alongside Culloden park and their right extending to the walls of an enclosure, which stood between them and the river. As they still had not moved, and it was now about one o'clock, the duke of Cumberland was asked whether his men could eat before they fought. "No," he is alleged to have said "They'll fight all the better on empty bellies. Remember what a dessert they got to their dinner at Falkirk." Instead he sent Lord Bury forward to try to discover the intentions of the rebels. He soon found out, for as he rode towards them a cannon ball whistled over his head. The battle of Culloden had begun.

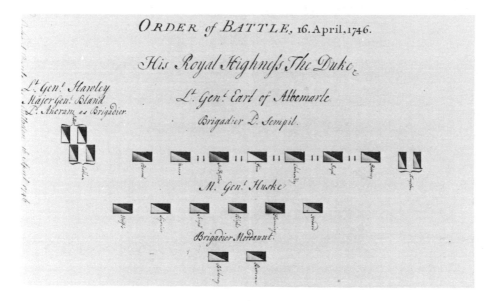

The order of battle of the Royal army at Culloden. The lines between the front line regiments indicate where Major Belfort positioned his guns, which decimated the rebels before and during their charge.

"It is not an easy task to describe a battle," Lord George Murray observed of Falkirk, and his words, as John Keegan has shown, apply to most battles.[13] Culloden is no exception. "Springs and motions escape the eye, and most officers are necessarily taken up with what is immediately near to themselves, so that it is next to impossible for one to observe the whole: add to this, the confusion, the noise, the concern that the people are in whilst in the heat of the action." Something of the confusion survives in the different accounts which participants left behind, making it difficult to reconstruct in due sequence exactly what happened. There are further difficulties for historians seeking the truth about this

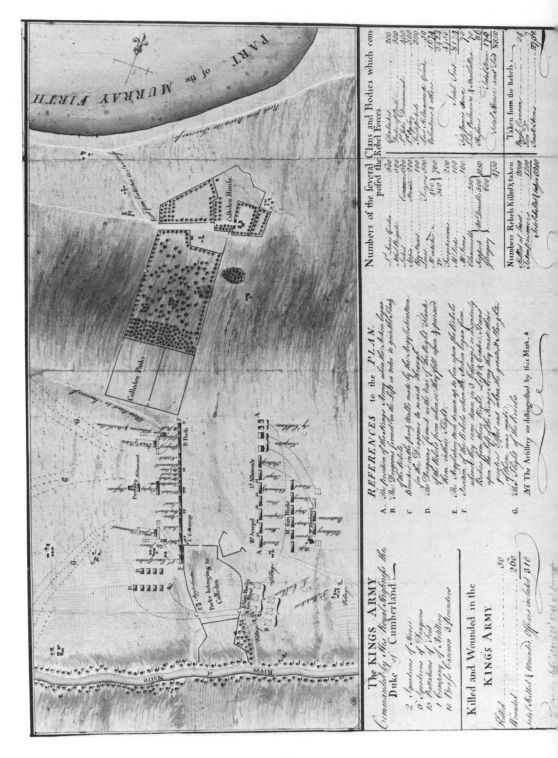

138

particular battle, for intense partisanship, more often than not on behalf of those who lost it, has coloured accounts, giving rise to legends of super-human bravery on one side, and subhuman barbarity on the other. There is even a legend involving the whereabouts of the duke of Cumberland during the action. Visitors to the battlefield today come across a boulder a good way behind what was the line of his forces, in one of the few clearings left by the Forestry Commission, which has engraved on it the words "Cumberland Stone". According to the legend the duke viewed the battle from the safety of this rock, when in fact he was observed by eyewitnesses in the midst of his troops, as one put it "riding from right to left all the time of the action with all the calmness and courage becoming a hero", while another stated that "during the engagement the duke was often riding through the lines, and sometimes among the dragoons on the right, observing with his spyglass the motions of the rebels."[14] There is no need to go to the other extreme of adulation, which an officer allegedly present at the battle wrote in a letter, claiming that "by his exposing his valuable person too much, it had often like to have cost us too dear; a battery of their cannon bore directly upon the place where he stood; it did little execution, for a particular Providence guards him, and he trusts to it: several shots nearly [narrowly] missed him, and one shot took off two men exactly before him."[15]

Even a historian who discounts all later versions of the events on the battlefield, and relies exclusively on eyewitnesses, finds that it is not an easy task to describe Culloden. To give an apparently trivial instance, the question did the rival armies shout battle cries before the action admits of two different answers, both from participants in the rebels' ranks. According to John Daniel: "We began to huzza and bravado them in their march upon us...But notwithstanding all our repeated shouts, we could not induce them to return one; on the contrary, they continued proceeding, like a deep sullen river, while the Prince's army might be compared to a streamlet running among stones, whose noise sufficiently showed its shallowness."[16] On the other hand, James Maxwell recalled that: "The highlanders, though faint with hunger and ready to drop down with fatigue and want of sleep, seemed to forget all their hardships at the approach of the enemy; it was surprising with what alacrity and spirit they returned the shout given by the duke of Cumberland's

(Opposite) Plan of the battle of Culloden, fought 16 April 1746, later pub-lished "by authority" in the London Gazette. *The claim that the rebel army numbered as many as 8,850 was a wild exaggeration. At most they were about 5,000, while Cumberland commanded some 9,000 men. The estimation that "at least" 2,000 rebels were killed, however, minimised Jacobite casualties.*

army."[17] It might not seem to matter which version one accepts; but if Daniel's is followed, the royal forces appear to be grim automata, whereas Maxwell's makes them more human; and that distinction can be vital in deciding whether or not the victors were capable of the butchery which the partisans of the vanquished accused them of, both at the time and since. It seems that Maxwell's recollection was more reliable, for another rebel, Lord Elcho, recorded that "when they came within cannon shot there was a great many huzzas passed on both sides".[18]

When even eyewitnesses on the same side could disagree, it is not surprising that accounts of the battle provided by men who fought in Cumberland's army sometimes differed widely from those given by their opponents. For example, according to rebel sources their men had nothing to eat or drink before the battle. Yet Michael Hughes, a soldier in the royal ranks, later claimed that they had "a double portion of oatmeal and whisky for incouragement", while Hugh Ross observed at the time that "graite many of the rebels that we took prisoners were drunk, and it is reported that most of their army drunk. Every man had so much spirits given before the battle begun."[19]

Predictably the most striking discrepancy occurs in estimates of the numbers of each army. According to Hugh Ross "our army did not consist of above 6,400 effective men that day, and the rebels were called fourteen thousand", though he himself believed that they only "had in the field of battle above 8,000".[20] Some "official" figures made the royal army precisely 7,197, consisting of 6,410 infantry and 787 cavalry, and the rebel army 8,880.[21] On the other side, John Daniel estimated that "of the twelve thousand men, who were actually in arms and in the pay of the Prince, not above four thousand were now with him", while he claimed that Cumberland had 12,000 men on the battlefield.[22] In fact, as far as it can be known, there were somewhere near 9,000 in the duke's army, and 5,000 in the Young Pretender's.[23]

As with estimates of total strength on each side, so with calculations of casualties, armies invariably minimise their own and maximise their opponents'. At first there was something of a competition among the victors in calculating how many rebels they had slaughtered. An early account which reached the lord justice clerk claimed that at least 1,000 had been slain.[24] The day after the action an officer in Monroe's regiment boasted that it alone had killed 1,600 on the spot.[25] One of his captains claimed that "seventeen hundred rebels were counted dead in the front of Barrell's and our regiment".[26] The duke of Cumberland's "official" report gave the figure of 2,000.[27] Hugh Ross thought that 3,800 were dead.[28] "They have not had such a thrashing since the days of Old Noll," an officer informed a correspondent in Newcastle, "and whatever the Jacobites may insinuate to lessen their losses believe them not."[29] It is significant that in the event the rebel side did not challenge these figures, though they did query the small numbers of only fifty dead and 260 wounded, which the royal army claimed for its own casualties. Even an officer in Wolfe's regiment admitted that "the insignificance of our loss, considering the fury and despair with which they attacked, is hardly credible."[30] Instead of minimising their casualties, according to the duke of Cumberland "by their own accounts they make their loss greater by two thousand than I have ventured to state it", i.e. 4,000. The carnage on the rebel side was too great for anybody to deny that there had been a most dreadful slaughter; but it is an almost unique feature of this battle that the defeated army put out an estimate of its slain even higher than the highest claimed by its enemies.

This peculiarity of Culloden gives rise to the greatest difficulty in accounting for what happened. The Jacobites claimed that Cumberland's forces were guilty of cold-blooded butchery, both on the field and in their pursuit of the rebels after the battle. These allegations, embroidered by romantic historians, have created an indelible impression of the behaviour of the royal army on that day. To avoid being unduly influenced by the biased testimony of hostile witnesses, the following narrative of the battle and its aftermath is based on accounts by contemporaries on the winning side. Far from showing a Jacobite bias, their partisanship was quite the reverse. Such evidence nevertheless demonstrates that there is no necessity to turn to suspect sources in order to document acts committed by the British army, which were outrages even by the standards of contemporaries, who were not remarkable for being squeamish. On the contrary, the very recreations of all ranks of society, from the foxhunting of the aristocracy and gentry to the cockfighting of the crowd revelled in the destruction of life for fun. The punishments meted out, even for what would now be regarded as petty crimes, were sanguinary, as the hangings on "Albion's Fatal Tree", the Tyburn gallows, bore witness. In a brutal age soldiers were probably the most brutalised. Ferocious floggings were frequent, and several of the men who fought for the king at Culloden had backs scarred by the lash. Arbitrary executions by orders of courts martial which were little more than kangaroo courts were not infrequent. Yet there was a rough and ready code even in that century. Hawley clearly crossed a recognisable line, or he would not have obtained his nickname of the Hangman. And that at least some of the ways in which the rebels were despatched on 16 April raised doubts in the minds even of the hardened soldiers of Cumberland's army can be substantiated from the victors' own versions of events.

James Ray, the Whitehaven volunteer, noted that when the rebel cannon began to fire "about one o'clock…at this instant the weather grew fair".[31] There was to be no repetition of the failure to fire muskets

A detail of a painting of the rebel attack on Cumberland's left wing at Culloden. The artist, David Morier, apparently used Jacobite prisoners as "models".

because of wet ammunition that had occurred at Falkirk. The royal artillery was also well placed on this occasion, in gaps between the front line regiments, under the command of Major Belford. Whatever the charms of his young wife might have been, they did not prevent him from doing his duty that day. When his guns replied to the rebels, they "made a great slaughter house of the rebels' battery". They withstood a murderous fire for between a quarter and half an hour before they "came running on in their wild way". As they charged Belford changed his shot from ball to case. This consisted of nails, bolts and virtually any old iron which could be placed inside a paper case and rammed down a cannon. Its mutilating effects as it spread upon being fired were so devastating that it was condemned in some military quarters. When the father of a wounded English prisoner taken at Fontenoy went to Lille to see him, the French there complained to him, accusing the British army of firing with iron grape. Whenever he fought the Marshal de Saxe Cumberland was punctilious about the conventions of warfare, and the visiting Englishman strenuously denied the charge.[32] The duke showed no scruples about using grape against rebels, however. "Their lines were formed so thick and deep," according to Michael Hughes, another volunteer in the royal army, "that the grapeshot made open lanes quite through them, the men dropping down by wholesale."[33]

The rebel left wing charged the royal right three times, running up to within 100 yards of their front line before retiring. Cumberland himself, who had taken up his position opposite them on the right, "imagining the greatest push would be there", observed that "the Royals and Pulteneys hardly took their firelocks from their shoulders, so that after those faint attempts they made off".[34]

The two armies came more closely to grips with each other on the duke's left, where Ray noted that "their whole first line came down". This was because the rebels in the centre were so decimated by musket fire from the regiments in the middle of the royal first line that they wheeled, to mingle with their own right wing in one confused body. Those on the extreme right sustained a devastating fire as they charged too, not just from the front line of the royal army, but also from the enclosure on their flank. A party of Campbells under Hawley had made gaps in the dry stone walls of the enclosure to let through some dragoons, and now fired into the ranks of the rebels as they charged. Wolfe's regiment too had lined up along the easternmost wall, and likewise shot at them as they ran past. Even so, many got through, outflanking Barrell's regiment on the extreme left of the front line, "which was drove back with the weight of them".[35] Cumberland reported that "the greatest part of the little loss we had was there". "We gave them an English reception," bragged an officer in Wolfe's regiment, "and plied them with continual fire from our rear and fixt bayonets in front."[36] The "smart fire" from the regiments in the second line, soon repulsed them, though not before some had dropped their muskets about 150 yards before the royal front line, in order to fight Barrell's men with broadswords. Their opponents retaliated with bayonets, and in the fierce hand-to-hand fighting which ensued, Lord Robert Kerr and about seventeen men were killed on the royal ranks. But "the rebels paid dear for this rash attack," according to Ray, "for of about 500 of them...I believe there was not a single man that escaped." Many were "spitted with bayonets".[37] "I dare say," claimed Cumberland, "there was neither soldier nor officer of Barrell's and that part of Monroe's which engaged, who did not kill their one or two men with their bayonets and spontoons." The newspapers were soon to report that "Barrell's regiment have gained the greatest reputation in the late engagement; the best of the clans having made their strongest efforts to break them, but without effect, for the old Tangierines bravely repulsed those boasters, with a dreadful slaughter, and convinc'd them that their broad sword and target is unequal to the musket and bayonet when in the hands of veterans who are determined to use them. After the battle there was not a bayonet in the regiment but was either bloody or bent." An officer in Monroe's regiment, which was immediately on the right of Barrell's, boasted that "our lads fought more like Devils than men...no one that attacked us, escaped alive, for we gave no quarter, nor would accept of any."[38] "They so fairly drove them back," concluded Cumberland's account of the fighting on his left, "that in their rage that they could not make any impression upon the battalions, they threw stones at them for at least a minute before their total rout began."

What caused the rebels to turn and run was the sustained firing of their opponents, across their whole front line. The right wing "gave their fire in so close and so full a manner that the ground was soon covered with the bodies of the dead and wounded, and the cannon being again loaded, these fired into the midst of the fugitives, and made a frightful carnage."[39] On the left an officer found it "incredible to believe the perpetual fire our troops made for five minutes, which caused the rebels to retreat, on which we made our pursuit, but could hardly march for dead bodies. Sure never such slaughter was made in so short a time."[40] There the retreating rebels again had to run the gauntlet of the Campbells inside the enclosure wall, who now came out to fight them as they fled. They also ran into the dragoons who had filed through the gaps in the walls to attack their second line. These now "rode in among the fugitives, and hacked them terribly with their broad swords, some had their brains beat out by the horses, so that only few of that wing escaped to the other side of the Nairn, where it was not practicable to pursue them."[41]

The rest of the royal cavalry converged in the middle of the field to give chase to the rebels who were fleeing towards Inverness. "Lord Ancram was ordered to pursue with the horse as far as he could," wrote Cumberland, who gave the order, "and which he did with so good effect, that a very considerable number were killed in the pursuit…Major General Bland… also made great slaughter and gave quarter to none but about fifty French officers and soldiers he picked up in his pursuit." "The dragoons and light horse pursued calling out 'Cut hard, pay 'em home', etc", claimed one who probably rode in Cobham's regiment after the rebels, adding "our men have really been pretty severe, and gave little quarter."[42] The relentless horsemen "cut down every thing in their way."[43] How many were hacked to death flying before them it is now impossible to ascertain, but the sight of slaughter was observable all the way down from the battlefield to Inverness, the streets of which were said to have "run with the blood of those killed in the pursuit". An eye witness wrote from the town two days later that "for near four miles from where the pursuit began, the ground is cover'd with dead bodies. Rebels, as they were, shocking even to look on!" Another observed that "the country is covered with their dead bodies." A newspaper report estimated that "1700 of them were buried from the field of battle; and in the pursuit…it appears in all that 3,600 have been killed." i.e. that nearly 2,000 bodies littered the road from the moor to the town, to say nothing of those who, though desperately wounded "crawled off and died in the woods", some many miles away.[44] A messenger who took a letter from Inverness to Lord Glenorchy at Taymouth two weeks later said "he saw near 500 of the rebels, most of them wounded and many dying in huts upon the way."[45] "The misery and distress of the fugitive rebels was inexpressible," admitted James Ray, "hundreds being found dead of their wounds, and thro' hunger, at the distance of twelve, fourteen or twenty miles from the field of battle."

While Cobham's dragoons and Kingston's light horse were galloping like furies down to Inverness, back on the moor behind them the smoke from the artillery, which thanks to the easterly wind had near blinded the rebel army, gradually cleared, uncovering a ghastly sight. "I never saw a field thicker of dead" stated a fusilier. A visitor to it early next morning "spent at least three hours in viewing the dead. The sight was something shocking, but the numbers of the slain made it familiar." An officer of Barrell's regiment also returned there the following day, "where lay 1500 of the flower of the Highland clans."[46] This grisly spectacle does not appear to have turned the stomachs of the royal infantry, who at last obtained some refreshment, Cumberland personally ordering each man some brandy and a biscuit. When they received these victuals "they advanced huzzaing, and throwing up not only their own hats, but some bonnets in the air, while the transports discharged a round for victory." They all called out "Now, Billy for Flanders".[47] After their delayed lunch

REBELL GRATITUDE.

Or a Representation of the Treachery and Barbarity of two Rebell Officers, at the Battle of Culloden, who had their Lives Generously given them by the Earl of Ancram, (Who had a considerable Command that Day) and by Captain Grosett Engineer & Aid De Camp to the General. The One attempted to shoot His Lordship behind his back with a Pistol, which He had kept conceal'd & which luckily, only Flash'd in the Pan, the Other, shot Captain Grosett Dead with his own Pistol, which happened Accidentally to fall from him as he was on Horseback under pretence of restoring the same to the Captain. These Rebells received the Just reward of their Perfidy, by being immediately cut to pieces by the Kings Troops, And it is generally believed that this their Ingratitude and Treachery greatly heightned the Slaughter that was that Day made of their Party. Captain Grosett left behind him a Distressed Widow, with Six young Children.

This Battle was fought the 16th of April 1746. Relative thereto to Act of Parliament Jan.ry 14. 1747.

146

they made their way down to Inverness, a journey which sobered them up a little, for "when near Inverness they appeared somewhat concerned at the case of the miserable people, whose carcasses lay strewed in the way."[48] The concern did not last long, however, for that night they ate the food which had been prepared for their rivals' suppers by the inhabitants of the town.

The rebels killed on the battle field were not slain in cold blood, the royal army having, on the contrary, what one officer called "full revenge in hot".[49] He alluded to the alleged butchery of their own colleagues in previous battles when the boot was on the other foot. It was widely believed that the rebels had indiscriminately slaughtered the wounded at Prestonpans, and that at Falkirk "they knocked them on the head, and slew them outright".[50] Even the slaughter in the pursuit was the work of men "warm in their resentment". The frustration, not only of the soldiers, but of all who felt resentful that their way of life had been disturbed by Highlanders who lived beyond the pale of civilisation, found vent in this dreadful bloodletting. A whig historian of the rebellion explained the slaughter, partly by referring to the memories of what the rebels were alleged to have done previously, but also with a curious reference to their strangeness: "the habit of the enemy was strange, their language still stranger, and their way of fighting unusual."[51] They were regarded widely as aliens, as barbarians intruding into polite society. The language used in addresses to describe their final destruction makes Culloden almost a national catharsis. York corporation sent in its congratulations on "the late glorious success over rebellious savages". The Merchant Company of Edinburgh spoke of the rebels as "the barbarous inhabitants of the more remote parts of the country". Ludlow called them "barbarians, enemies to all civil society". Southwold thanked Cumberland for freeing them from "wolves and tygers, maugre the fierceness of those mountain savages". The process of dehumanising the rebels by calling them 'animals' and 'vermin', which started when their pursuit through England was compared with a chase, continued as Cumberland pursued them to the north of Scotland, which Sir John Ligonier called "the disagreeable hunting of those wild beasts".[52] The chase culminated at Culloden. A private in the Royal regiment described their charge in words which summed up this whole attitude, writing to his wife that "they came running upon our front line like troops of hungry wolves".[53] And like a pack of wild beasts they were hunted down and killed as they fled from the field.

(Opposite) As counter-propaganda to the atrocity stories circulated after Culloden, the actions of the British troops were 'justified' on the grounds that they were reacting to "the treacherous behaviour of some of the rebels who, after quarter given, fired at the officers who had given it".

The day after the battle a more sinister justification for harsh measures was added to the catalogue of grievances, real or imagined. The Orders of the Day issued by the duke of Cumberland on the 17th instructed a captain and fifty infantrymen "to march directly and visit all the cottages in the neighbourhood of the field of battle and to search for rebels," adding grimly, "the officer and men will take notice that the public orders of the rebels yesterday was to give us no quarters."[54] This is usually taken to have been a licence to kill. The only alternative explanation which has been offered, though even it admits that the wording of the order may have been unfortunate, is that "the intention may well have been to warn those detailed for the work that they had to deal with desperate men from whom no quarter was to be expected."[55] Now it is true that some accounts of the severities of the previous day accounted for them in part by "the treacherous behaviour of some of the rebels who, after quarter given, fired at the officers who had given it."[56] This was attributed at the time to their endeavouring to comply with the order to give no quarter even when they were near to death. But this 'clarification' of Cumberland's orders is not entirely convincing, since it was apparently neither intended nor taken that way. Those officers who gave quarter to the rebels after the battle got no thanks from the duke. "Major McKenzie has not yet been allowed to see the Duke," Alexander Brodie informed Lord Loudoun on 29 April, "for he is angry at all officers that give their parole to rebels."[57] When news of the order he issued on the 17th reached London some read it as being one to give no quarter. Lord Bury, whom he had sent with the news of the victory, was challenged about this at a masquerade on 1 May. He was asked "in broad Scotch...Did the Duke make order that no quarters should be given? To which he answered, No, but that, their men knowing the day before the action the orders of the rebel generals [he] believed they gave the rebels no quarter, and that for his own part as long as he wore a sword he never would give quarter in the field to a rebel."[58] Although this can only be a garbled version of what Bury said, it is clear enough how he took the duke's order. As for the way in which others interpreted it, a letter from Wolfe's regiment complained that they had taken more prisoners than they "should have done, had we known their orders, which was to spare neither man, woman or child".[59]

"Their mock Prince gave out orders not to give quarters to the English," William Oman wrote from Inverness on 23 April, "which have caused a great many lives to be taken."[60] Besides sending fifty men up to the moor Cumberland ordered a detachment of 500, led by Lieutenant Colonel Cockayne, to go to Lady Mackintosh's house, about twelve miles from Inverness, and bring her back as a prisoner. On their way "they found several wounded, and others endeavouring to hide themselves, all which were shot directly."[61] When Captain Thomas Davis heard that parties were out searching for the Young Pretender and his adherents, he exclaimed "pray God they may have success, in hopes of having revenge for the unnatural orders he gave out in the morning before the action not to give a man of us quarters, which writing orders have been found upon them."[62]

Whether such orders were in fact issued by the rebels has been a matter of dispute ever since. Lord Balmerino denied in his speech from the scaffold before laying his head on the block that any had been. On the other hand Lord Kilmarnock acknowledged that when he was a prisoner at Inverness he had heard officers refer to some being in the duke of Cumberland's possession. There were many stories circulating in the days after the battle about these alleged orders. "Those rapacious villains thought to have destroyed their prisoners," Enoch Bradshaw, a soldier in Cobham's dragoons wrote to his brother, "and by their orderly book had they got the better we were to have been every soul cut off, and not to have had one prisoner, and for the Duke he was to have been cut as small as herbs for the pot."[63] "There was one of their orderly books found after the battle," Hugh Ross informed a Newcastle correspondent, "wherein their orders the night before we fought was to not give quarters to man woman or child and to cut all our prisoners throats and murder every one from this to London."[64] A "copy of the rebels orders" was even published in the press before the end of the month, containing the statement, "give no quarter to the Elector's troops on any account what-soever".[65] In some versions the orders were also said to have been signed by Lord George Murray.[66] The authenticity of this copy, however, has been called in question. Cumberland has even been accused of fabricating "an impudent forgery of an order from the Prince to give no quarter...for no other purpose but to execute what was intended, and to divest the common soldiers of all sentiments of humanity and compassion and harden them for the execution of such bloody designs."[67]

Several copies of orders actually signed by Lord George Murray have survived, none of which contains the notorious phrase.[68] They give the pass word 'Rie James' (King James) and continue:

> It is His Royal Highness positive Orders that every person attach themselves to some Corps of the Armie and to remain with that Corps night and day till the Battle and persute be finally over, This regards the Foot as well as the Horse.
> The Order of Battle is to be given to every General officer and every Commander of Regiments or Squadrons
> It is required and expected that each individual in the Armie as well officer as Souldier keep their posts that shall be alotted to

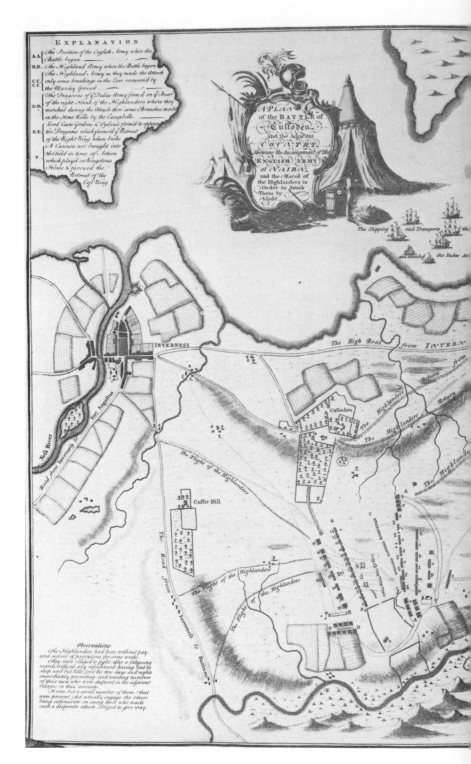

The terrain between Nairn and Inverness, showing the routes of the rebels on

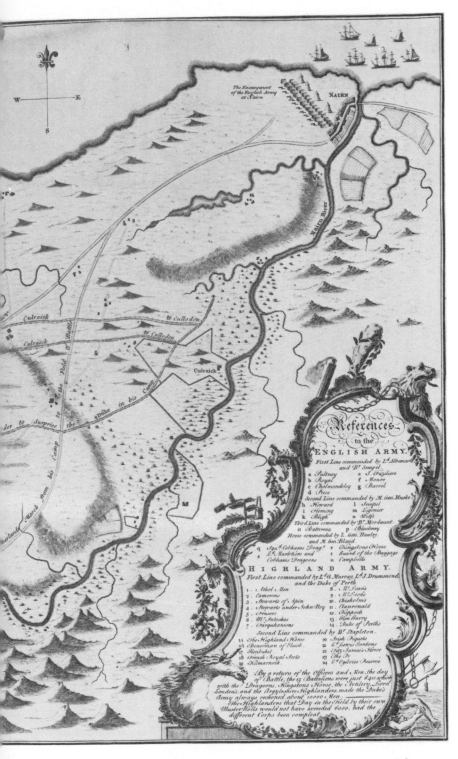

Within the map illustration:

W E (compass with) S

The Encampment of the English Army at Nairn

NAIRN

Nairn River

Culraick

Culraick

To Culloden

To Culloden

Culraick

the Duke in his Camp

order to Surprise the

March from his Camp

References to the ENGLISH ARMY.

First Line commanded by Ld Albemarle and B.^r Sempel.
a . Pultney
b . Royal
c . Cholmondeley
d . Price
e . S. Fraziliers
f . Monro
g . Barrel

Second Line commanded by M. Gen. Huske.
h . Howard
i . Fleming
k . Bligh
l . Sempel
m . Ligonier
n . Wolfe

Third Line commanded by B.^r Mordaunt.
o . Batterau
p . Blackney

Horse commanded by L. Gen. Hawley, and M. Gen. Bland.
q . Squ.^d Cobhams Drag.
s . Ld Markhew and Cobhams Dragons
r . Kingstons Horse
t . Guard of the Baggage
u . Campbells

HIGHLAND ARMY.
First Line commanded by Ld G. Murray, Ld J. Drummond, and the Duke of Perth.
1 . Athol Men
2 . Camerons
3 . Stewarts of Apin
4 . Stewarts under John Roy
5 . Frissors
6 . Mc Intoshes
7 . Farquharsons
8 . Mc Leans
9 . Mc Leods
10 . Chisholms
11 . Clanronald
12 . Keppoch
13 . Glen Garry
14 . Duke of Perths

Second Line commanded by B.^r Stapleton.
15 . The Highland Horse
16 . Bannerman of Elsick
17 . Hindsket
18 . French Royal Scots
19 . Kilmarnock
20 . Irish Piquets
21 . Ld Lewis Gordons
22 . Ld J. James's Horse
23 . The Pr.
24 . Ld Ogilvies Reserve

By a return of the Officers and Men the day of ye Battle, the 15 Battalions were just 6400 which with the Dragoons, Kingstons Horse, the Artilery, Lord Londons, and the Argyleshire Highlanders, made the Dukes Army always reckoned about 10000 Men.
The Highlanders that Day in the Field by their own Muster-Rolls would not have exceeded 6000, had the different Corps been compleat.

the night of 15 April and of the royal forces on the morning of the 16th.

Original Orders, under
Lord George Murray's own
Hand; from April 14: to 15:
1746.

Orders from the 13th to the 15th April
1746

Rie James (in English King James)

It is His Royall Highness posetive Orders that
every person atatch them selves to some Corps of the Armie
& to remain with that Corps night & day till the
Batle & persute be finally over; This regards the
foot as well as the Horse

The Order of Batle is to be given to every
Ginerall Officer & every Comander of Regiments
or Squadrons.

It is requierd & expected that each indevidual
in the Armie as well Officer as Souldier keep
their posts that shall be alotted to them, & if
any man turn his back to Run away the nixt
behind such man is to shoot him.

No body on pain of Death to strip the
slain or Plunder till the Batle be over.
The Highlanders all to be in Kilts & no body to throw
away their Guns; by H: R H Command George Murray

*The genuine orders of Lord George Murray issued to the rebel forces for
"the 14th to the 15th April 1746".*

152

them, and if any Man turn his back to run away the next behind such man is to shoot him.

No body on pain of Death to strip the Slain or plunder till the Battle be over.

The Highlanders all to be in kilts and no body to throw away their Guns; by H.R.H. Command.

There is a document in the papers of the duke of Cumberland which virtually reproduces these orders, apart from inserting the words "and to give no quarters to the Electors troops on any account whatsoever" between the first and second sentences, i.e. between "over" and "This".[69] This is the alleged forgery, though it certainly was not written by Cumberland himself, nor is the handwriting that of his secretary or any of his aides de camp. Needless to say, it is not in Lord George Murray's handwriting either. Whoever wrote it cannot seriously have drawn it up with a view to passing it off as genuine orders issued by Lord George. The orders occupy only the bottom half of one side of a single sheet of paper. The top, written by the same hand, duplicates the Declaration published by Lord John Drummond at Montrose on 2 December 1745, and is even signed "J Drummond", though he did not write it. Moreover the controversial clause is not the only difference between Murray's genuine orders and these. For one thing these are not signed. For another, Lord George dated his "from the 14th to the 15th April", while the document is dated "Culoden April 15th". There are also several minor differences.

This sheet of paper poses problems which will probably never be solved.[70] It could have been picked up from a rebel on the battlefield, even though it is not included in the list of captured documents which Cumberland sent to the Secretary of State, for neither is the sheet signed by Lord George Murray.[71] Nor is it an orderly book, which some versions claimed had been found. Another version, however, and one which was given to the press, was that the orders had been "found in the pocket of one of the prisoners". Certainly the paper would fit into a pocket, and has indeed been folded at some now unascertainable stage in its existence, unlike Murray's orders. If it was written by a rebel, and not forged by a royalist, it could be an updating of the orders for 14—15 April, not for the battle of Culloden, but for the night march to Balblair. Although Cumberland's order book on 17 April refers to "the public orders of the rebels yesterday", while other sources relate them to the morning of the battle, they are in fact dated the 15th, and Hugh Ross heard that they were issued, "the night before we fought". Now on the night march, according to John William O'Sullivan's testimony, "everybody agreed to what was said. Sullivan was commanded to give the orders, and explain what he said in them. Lord George answered that there was no need of

Declaration Lord John Drummond, Commander in Chief of his most
Christian Majesty's Forces in Scotland

We Lord John Drummond Commander in Chief of his Most Christian Majesty's
Forces in Scotland, Do hereby declare that we are come to this Kingdom
with writer Orders, to make War well against the King of England Elector
of Hanover and all his Adherants, and that are the possitiv orders we
have from his most Christian Majesty are to Attack all his Enemies
in this Kingdom, whom he has declared to be those, who will not immediately Join, or assist as far as will ly in their Power, the Prince of Wales
Regent of Scotland &c, His Ally, and whom he is resolved, with the
Concurrence of the King of Spain, to support in the taking of Scotland
England & Ireland, if Necessary at the expence of all his Men and money
he is Master of, to which three Kingdoms, the Family of Stewart, have
so just and indisputable a Title, and his most Christian Majesty's
Positive Orders, are, that his Enemies should be used in this Kingdom
in Proportion to the Harm they do or intend to his R. H. Cause

Given at Montrose yᵉ 2ᵈ of Mir 1745 Years
J. Drummond

Caladon April 15ᵗʰ 1746
Parol / Hay Comes

The R. H. Resolves orders that every Person, Attack themselves to some Corps of this
Army, and to remain with that Corps Night and Day until the Battle and Persuit
be fully over, And to give no Quarters to the Electors Troops, on any Account
whatsoever, This regards the Foot as well as the Horse &c

All order of battle to be given to every Genᵉ Person and every Commander of Regimᵗ
and Squadrons
It is required and expected that every Individual Person in the Army as well
Officer as Soldier to keep their Post as shall be Allotted them
And if any Man turn his Back, or run away the next Man behind him is to
shoot him Dead
No Body to Strip the Slain or Plunder till the Battle be over on pain yᵗ of it
The Highlanders to be in Kilt — and no body to throw away his Arms
By his Royal Highness Command

154

orders, yt everybody knew what he had to do."[72] This is an unfortunately cryptic statement. Lord George Murray was plainly against issuing
any orders, since the men knew what was required of them. What that was
has never been given its due significance. They were to march across the
moor at dead of night in order to kill the royal army as it lay asleep by
stabbing the soldiers with broadswords in cold blood. An officer who took
part in the abortive attack recorded that they were forbidden "to make
any use of our firearms, but only of sword, dirk, and bayonet, to cut the
tent strings and pull down the poles, and where we observed a swelling
or bulge in the fallen tent there to strike and push vigorously."[73] "As for
their numbers," noted a pamphleteer, "tho' not half that of the enemy,
they might very probably have succeeded, for had they made the attack
undiscovered, so as to have got in sword in hand, they had undoubtedly
cut the enemy to pieces".[74] When they knew that there were at least
twice as many men in those tents as were on the raiding party, then
whether the order was issued or not, it was as plain as a pikestaff that for
the raid to stand a chance of success they could afford to give no quarter
"on any account whatsoever". It is not clear whether O'Sullivan gave
such an order, orally or in writing. But if the duke of Cumberland is to
be found guilty or not guilty of forgery on the basis of this document
and the circumstances surrounding it, then he must be given the benefit
of the doubt: it could have been picked up from a rebel after the battle
of Culloden. Since the alleged offence of forging it took place in Scotland,
the best verdict is perhaps 'non proven'.

There can be no doubt that Cumberland was utterly convinced that
the rebels must be extirpated to prevent another rebellion breaking out.
He had already gone beyond the strict limits of the law in pursuit of what
he saw as his duty; and he was to go much further in the weeks that lay
ahead. He believed in "military execution", and thought that lenity after
the 1715 rebellion had kept treason alive. Yet there is nothing in his
character to support an accusation that he was capable of deliberately
fabricating false rebel orders, in order to ensure that his policy would be
relentlessly executed. Nor could he have done so without his colleagues
aiding and abetting him. Sir Everard Fawkener, the duke's personal secretary, Philip Yorke and Colonel Napier, his aides de camp, must at the very
least have been implicated. Unless we are to accuse the high command of
a diabolical conspiracy to denigrate their opposite numbers in the rebel
army, after they had been well and truly defeated in battle, in order to

*(Opposite) The controversial "copy of rebel orders" dated "Culoden April
15th 1746" in the duke of Cumberland's papers. Cumberland has been
accused of forging Murray's orders by adding to them "and to give no
quarters to the Elector's troops on any account whatsoever".*

justify a policy which to them needed no justification anyway, then in the light of the available evidence the duke of Cumberland must be cleared of the charge of forgery.

The allegation that goes along with it, however, namely that he authorised savage reprisals against the rebels, has stuck, along with his grim nickname, "The Butcher". What is more, both were associated with him shortly after Culloden, even among those who were relieved that the battle had brought an end to the rebellion.

At first the relief was so overwhelming that few questions were asked about the means by which domestic peace had been re-established. "The victory of Culloden gave birth to an inexpressible joy throughout the extensive dominions of the British Empire," enthused Andrew Henderson. "Not only Europe and Africa, but the two Indies joined in the shout, and gave joyful acclamations."[75] The news arrived in London ahead of Lord Bury who had been despatched with it from the battlefield. Unfortunately the ship he took from Inverness was blown off course and spent five days at sea before putting in to North Berwick. He then proceeded overland, but the news travelled ahead of him, arriving in the capital on 23 April, a day before he did. Apart from the issue of an extraordinary *London Gazette* on the 23rd, official celebrations awaited his arrival. When he was introduced to the king, George asked him 'What's become of my son?", and on being assured that the duke was well replied "then all is well with me". He then ordered Bury a present of 1,000 guineas and withdrew, being "unable to speak for joy".[76] Ordinary citizens, however, did not wait until the guns in Hyde Park and the Tower saluted the victory on the 24th before demonstrating their joy. "This town has been in a blaze these two days," Sir John Ligonier wrote to Cumberland on the 25th, "Return as soon as you please. No lady that prides to the name of an English woman will refuse you."[77] Horace Walpole wrote to Sir Thomas Mann on the same day, "the town is all blazing round me, as I write, with fireworks and illuminations."[78]

Probably every town in the country celebrated the victory too. One of the first was Newcastle upon Tyne where the news arrived on 21 April. The *Newcastle Journal* reported that it:[79]

> ran thro' this town like a torrent, and in a few minutes was spread into every corner of it; all business was immediately suspended and every man hastened to congratulate his neighbour and his friend on the joyful occasion; so that the streets were quickly crowded and echoed with repeated shouts and acclamations; the bells at the same time rung their peals from all the churches and the guns incessantly thundered from the ships and around the walls. About five in the afternoon, the Marquis of Granby's

General James Wolfe, who took Quebec in 1759, was a brigade-major at Culloden, although he was then only 18. There is a legend that the duke of Cumberland ordered him to shoot a wounded rebel on the battlefield, and when Wolfe refused got another to obey the order. Although the story is almost certainly false it contributed to Cumberland's reputation as "the Butcher".

regiment was drawn up on the Sandhill, where the Right Worship-
ful the Mayor and the rest of the magistrates of the corporation
were present. The regiment made three excellent fires and betwixt
the vollies many loyal healths were drunk by the magistrates,
officers, and other gentlemen, amidst the loudest huzzas of the
people; after which the mayor made a handsome present to the
soldiers to drink his Majesty's health, etc. In the evening bonfires
were lighted in the streets, and the windows both of the houses
and the churches in the town, thro' every lane and alley, to the
extremities of the suburbs, and the ships in the river, were more
generally and splendidly illuminated than ever was known on
any occasion. Nor were the rejoicings confined to the limits of
Newcastle, but equally manifested by all possible demonstrations
in every town and village, nay, even thro' the country, and in
private houses, as far as the news had reached.

Similar celebrations occurred throughout the land. As with the addresses
and Associations which preceded the campaign in England, so with the
rejoicings subsequent to the battle of Culloden, the lead was taken by
Court whigs. Thus Cholmley Turner, MP for York, organised a celebratory
buffet at his house, which was attended by no fewer than 2,000 people.
Those at dinner drank ten healths, including one to "the archbishop of
Canterbury, the duke of Newcastle, the Lord Chancellor and Mr Pelham".
   Like the previous manifestations of loyalty, the demonstrations after
the battle cannot be dismissed as contrived set pieces stage managed by
the Court; they too brought together all parties and classes to attest their
allegiance. At Preston "both sexes of all ages and ranks made addition
to their dresses suitable to the day" on 28 April. "The men had cockades
in their hats of green and red, the colours of the Duke's livery, and the
medal struck on the Duke's retaking Carlisle fasten'd thereto; the women
had ribbands and breast knots of the same colour, but they had besides
red ones stampt with 'For King George and the Protestant Succession'."[80]
The bells of the established Church rang for days, while the dissenters
demonstrated their joy rather more quietly. The minutes of the first
Independent Church in Bedford record how on 30 April "besides the
supplications which were now made on the account of our national
troubles, there were praises and thanksgivings offered up for the complete
victory over the rebels in the battle of Culloden, near Inverness, under
his Royal Highness the Duke of Cumberland."
   At the very end of April both Houses of Parliament addressed the king
with their congratulations for the suppression of the rebellion. On the
29th the Lords presented theirs, which included a passage praising the
duke of Cumberland:

It is with the greatest pleasure and admiration we behold in how eminent a manner this signal victory has been owing to the valour and conduct of His Royal Highness the Duke: if anything can add to our joy on such an event, it is to see a prince of your majesty's blood, formed by your example and imitating your virtues, the glorious instrument of it; and happy should we be in any opportunity of testifying the high sense we have of such illustrious merit.

Next day the Commons followed suit, praising Cumberland rather less fulsomely, though more practically offering to give him a mark of public gratitude, an offer they followed up with a grant of £25,000 a year in addition to the £15,000 allowed him in the civil list.

But while his praises were being sung and honours were showering upon him, some discordant notes were also being struck. It was on 1 May that Lord Bury was asked at a masquerade if the Duke had ordered his men to give no quarter to the rebels. "Tom Curious" wrote a letter to the author of the *National Journal* observing that, in all the lists of prisoners taken at Culloden, none were described as wounded, and wished to be informed "what became of the rebels that were left wounded in the field at that battle?" This alluded to ugly stories that were circulating that they had been systematically put to death. The Revd Robert Forbes devotedly collected accounts of the atrocities allegedly committed by the royal forces in some ten manuscript volumes which he called *The Lyon in Mourning*. These are a mine of information for those seeking to dig up evidence that the duke of Cumberland was the 'Butcher' of legend. They are also a minefield, for many of the dark deeds which Forbes faithfully chronicled blow up if they are not handled carefully. One of the more horrific of them was challenged by contemporary testimony. It concerned one John Fraser, an Ensign in Lovat's regiment, who was shot through the thigh by a musket ball at Culloden, and taken prisoner after the battle. He was carried to Culloden house, where, he claimed, "a multitude of prisoners, all gentlemen, lay under strong guards". According to Fraser, they were left for two days with undressed wounds "in great torture", until on the third day he and eighteen others were taken from the house in carts. They at first thought that they were being taken to Inverness for medical attention, but were soon disillusioned; for when they reached a park dyke the carts stopped, they were dragged out by their guards, and shot in cold blood. The guards proceeded to knock out the brains of those who were not quite dead, one of them, observing signs of life in Fraser, striking him in the face with the butt end of his gun, dashing out an eye and breaking his nose. Though he was left for dead, he survived and managed to crawl away from the charnel pit of the dyke, until a good

A romantic representation of the atrocities allegedly committed by Cumberland's troops against wounded rebels, and even their women and children, after the battle of Culloden. Such accusations also fostered "Butcher" Cumberland's notoriety.

Samaritan saw him and took him home, where he revived.[81]

His story first appeared in print in a pamphlet published in 1749 with the title *An account of the signal escape of John Fraser.* When he read it, the Revd Henry Etough wrote to Sir Everard Fawkener to inform him that he had shown it to two officers of Dejean's regiment who had fought at Culloden, and "they both assured me of the representation being absolutely false and groundless".[82] One of them had himself been wounded in the battle, and taken to Culloden house, where he had stayed for fourteen weeks. "He averreth that to his certain knowledge none of the wounded rebels were carried to Culloden house; that a few of the common soldiers were there and two serjeants but not one Ensign nor any of superior rank. He added that not one of those had received any hurt and that they did not remain in the House above two hours."

If stories of systematic butchery of the rebels cannot be sustained, a milder version of their treatment, namely that they were left for two days up on the moor by way of reprisal for their alleged neglect of royal troops wounded after other battles, appears to be more well grounded. Indeed even wounded soldiers in the duke's own army seem to have been neglected, though in their case more through carelessness than calculation. At all events on Saturday 19 April, three days after the battle, a serjeant and six men were ordered to take fifteen or twenty carts "as soon as possible to the houses in the neighbourhood of the field of battle in order to bring to the hospital here [Inverness] the poor wounded soldiers who thro' the negligence of the officers and surgeons were left there without care."[83] This order might be taken to refer to the rebels, and to show Cumberland's concern for them, if it did not end "and to report the number and regiment they belong to". His contempt for the defeated rebel army was such that in the days after Culloden he was heard to abuse them "for being dastardly cowards for allowing him so compleat a victory so cheap".[84] He even arranged for the standards captured in the battle to be burned in Edinburgh rather than taken to London in triumph, a task performed by the town's chimney sweeps. He was not in a mood to regard it as a regular force with distinct regiments after his total victory. The duke would only give such an instruction to care for his own men. If they could be treated so callously, then the stories that their wounded enemies were deliberately left untreated gain credence.

Such reports reaching London from Scotland after the battle carried sufficient credibility for a newspaper to report, before the end of May, that when the duke came back to the capital he was to be made a freeman of the Butchers' company. As Hume Campbell, who sent this news to his brother, commented "you understand what this means to signify".[85] The conceit was to become commonplace over the summer. On 1 August Horace Walpole retailed a more well-known version of the story to Sir

161

Horace Mann, telling him that, when "it was lately proposed in the City, to present him with the freedom of some company; one of the aldermen said aloud, 'Then let it be of the Butchers!'"[86] Within weeks of the action of Culloden, the duke of Cumberland had been dubbed with the title he was forever to be known by: 'the Butcher'.

CHAPTER SEVEN

"They in rebellion shall arise no more"

Enter Duke of Cumberland, Generals Hawley and Huske,
with Major Lockhart, victorious.

Duke: Beyond our hopes our foes are put to flight
Come tell me soldiers have I acted right?

Hawley: Your courage or your conduct who dare blame?
For now immortal is great William's name.
Methinks I hear the royal youth cry out
Now soldiers now we've put 'em to the rout
Kill all the wounded, see their latest breath,
And let them feel our mercy by their death.

Duke: You heard me then, I hope I was obey'd.
Curst be the heart who for the wretches plead.

Lockhart: With joy I obey your just commands
And seventy eight were finished by my hands.

Duke: Well done my Lockhart, worthy of they self,
Who fights for Glory and despises self.
The Protestant Religion is the cause,
We'll that maintain, our Liberty and Laws.
For thy reward I give thee this command,
Go then, and plunder all the Northern land.
You'll not be mov'd by wretched women's cries,
Altho' their shrieks do rent the affrighted skies.
First burn their houses, put themselves to flight,
Then we'll be safe, if this is acted right.

Lockhart: Your Highness's command I will obey,
I take your orders in this glorious day.
They in rebellion shall arise no more,
Their babes and sucklings die in blood and gore.

Anonymous (?Jacobite), fragment of a tragedy[1]

"I think I may upon the best and surest grounds rejoice with your Grace that the head of that Monster Rebellion was quite crushed on the glorious field of Culloden.", Sir Everard Fawkener wrote to the duke of Newcastle early in May 1746.[2] "The dispersed members will by degrees be quite picked up, so that nothing may remain of that Fury let loose from Hell upon us to disturb these kingdoms any more." In the weeks following the battle the government embarked upon a whole series of measures designed to ensure that another year would not share with 1715 and 1745 the dubious distinction of designating a Jacobite uprising. The army was employed in Scotland "to bruise those bad seeds spread about this country so as they may never shoot again";[3] parliament passed laws aimed at removing the capacity for starting another rebellion; and the judiciary dealt with those who had already been implicated in the uprising.

The duke of Cumberland remained in Scotland until the middle of July, sending our search parties in pursuit of the Young Pretender, and "to pursue and hunt out these vermin amongst their lurking holes".[4] Brigadier Mordaunt went with 900 volunteers into the Fraser country alongside Loch Ness "to destroy all the rebels he finds there".[5] Lord Loudoun was ordered to march from the Isle of Skye to Fort Augustus with instructions to "drive the cattle, burn the ploughs and destroy what you can belonging to all such as are or have been in the rebellion, and burning the houses of the chiefs."[6] Before proceeding to Fort Augustus he was further instructed to scour the coastline, with the doubtless unnecessary reminder "you will constantly have in mind to distress whatever country of rebels you may pass through, and to seize or destroy all persons you can find who have been in the rebellion or their abettors."[7] Lord Ancram was dispatched to Aberdeen, from where he reported that since leaving Inverness "I have burnt two Roman Catholic meeting houses and five episcopal, not forgetting two libraries of Popish and Jacobite books; in the house of one Gordon a priest I found several hundred volumes all upon that religion."[8] William McKenzie vied with Ancram in wreaking destruction between Inverness and Strathbogie, boasting that he had "burnt the Popish academy at Scala, four mass houses and two priests houses. Upon these occasions I always employed Sir Harry Monro, as I know he has a particular regard for that sect, for which I have christened him Flagellum Ecclesiae Romanae."[9] Besides Catholic chapels, one of the main targets of the raiding parties were the meeting houses of the episcopal nonjuring clergy, who were rightly regarded as being the most ardent supporters of the house of Stuart. Ancram stripped them of all their timber to provide firewood for the dragoons.[10]

Despite these expeditions, which were sent out immediately after the battle of Culloden, the *Scots Magazine* claimed that "the Duke began with the rebels in a gentle, paternal way, with soft admonitions and a promise of pardon and protection to all common people that would bring in their arms and submit to mercy."[11] There was indeed a policy of distinguishing between rebels who continued to resist the royal forces and those who voluntarily surrendered with their weapons. "Those who are found in arms," recorded Colonel Whitefoord "are ordered to be immediately put to death, and the houses of those who abscond are plundered and burnt, their cattle drove, their ploughs and other tackle destroyed."[12] To assist in the discovery of rebels "the clergy were desired to give in lists of all those in their respective parishes that had, or had not, been in the rebellion."[13] Naturally some were reluctant to do this, either through pity for the rebels or fear of reprisals. At one stage the lord justice clerk suggested that it might make their task easier if they were simply asked to list those of their parishioners who had not been 'out': "this sounds well and yet will be of the same use because lists of the whole parish can be got at any time."[14] Although some ministers, led by the Edinburgh clergy, objected that the well-affected might suffer "from any unjust suspicions on occasion of this rebellion", Cumberland insisted on the production of lists of rebels too, since "an ill-judged lenity is the greatest cruelty".[15] A guarantee of confidentiality procured a great many parochial compilations, which gave the government a sort of index to the rebels throughout much of Scotland.[16]

When men came in to surrender their weapons the policy was to detain their leaders, while "private rebels...receive certificates and return unmolested to their homes until his Majesty's further pleasure is known."[17] How far this was carried out, however, depended to a large extent upon the attitudes of the officers who had to enforce it. Major General John Campbell implemented it strictly, giving orders "to receive such arms as were brought in, taking down the names and places of abode of such as surrendered, that the common people should be allowed to return home. But if any gentlemen come in they shall be civilly treated but kept prisoners till such time as I should know H.R.H's pleasure concerning them."[18] On the other hand General Bland ordered the commander of the men who were sent to demolish Cameron of Lochiel's house "to destroy as many of them as he can, since prisoners would only embarrass him; and in case the country people did not come in immediately, deliver up all their arms and submit to the king's mercy, he was to burn and destroy their habitations, seize all their cattle, and put the men to death, being pretty well assured it will be difficult for him to shed innocent blood on that count."[19] Scottish officers tended to treat their fellow countrymen more leniently than did the English. Lord Loudoun, for example, was scrupulous in his dealings with rebels who surrendered, while Hawley disdained the humane approach. The 'Hangman' indicated his attitude to the duke of Richmond, writing from Fort Augustus in

June that "if his Majesty would leave me the foot here and the parliament give the men a guinea and a pair of shoes for every rebel's head they brought in I would still undertake to clear this country…There's still so many more houses to burn, and I hope still some to be put to death, tho' by computation there's about seven thousand houses burned already, yet all is not done."[20] Nationality did not necessarily divide the humane from the brutal, however, for the men who acquired the most unsavoury reputations in these weeks were lowland Scots such as Major Lockhart and Captain Caroline Scot. Lockhart ignored the protection which Lord Loudoun had promised to rebels who surrendered their arms in accordance with the procedures laid down by the duke of Cumberland, and which his lordship had guaranteed by issuing them with warrants. The brutal Major maintained "that because of their many wicked, inhuman acts, both of a publick and private nature, if they were to show him a warrant from Heaven, it should not hinder him from following his orders."[21] Lord Ancram also disregarded protections which the civil authorities gave to "abettors in this rebellion". In Dundee he came across a case of a man released from prison by order of the lord justice clerk "because he was ill". Although, given the conditions in prisons, he must have been near death's door, Ancram would have none of it. "If these things are allowed," he complained "they will soon take care all to be ill."[22] By contrast there were some "officers of all ranks", as the Jacobite James Maxwell of Kirkconnell conceded, "whom neither the prospect of ingratiating themselves, and making their fortunes, nor the contagion of bad examples, were able to corrupt. Some of those that had done the Government the most essential services were as conspicuous now for their humanity as formerly for their courage and conduct. It might be indiscreet to be particular at present," he concluded darkly, "but their names…are already known."[23]

Much depended also on the frame of mind of the commander in chief. Cumberland did not licence indiscriminate looting, ordering his troops "to behave with discretion, and to plunder none but by order, and then there is an officer and a party to do it."[24] Apart from severely disciplining blatant offenders, however, he does not appear to have exercised a great deal of control over the activities of his army. Certainly the senior officers were given a free hand to interpret his orders how they wished. Thus Bland complained that his colleagues showed little appreciation of the distinction between licensed and unlicensed plunder, "and their example descended to officers of a lower station and from them to the private men, which drew on all the licentiousness we have all seen."[25]

While Cumberland was in Inverness, where he stayed until 23 May, he was joined by Lord President Forbes whose sage legal counsel seems to have greatly influenced his views on how to deal with the aftermath of

Duncan Forbes of Culloden House, Lord President of the Scottish Court of Session. When he interceded with Cumberland, urging clemency for Jacobites captured after the battle, the duke was said to have dismissed him as "that old woman who talked to me about humanity".

167

the rebellion. A memorandum which Forbes drew up for the duke's consideration began "No severity that is necessary ought to be dispensed
with, the omitting such severities is cruelty to the king and kingdom.
Unnecessary severities create pity, and pity from unnecessary severities
is the most dangerous nurse to disaffection, especially if continued for any
time".[26] It was necessary to be severe with the leaders of the Forty-five
"since the abuse of the lenity shown in the prosecution of the last rebellion aggravates their guilt and shews it to be unsafe for the public to trust
to that gratitude which may be expected from mercy shewed to men of
such principles." On the other hand it was unnecessary to deal severely
with the common people. Quite the reverse, for if they were "sought
after, and to a man destroyed, tho' the Pretender will thereby have lost
so many hands, it is a question whether the complaints of the disaffected
may not furnish a much stronger recruit to that villainous cause in a short
time." The lord president recommended the transportation of whole
clans to the American colonies, a policy which appealed strongly to
Cumberland "because it is feared, and I believe with great reason, that
while they remain in this island their rebellious and thievish nature is
not to be kept under without an army always within reach of them."

Then in the last week of May the duke moved to Fort Augustus, where
the army regarded itself as being in the heart of enemy country. "We are
now in the very centre of their fastnesses," wrote his secretary shortly
after their arrival, "which have hitherto been deemed inaccessible to
an army."[27] Here Cumberland's policy changed from pacification to
punishment. He was determined to maintain a high military profile in the
mountains to teach the Highlanders "that it is as much in his Majesty's
power to march his forces into that country which they have hitherto
boasted as inaccessible as into any other part of his dominions."[28] In
Fort Augustus he seems to have reappraised the policy of distinguishing
between those who surrendered their weapons and those who remained
in arms. "I hope his Majesty will not imagine that by these people's
laying down their arms the country is a jot surer from any fresh rising,"
he warned Newcastle, "for at this time almost every Highlander is possessed of two or three sets of arms."[29] *The Scots Magazine* was persuaded
that equivocal surrenders of old rusty weapons, while proper arms were
concealed, led Cumberland "to lay the rod more heavy upon them, by
carrying fire and sword through their country, and driving off their
cattle."[30] There were certainly some instances of punishing such equivo-
cation. "The people of Glenmoriston and the McDonalds in Glengary
trifled," Sir Everard Fawkener wrote in a letter to Lord Chesterfield,
"and their country has been laid waste and the cattle drove away."[31]

"In order to root out the remainder of the rebels", including if possible the Young Pretender, Cumberland visited Fort William at the end

of May, and sent out four raiding parties into the remotest parts of the Highlands. Lord George Sackville took 500 men across the country from Fort Augustus to Glenelg; Lieutenant Colonel Edward Cornwallis went with 300 along Loch Lochy and up Loch Arkaig to rendezvous with him; Captain Caroline Scot was directed to go from Fort William around Loch Eil; and, "that no part of the country may pass unexamined," Major General John Campbell was sent "to sweep everything that lies in Sunart and Morven." Meanwhile Captain John Fergusson threaded his way through the western isles in the *Furnace*, hunting for fugitives.[32]

These expeditions have become legendary for their brutality and bloodlust.[33] Even loyal Highlanders suffered from their depredations. Lord Fortrose protested that Sackville's men had attacked his country of Kintail, where his tenants had been beaten up and taken prisoners, "their houses plundered and burnt to ashes, their wives and daughters ravished, the whole of their cattle violently carried away, and even a little house I had there for my own conveniency first rifled and then hacked to the ground."[34] Major General Campbell confiscated cattle in Strontain although he admitted that "the people have and are delivering up their arms, submitting to his Majesty's mercy", yet he claimed he had "a very just pretence for so doing" because they were the duke of Argyll's tenants and owed his Grace two years' rent![35] The confiscation of their cattle and movables laid the greater part of Morvern waste. When such treatment could be meted out to loyal clans, or to people who surrendered in accordance with Cumberland's conditions, then those who offered any resistance to the raiding parties could expect no mercy. A reprisal raid by soldiers stationed at Fort William on Archibald Cameron's land left his mansion house and his tenants' houses rifled and burned with all their contents, their wives stripped and raped, and their livestock confiscated, so that he was utterly ruined and his tenantry "quite depauperated". His wife and five small children, as he explained to John Campbell, "were obliged to betake themselves to the wild hills...exposed to both cold and hunger, and yea thereby one of my children perished in the mountains, whose corpse I could not get decently interred in a Christian burial ground."[36] Such stories could be repeated many times over, and were, losing nothing in the telling when told to more sympathetic ears.

While Highlanders fled before the troops to starve in the hills, their tormentors fattened on their booty. A soldier stationed at Fort Augustus observed that "whilst our army stayed here we had near twenty thousand head of cattle brought in, such as oxen, horses, sheep and goats taken from the rebels (whose houses we also frequently plundered and burnt) by parties sent out for them, and in search of the Pretender; so that great numbers of our men grew rich in their shares in the spoil."[37] There was in fact a great market for livestock at the Fort, with drovers going to it from as far away as Yorkshire to take advantage of the ridiculously low prices the army were asking for the beasts they had rounded up in their raiding sorties. Nor were soldiers the only depredators in the highlands. It is clear from Captain Fergusson's log of his cruise about the isles that he wreaked havoc and misery upon their inhabitants.[38]

He failed, however, in his ultimate aim of locating the Young Pretender, though he did discover Lord Lovat "concealed in the trunk of a tree in a wood", after whipping one of his servants until he agreed to disclose his whereabouts.[39] The duke of Cumberland was so hopeful of his search parties finding Charles Edward that he stayed at Fort Augustus longer than he had originally intended. Since the barracks there had been burned down by the rebels "they made a pretty place for the Duke to reside in", in the words of Michael Hughes, who described it as "a fine hut with doors and glass windows, covered at the top with green sods and boughs", though another soldier thought it was more like "a Scotch palace built on purpose of turf...for his levee room is nigh thirty foot square".[40] To while away the time he gave prizes to the winners of races run on Galloway horses, "little larger than a good tup". There were events for both men and women, who rode these steeds bare back, while General Hawley and Colonel Howard also raced each other for a bet of twenty guineas, the "Hangman" winning by about four inches.[41] "It was necessary to entertain life in this manner," one participant considered, "otherwise by the constant view of mountains surrounding us, we should have been affected with hypochondriacal melancholy"![42]

Charles Edward eluded his pursuers until September, when he escaped to France. Meanwhile Cumberland had decided to quit Scotland too. He left Fort Augustus on 18 July, stayed overnight in Edinburgh on the 21st, and reached London on the afternoon of the 25th. He arrived to a hero's welcome, the capital celebrating his return as enthusiastically as it had done the news of his victory at Culloden. "All the bells in the City of London and Westminster rung, and at evening were illuminations and bonfires, with continual firing of guns for several hours, and all other demonstrations of the greatest joy from people of all ranks."[43] At a thanksgiving service in St Paul's cathedral the congregation was treated to the first performance of Handel's "The Conquering Hero", composed specially for his Highness.

Cumberland left behind him in Scotland the strongest military presence the country had ever seen. The earl of Albermarle was his reluctant successor as commander in chief, protesting that he was being "kept in the worst country existing".[44] Major General Blakeney commanded "from Fort William along the chain by Inverness and coast to Speymouth," with regiments in every major fortress. The Highlands were virtually occupied territory. It was felt to be necessary to maintain a high military profile "till Forts shall be built". The government embarked on a programme of strengthening the chain, the most ambitious aspect of which was the construction of a whole new fort to replace the one destroyed by the rebels at Inverness. When it was completed the new structure, named Fort St George after its predecessor though it was built by the sea to the east of Inverness, was one of the most impregnable in Europe. It remains to this day a monument to eighteenth-century engineering, a symbol of the hard line which the government adopted after the Forty-five. Cumberland, the main architect of that policy, also left behind a great deal of both good and ill will. His soldiers loved him. "I am sure I speak the sentiments of the whole army," wrote one of them, "we shall certainly regret him, when he is from us...our fellows will never fight with so much coolness and firmness as under his eye and command."[45] The Highlanders hated him. When they learned that an English flower had been renamed Sweet William in his honour, they nicknamed one of their most noxious weeds Stinking Billy.

Before he left for London Cumberland perused a "sketch of regulations to be made in Scotland", which the duke of Newcastle had sent to him for his comments.[46] This was in fact a complete package of six bills which the government proposed to lay before parliament to deal with what were regarded in Whitehall as the root causes of disaffection in the northern kingdom. One would have set up a commission of inquiry into the behaviour of the clans within certain districts throughout the rebellion. Another was "to abrogate and take away such superiorities and tenures in Scotland as are oppressive and give opportunity for oppression." A third was "to prevent the mischiefs arising from the private jurisdictions in Scotland." The fourth was aimed at the more effectual disarming of the Highlands, the abolition of highland dress, and the suppression of the very names of "some of the clans most notoriously concerned in the rebellion, viz. Cameron, Macpherson, etc." The fifth was "to suppress all meeting houses and conventicles for religious worship in Scotland where the king and the royal family shall not be prayed for by name", i.e. the nonjuring chapels. The sixth was to vest forfeited Highland estates in the Crown.

Though he was not prepared to gloss the last two, since he was "not enough conversant in the Scotch laws" to do so, the duke did comment on the first four of these proposals. Some of his reflections throw an interesting light on his and the government's thinking about the conditions in Scotland which gave rise to rebellion, and how they could be changed by legislation.

The bills to abolish private Scottish courts distinguished three sorts: regalities; barons' jurisdictions; and those enjoyed by all heritors of land. There were about 160 courts of regality, not all of them presided over by rebels. Indeed the greatest was owned by the duke of Argyll. They would

THE HIGHLANDERS MEDLEY, or THE DUKE TRIUMPHANT

A Loyal SONG.

Sung by Mr. *Beard* at the Theatre
Royal in Covent-Garden

FRom barren *Caledonian* Lands,
Where Famine, uncontroul'd com,
The Rebel Clans, in search of Prey, (mands,
Come over the Hills and far away.
O'er the Hills and far away,
O'er the Hills and far away,
The Rebel Clans, in search of Prey,
Come over the Hills and far away,

Regardless, whether wrong or right,
For Booty (not for Fame they fight)
Banditti-like, they storm they slay,
They plunder rob and run away,
O'er the Hills &c.

With these a vain Pretender's came
and perjur'd Traytors Dupes
termin'd all, without Delay
Conquer, Die,
O'er the

The Royal Highness   Wm D. of Cumberland.

Britons, behold the Royal Youth, 'tis he
Who fights your Battles, sets your Country free
The Rebels hear, & tremble at his Name,
And Ch—s with Envy, eyes his rising Fame.

See there the Highlanders, in fearfull flight,
On Carrion Horses make a hasty flight,
Satan has caught 'em in his Net, & see
He drags 'em onward to the triple Tree.

According to Act of Parliament. 1746.   price 6.

172

require some sort of compensation. Nevertheless Cumberland was convinced that all regalities should be swept away in Scotland, "and the course of justice free and open to any one as in England, which cannot be without the expence of lawsuits be lessened and that there be more frequent circuits." There were even hereditary sheriffs in Scotland, which he thought to be "very dangerous to the crown and oppressive to the subject and at present they are sold like private property". As for the baronial courts and other heritable jursidictions it was proposed to abrogate all their powers and vest them in other courts, save only their right to arraign tenants for arrears of rent. The duke thought that even this should be circumscribed, "for if they should have but a shadow of power left to oppress their people they will intimidate them at first as much as ever."[47]

His comment on the disarming clause in the fourth bill was that "the only effectual method for disarming the Highlands appears to be by the proposed annual visitation and by death or transportation being the punishment to be inflicted on all who may be found armed, or to have arms concealed, in or near their habitations, and that at every circuit one should be brought to his trial that shall have been seen with arms. N. B. swords to be named particularly as they won't understand them to be arms." He approved of the proposal for prohibiting Highland dress. "The abolishing their habit after a proper time will be of infinite use, but should they pretend that this mountainous country requires their habit (which I am not at all convinced of) then the use of tartan or plaids should be particularly forbid as that is what makes their uniform." He was, however, dubious about the practicality of suppressing the names of clans, since it had been tried before in the case of the McGregors, but they "continued always to be called so in the hills and on all troubles publicly took up that name again, and it is to be feared that nothing but transplanting can succeed."

Most of these proposals resulted in legislation. Those abolishing oppressive tenures and private jursidictions in Scotland ran into legal complexities which delayed their enactment until 1747, but the measures for disarming the highlands and suppressing nonjuring meeting houses both received the royal assent on 12 August 1746.

The Disarming Act stiffened previous laws aimed at depriving people who lived in the Highland zone of weapons of war.[48] Anybody, man or woman, who carried or concealed arms was liable to be fined. As Cumberland had recommended, the illegal arms were specified and included broad swords. Until the fine was paid they could be jailed for one

(Opposite) "The Martial Boy": Cumberland as the centre piece of a patriotic print extolling his defeat of the rebels at Culloden. The inscription on his sword reads "for father and fatherland".

month, and then, upon continued non-payment, men fit for service could be drafted into the army for service in America, while others were liable to spend a further six months in prison. There was no provision for an annual visitation, the continued presence of the army presumably making this unnecessary. Searches for concealed weapons, however, could be made at any time, day or night. This Act also made it illegal after 1 August 1747 for anybody not in the army to wear Highland clothes, or even to use "tartan or party-coloured plaid" for great coats, which was also in line with the duke's recommendations. Henry Pelham referred to the bill as "one for disarming and undressing those savages".[49] There was some murmuring against this by loyal Scots, who asked "what crimes had the Campbells, Sutherlands, McCleods, Munros, McKays etc been guilty of, that they should be punished by the legislature whilst they were in arms for the Government?" An attempt to exempt such clans from the provision was rejected as being impractical, and in the end they acquiesced since it was "no more than a chip in porridge, which, without disarming, signifies not one half penny."[50] The Act did not proscribe the names of any disaffected clans, the proposal doubtless being dropped since, as Cumberland had pointed out, an earlier measure to deprive the McGregors of theirs had been totally ineffectual. Nothing was done, though, to implement his own more drastic solution of transporting whole clans to the colonies.

The Act to suppress nonjuring meeting houses insisted that episcopal ministers should duly qualify themselves by taking the oaths and that they should pray for King George by name.[51] Failure to fulfill these requirements had "greatly contributed to excite and foment a spirit of disaffection amongst numbers of people in that part of the kingdom against his Majesty's person and government; which hath been one of the causes of the wicked and unnatural rebellion lately raised and carried on against his Majesty." Certificates recording that they had sworn allegiance to George II were to be fixed to the doors of their meeting houses and displayed prominently inside. So far as whig politicians like Lords Stair, Tweeddale and Winchilsea were concerned the most important provision of this statute was that which declared it to be

> just and necessary to provide that those who give reason to suspect their being disaffected to his Majesty's person and government, and the present happy Establishment, by their frequenting or resorting to such illegal meeting houses, where his Majesty is not prayed for in express words, should be restrained from the power of hurting that Establishment to which they shew such disaffection.

They wanted to deprive of their employments all office holders who had been twice to a nonjuring meeting house since September 1745.[52] Instead, by the Act, anybody who went to an episcopal service disallowed under it was to be deprived of his civil rights, as well as paying a fine of £5 and risking imprisonment for six months if it were not paid. Thus Scottish Lords could neither be candidates nor vote in elections for the sixteen representative peers for Scotland in parliament, while others could not stand or vote in parliamentary, county or borough elections.

A stipulation that masters in private schools should also qualify themselves by taking the oaths and obtaining a certificate, and that they should pray for the king by name, was for some reason incorporated not in this Act but in that for the more effectual disarming of the highlands. Its purport was quite plain, "to prevent the rising generation being educated in disaffected or rebellious principles." Schoolmasters who defied its provisions ran the risk of being transported to the colonies for life, while even parents or guardians who knowingly put children in their care could be imprisoned for two years.

After these provisions had been agreed in the Lords the chancellor explained that the bill concerning heritable jurisdictions would have to be delayed until one could be prepared by the Court of Session in Scotland, which was also required to submit a list of them to parliament. Hardwicke "could not help thinking from the two formidable Rebellions, which have broke out there within about thirty years past, that the cause must arise from some peculiar defect in the Constitution and Government of that Kingdom." Private courts, which gave landlords judicial powers over their tenants, he considered to be one such defect. It could only be remedied by abolishing them, with due compensation, so that the two nations would be "reduced under one system of laws, as Wales was under that of England". Henry Pelham agreed with him that "till they are govern'd in the same manner as in England it is not to be presumed that they will entirely become a civilised people, and till they are so they will always be a nuisance to a free government."[53] Some of the chief supporters of the government north of the border were not impressed by these arguments, and when the Upper House agreed to refer the matter to the Court of Session, the duke of Argyll "sat by in a corner silent, and complained of the headache".[54]

A major difficulty for the ministry was that heritable jurisdictions had been guaranteed by the Act of Union in 1707. This was the main reason why the Court of Session refused to co-operate in drafting a bill to abolish them. When one was nevertheless introduced in February 1747, several Scots protested at the violation of what the duke of Queensbury and Dover called "the most sacred treaty that ever was executed between two free and independent nations". He conceded that if there were people "possessed of heritable jurisdictions who, contrary to law, and every true principle of government, have kept the common people there in such a state of bondage, and erected themselves into petty tyrants over them, as to have been able to compel them into a rebellion...under the threat of fire and sword...such guilty wretches deserve every degree of punishment the law inflicts." He nevertheless objected that he had not abused his own powers, and that the bill was punishing the innocent along with the guilty. Others defended the jursidictions on the grounds that they were more suitable for the remote Highlands than a system based on Westminster. Heritable sherifdoms, it was even argued, were better than those appointed by the Crown, since they acted as returning officers in parliamentary elections and unlike government appointees were independent of the Court.

None of these objections overcame the government's basic contention that the private courts gave their proprietors power over their inferiors which could be used to set up an interest opposed to that of the Crown. Even the argument that it was against the spirit of the Union to abolish them was swept aside. George Lyttelton professed incredulity that the measure could be regarded as an attack upon it. "Can there be a better or happier fruit of the Union than an active communication of the generous, free and noble plan of the law of England," he asked, "in the room of those servile tenures and barbarous customs which in Scotland deform the system of government: and by the effects which they have over that part of the people which being least civilised is consequently more prone to disorder, disturb the peace and endanger the safety of the whole constitution?" The tories, most Scots and even some worried whigs were nonetheless opposed to the measure. William Pitt stayed away from crucial debates on it, complaining of gout, though some said he had it on the orders of the duchess of Queensberry. The bill took from February to June to go through all its stages, and in the process some of the government's proposals were watered down.

Regalities were abolished and their jurisdictions vested in the king's courts, while heritable sherifdoms were resumed and annexed to the Crown, so that in future all Scottish sheriffs were to be appointed annually as in England. Baronial courts, however, survived with rather more extensive powers than Cumberland had envisaged. They could no longer try capital cases, but their jurisdiction over criminal offences was not entirely swept away, though it was restricted to assaults and "smaller crimes". They continued to try civil cases where the sums involved did not exceed 40s., while in arraigning tenants for arrears of rent there was no such ceiling. Clearly the government had to take notice of some of the objections to the measure, if only in the interests of relatively cheap and efficient justice, in cases which not even the most suspicious minister could interpret as perpetuating the rule of overmighty subjects in Scotland. It nevertheless got its way on the main issue, bringing the judicial system in Scotland into line with that of England from 25 March 1748. Recently it has been argued that "this is a date which should rank with the Union of the Crowns in 1603 and the Union of the Parliaments of 1707 in the slow destruction of the traditional Scottish polity."[55] If so, perhaps the date to commemorate is 17 June 1747, since the bill received the royal assent on that day. George II also consented at the same time to a bill taking away the tenure of ward holding in Scotland, by which the tenant could be called out for military service, a system obviously open to abuse if the landlord participated in a rebellion against the Crown.

Another Act vesting forfeited property in the Crown completed the legislative programme which the government had outlined to the duke of Cumberland as a package to eradicate the potential for rebellion in Scotland. There were even signs that the ministers felt that they could afford to relax their grip. The deadline for the wearing of highland clothes was extended to 1 August 1748. An Act "for the king's most gracious, general and free pardon" was also passed. Since this indemnified all subjects from prosecution for crimes committed before 15 June 1747 there was of necessity a long list of exceptions to the pardon, though some were perhaps unnecessary, including "all and every person and persons of the name and clan of MacGregor".

By then the judiciary had also virtually finished its work. Over 3,000 rebels had been dealt with by the courts, including the high court of parliament.

Parliament dealt with the more prominent rebels. An Act of attainder against forty-one individuals was introduced on 2 May 1746 and received the royal assent on 4 June. This was the most summary form of jurisdiction possible, for those named were simply declared guilty of treason and could be executed without further process if apprehended, while their titles were annulled and their properties confiscated. A similar Act had been passed in 1716 after the previous rebellion in which the third earl of Derwentwater had been attainted. When his brother Charles Radcliffe, who had assumed the title, was captured on board a ship sailing for Scotland, and was subsequently sentenced to death for treason, he ought technically to have been executed as a commoner rather than as a peer because of the attainder, but instead, by a quaint dispensation, he was granted the privilege of decapitation rather than hanging.

Radcliffe had in fact been involved in the Fifteen, and had escaped after being found guilty and condemned to death, so that the only judicial process necessary in his case was an appearance before the Court of King's Bench to establish that he was the man who had previously been convicted. Full scale trials before the high court of parliament were necessary, however, to establish the guilt of four peers involved in the Forty-five:

Lords Balmerino, Cromartie and Kilmarnock, who were tried by the Upper House in July 1746; and Lord Lovat, who was impeached by the Commons in March 1747.[56] All four were inevitably found guilty. Balmerino and Kilmarnock had been captured at Culloden, while Cromartie had been taken, the day before the battle, at Dunrobin by the earl of Sutherland's militia. Lovat's treason was less overt, but his correspondence with leading rebels was disclosed at his trial by his own secretary and Charles Edward's, John Murray of Broughton, who turned King's evidence. Before testifying against Lovat Murray, who drank "like a fish", fortified himself with a whole bottle of wine "and would have had brandy if it had been to be come at".[57]

Cromartie escaped execution, his wife's emotional intercession with the king when she fainted theatrically at the royal feet procuring him a reprieve. The others, however, all went to the block. Both Balmerino and Kilmarnock, in their different ways, made profound impressions at their executions. Kilmarnock, a stately, tall man, solemnly dressed in black, behaved with such decorum that he brought tears to the eyes of nearly all the thousands of spectators present on Tower Hill to witness the spectacle on 18 August, including hardened veterans of Fontenoy. Even the executioner cried, and had to be braced for his job with spirits. Balmerino played it nonchalantly, taking the axe out of the executioner's hand to feel its edge with his thumb before laying his head on the block. His dying speech was boldly defiant, beginning "I was brought up in true, loyal and anti Revolution principles," and denying to the end that the Young Pretender had ordered no quarter to be given before the battle of Culloden. Lovat, the last of the lords to be executed, generated even more sympathy. At his trial he had appeared as something of a buffoon. At one stage, after Sir Everard Fawkener had testified against him he was asked "if he had anything to say to Sir Everard? He replied, 'no; but that he was his humble servant, and wished him joy of his young wife'." Fawkener was nevertheless impressed by his defence that a statute of George I's reign debarred a vassal or a tenant in Scotland from testifying against his lord in Scotland. "It is remarkable that none of the House of Commons lawyers knew of this Act," he observed, "so that if Lovat could have made out his facts, they would have been deprived of very material evidence."[58] On the scaffold Lovat rose to the occasion. Although by all the rules of the game in the eighteenth century he thoroughly deserved his fate, his great age and infirmities, and his stoical attitude on the brink of death, excited pity when justice at last caught up with "the life and soul of the Pretender's cause for 40 years successively."[59]

Lesser lights were dealt with by less prestigious tribunals. The officers of the Manchester regiment who had surrendered to the king's mercy at Carlisle were tried in the Court house on St Margaret's Hill, Southwark.

Although their offences had been committed miles from Surrey, an Act had been hurriedly placed on the Statute book enabling the king to appoint places for the trials of those implicated in the rebellion wherever he wished. The government was determined to make an example of the leaders of the few Englishmen who had joined the rebel army, and wanted show trials near the capital rather than in the remote provinces. One of the more unsavoury aspects of these trials was the testimony of the star witness for the Crown, Samuel Maddox, a Manchester apothecary's apprentice, who had turned King's evidence to save his own skin. His word was instrumental in sending eight men to the grisly death of a traitor. Unlike the Lords, who died on the block, they were first hanged, but kept alive, at least in theory, until their bowels were cut out and burned before their eyes, after which their heads were severed and their bodies quartered. In practice the executioner made sure they were dead before he disembowelled them. Maddox had a grudge against the commander of the regiment, Francis Townley, claiming that when he (Maddox) had an inclination to leave it, he was threatened "and told that if he did he would have his brains knocked out". He was also said to have another against Thomas Chadwick, having fought with him over some sausages in Carlisle, when provisions were scarce. But he denied this, declaring "I would not swear any man's life away for a sausage." He insisted that Chadwick had played "the king shall enjoy his own again" on the organ of Lancaster church. James Bradshaw's plea of being non compos mentis was not allowed, although he was almost certainly deranged. He declared after his trial that "Mr. Maddox perjured me, and I am afraid that he is so immersed in wickess that it would be difficult for him to forbear it."[60]

These were the first in a whole series of trials and executions. "As a lady said, we gave them a good bleeding in the battle, and since a good purging."[61] Besides the proceedings in London, special courts were held in Carlisle and York. Originally it was intended to hold them in Newcastle upon Tyne and Lincoln also. When the government decided "that all the rebel prisoners in Scotland be tried at Carlisle or Newcastle", however, the authorities on Tyneside protested that they could not guarantee the security of prisoners sent there, so they were shipped to London instead.[62] Those prisoners held in Lincoln were eventually tried at York along with those imprisoned there.

Many of the 315 arraigned in Carlisle had been captured when the town fell to the duke of Cumberland, though several were sent there from Scotland and from other towns in England. The special court was presided over by Sir Thomas Parker, Lord Chief Baron of the Exchequer, while three colleagues from the Courts of Common Pleas, Exchequer and King's Bench also officiated as judges.[63] The proceedings were scheduled to start on 12 August and it was expected that the Grand Jury would only take until the end of that week to sift the evidence and decide which prisoners should be formally charged. The complexities of presenting the evidence to them, however, made this timetable impossible. On 14 August Philip Cateret Webb, the Crown solicitor, confessed to being "an utter stranger to the evidence against these prisoners from Scotland, which consists of many large volumes in folio, which I must begin to read." On 21 August, therefore, Parker and Sir Thomas Burnett moved to York to open the special Court there, leaving the other two justices to continue the proceedings in Carlisle. When they returned on 8 September the Grand Jury had still not finished its work, and it was not until the 10th that it could be discharged. The trials proper began on 12 September and ended on the 26th. Next day the judges set out for York, passing through the English gate under the heads of Thomas Chadwick and Thomas Berwick, which had been set up there by the sheriff of Cumberland a week before as a gruesome warning of the risks run by rebels.

Seventy-five men were indicted at York, of whom only five were acquitted, the rest being sentenced to death. Addressing the condemned men Lord Chief Baron Parker rammed down their throats the government's attitude to those who had taken part in the rebellion:[64]

> The horrid nature of high treason, which involved in it many other heinous crimes; particularly wilful perjury in all those who have taken the oaths to the government; and also murder; for that all those concern'd in this unnatural rebellion were answerable for the deaths of those brave and gallant men who fell in the cause of their king, their religion, their laws, their liberties, their properties, in the battles of Prestonpans, Falkirk and Culloden. That the heinousness of the late rebellion was greatly aggravated, in regard there was no sort of foundation or even the least pretence to be made for it; his present Majesty having never invaded, nor so much as attempted to invade, any of his subjects liberties or properties in the least degree, or in one single instance, during a reign of near twenty years; That therefore an attempt calculated to depose and murder so gracious a Prince, one of the best and most merciful monarchs that ever sat on the English throne, and to destroy his illustrious family, was a crime of so flagrant a nature that he wanted words to express.

Several pleas made on behalf of the rebels in attempts to mitigate the full severity of the law were disallowed by Crown lawyers. The rebels taken at Carlisle pleaded that they had surrendered in expectation of saving their lives. This was waived on the grounds that the duke of Cumberland had merely spared them from being put immediately to the sword. Some claimed commissions from the king of France, and that they should therefore be treated as prisoners of war rather than as rebels. It was ruled that while those born in France could be regarded as special cases, native born Englishmen could not evade the penalties for levying war against the king by enlisting with a foreign monarch. Others insisted that they had been forced to participate under threat of reprisals if they did not join the rebels. Much of the legislation aimed at curtailing the powers of Highland chiefs was in fact based on the assumption that they could abuse them in order to drag their vassals unwillingly into rebellion. Yet this plea was looked upon with deep suspicion by counsel for the Crown, who were adamant that "in point of law it must be proved in the clearest manner...there must be...a total disinclination to the cause, a laying hold of the first opportunity to desert from it." One who successfully pleaded thus was John Ballantine, who was tried at York.[65] He had been a piper in Captain James Stewart's company in Lord George Murray's regiment, but nevertheless pleaded 'not guilty' on the grounds that he had been forced into service by a party of rebels, who dragged him out of bed, and afterwards placed a guard over him to prevent him escaping. When the jury acquitted him "the poor fellow was in such a transport of joy that he threw up his bonnet to the very roof of the court, and cry'd out, my Lords and Gentlemen I thank you. Not Guilty! Not Guilty! Not Guilty! Pray God bless King George for ever. I'll serve him all the days of my life. And immediately ran out into the Castle Yard, with his irons on, took up a handful of channel water, and drank his Majesty's health."

The macabre fascination of the state trials, and grim spectacle of death on the block or the gibbet, with its attendant theatre of last meals, mob-lined processions, dying speeches and heads impaled on gateways, can give an undue emphasis to the axe and the rope in the aftermath of the Forty-five. In fact only 120 rebels were put to death, out of a total of over 3,100 who were taken prisoner. Moreover no fewer than forty of these were deserters from the army who had joined the Young Pretender and whose summary execution was in line with contemporary notions of military justice. The civil government in eighteenth-century Britain made a show of tempering justice with mercy, and, apart from the treatment of the Manchester regiment, even dealing with rebels found guilty of treason proved no exception. The authorities were after the ringleaders rather than the lesser fry anyway, as the treasury solicitor made clear when he divided the prisoners up on a rough and ready basis into four categories: really gentlemen; not properly gentlemen but above the rank of common men; a lower degree than the preceding; and common men. One curious feature of this discrimination was that rebels below the rank of gentlemen or men of estates, who had not "distinguished themselves by any extraordinary degree of guilt", were allowed to draw lots, so that only one in twenty found themselves facing the prospect of capital punishment. The rest, provided they pleaded guilty and petitioned for mercy, were generally transported to the colonies for life. Ironically, since most of those sentenced to death had their sentences commuted to transportation, the bulk of the 'unlucky' ones were sent there too. There is even evidence to suggest that the lots were 'fixed' so that they fell on suitable subjects for the exercise of the prerogative of mercy. A large proportion of those who drew lots to face trial were either young or feebleminded or both. Some were even acquitted. John Thoirs, for example, "a little deformed boy", despite having told Charles Edward "Sir, tho' my body is small my heart is as big as any man you have", was "acquitted by favour of the King's Counsel". Others were banished, a few were pardoned, and fewer still escaped.

The appalling filthy and disease-ridden prisons in which the rebels were held certainly killed off over eighty prisoners, and probably most of the 684 who cannot be accounted for otherwise. For this the decision to transport those originally destined to be tried in Newcastle to London instead was largely responsible. The long voyage in crowded hulks, and their longer stay in the Thames, either still on board ship or in Tilbury fort, in overcrowded and insanitary conditions, quite apart from the alleged brutality of their guards, guaranteed that many died before they could be brought to trial. Their treatment aroused indignation at the time, and still can.

Yet when all is said and done the treatment of the rebels cannot be regarded by the standards of the age as unduly harsh, especially considering that the government itself was determined not to be accused of lenity, on the grounds that mildness in 1716 had kept alive the spirit of disaffection which returned to haunt the country in 1745. On the contrary, Horace Walpole commented that "popularity has changed sides since the year '15, for now the city and generality are very angry that so many rebels have been pardoned."[66] If the government was being unduly severe, many of its own subjects did not think so. A French appeal for clemency was counter-productive, it being held that the French had ulterior motives in intervening on behalf of people who had expected more material help from France.[67] Nevertheless 1,287 prisoners, over a third of those captured, were set free, including 382 who were exchanged for prisoners of war taken by the French. Although the spotlight of history usually ignores these, and picks out those who were harshly treated, ministers doubtless felt that even the repressive measures they had adopted to deal with the rebels after the battle of Culloden were justified, since Jacobitism failed to survive as a real threat to the regime after 1746.

CHAPTER EIGHT

"King George reigns in the Hearts of all"

To conclude; I have taken Care, through the Whole of my History, to relate Facts with the greatest Perspicuity and Exactness; and will only add, that, when the Nation became rouz'd from its Lethargy, never was there a greater Spirit of Love and Loyalty than appear'd amongst all Ranks of People (some Malecontents excepted) which plainly shews, that his Majesty King George reigns in the Hearts of all his faithful Subjects.

James Ray, The Acts of the Rebels *(1746), p. ix*

The fact that there never was another Jacobite rebellion after 1745 owed more to a disinclination to rebel than to the government's repressive measures. Indeed the ravages in the glens, the disarming of the Highlanders and proscription of the plaid, together with the treatment of the prisoners, did not exorcise the spirit of Jacobitism but kept it alive, at least as much as any romantic attachment to 'Bonnie Prince Charlie' did. The truth was that, despite his spectacular success, he had not been able to attract many to his cause.

Even in Scotland the Young Pretender's appeal was strictly limited. He did not get so much support there as the earl of Mar had done in 1715. "It is worth stressing," concludes the latest and most scholarly survey of the Jacobite movement, "that no really great Scottish magnate ever committed himself to the '45."[1] It is moreover misleading to assume that the rebellion divided Scotland geographically, with the north solidly for the Pretender and the south generally opposed to him. While it is true that southern Scots showed little or no inclination to join him, plenty of their northern brethren were equally reluctant to commit themselves to his cause. The author of some astute "considerations on the rebellion in Scotland" noted that the rebel strength was confined to the area north of

Stirling and south of Inverness, only about a third of the Scottish land mass.[2] Moreover this by no means included a third of the inhabitants. "According to the best computation that I have met with," he continued,

> there may be in the whole Kingdom about a million of people, and of these I reckon the Highlanders may be a sixth part, and I am persuaded this is rather more than less than they are. But let us take them at one hundred and sixty thousand men women and children. And then if every person capable of bearing arms were brought into the field, they might amount to twenty five thousand men; but then if we consider that at least one half of the Highland clans are either neutral or well affected, and that there are fewer chiefs in this, than there were in the last rebellion, we may very fairly and justly conclude on these grounds that the rebels can hardly bring twelve thousand men into the field; but at the most, and by all the methods they can use, supposing they do not leave a serviceable man at home, not above fifteen thousand men, whatever we may have heard to the contrary.

An estimate of the rebellious and loyal clans drawn up in June 1746 calculated that those who rose in rebellion could mobilise 9,720 men as opposed to 8,350 on the government's side.[3] They were not quite so evenly divided as this implies, for twenty-two clans were 'out' for the Pretender, and only ten for the government. Moreover the loyalists included the duke of Argyll, whose followers were computed at 3,500 or forty-two per cent of the total. The compiler left out of his account altogether Lord Seaforth and the Grants, and with good reason, for, as another analysis of "the highlands chiefs with the number of men they can raise" recorded, "few or none of Seaforth's followers would join him this year for the government, being all Jacobites", while the Grants, though "mostly Revolutionists", had "acted an indifferent part this year."[4] The Grants had in fact signed a treaty of neutrality with the Young Pretender, which incensed the duke of Cumberland, who regarded them as "traitors for corresponding with the rebels".[5] Nevertheless Charles Edward did not carry all the clans with him. Besides the Campbells the government could count on the followers of Lords Moreton, Rae and Ross, the earl of Sutherland, Sir Alexander McDonald, Sir Robert Monroe, the McKays and the McCleods. Measured in wealth rather than in numbers the government had the more prosperous clans on its side. 'Scoto-Britannus', writing in the *Caledonian Mercury*, claimed that "the yearly income of the clans which brought the 4,000 highlanders to Perthshire does not exceed £1500, which divided equally among them is only 7s 6d a year each, not a farthing a day."[6] The Young Pretender, although his army virtually conquered Scotland, never enjoyed mass support. By and large he appealed to those parts of the country which had not benefited economically since the Union. An exception was the Jacobite port of Montrose, the magistrates of which received a stern lecture from Sir Everard Fawkener.[7] "It is a very just as well as heavy reproach on the town of Montrose," he told them, "that tho' there is hardly an instance of any town in these Kingdoms that has received, within this same space of time, so great improvement and increase as that has since the accession of his late Majesty [George I] to the throne of these Kingdoms (all which are the effects of a good and a just government); yet the inhabitants should be so indifferent about, if not averse to, the preservation of that Establishment to which they owe so much." Yet Charles Edward dared not risk holding borough elections, and nominated governors to the towns he controlled. His control of Edinburgh lasted no longer than his army remained in the city. When it visited Glasgow on its return from England its reception was frankly hostile.

During its expedition south of the border the rebel army had attracted an insignificant handful of people. Charles Edward appealed to none of the English aristocracy or substantial gentry. In Northumberland "only two gentlemen joined him", besides a few tenant farmers.[8] One or two professional men and several tradesmen were recruited in Manchester. Otherwise everybody commented on the mean extraction of those who were raised there. According to James Ray the Townley regiment consisted of "mostly people of the lowest rank, and the vilest principles; which occasioned him, who called himself the Duke of Perth to say, 'that if the Devil had come a recruiting and proffered a shilling more than his Prince, they would have preferred the former'."[9] The overwhelming majority of all classes in the counties through which the Highland host marched, including even the Catholics, steadfastly refused to join them.

The fact that the Jacobite forces were mostly drawn from the Highlands of Scotland led them from the start to be depicted as men beyond the pale of civilisation. 'Scoto-Britannus' wrote of the Young Pretender having stolen like a thief into the most remote and obscure recesses of the island "there to hatch his dark treason amidst dens of barbarous and lawless ruffians...men without property or even any settled habitation; a hungry rapacious and uncivilis'd crew...of ungrateful villains, savages, and traitors." Addresses to the king from his Scottish subjects also dwelled on his appeal to their less enlightened fellow citizens in the Highlands. This kind of language was readily resorted to by Englishmen who referred to the rebels as barbarians and savages. *The Craftsman* called them "a ragged hungry rabble of Yahoos of Scotch Highlanders".[10] A letter allegedly written from a gentleman in Derby who had been forced to billet six rebel officers and forty privates in his house laid heavy emphasis on these characteristics.[11] "My hall" he claimed

> stunk so of their itch and other nastinesses about them, as if they
> had been so many persons in a condemn'd hole, and 'twill be very
> happy if they've left no contagion behind them...Their dialect
> (from the idea I had of it) seemed to me, as if an herd or hot-
> tentots, wild monkies in a desert, or vagrant gypsies, had been
> jabbering, screaming and howling together, and really this jargon
> of speech was very properly suited to such a sett of banditti

Such emotive language was calculated to denigrate the rebels. When the
archibishop of York described them as "wild and desperate ruffians" a
Jacobite protested that this was deliberately designed "to convey into
your audience a very unfavourable idea of those men, and to strike the
utmost abhorence".[12] English observers of the Young Pretender's followers could even slip quite easily into identifying them indiscriminately
with any old Scots. A correspondent wrote to the Chancellor of Carlisle
during the second siege of the City "I cannot but take part with you in
your sufferings amongst such a parcel that seem to be the collected scum
of the country they have passed through."[13]

Unfortunately this denigration of the supporters of the Young Pretender
coincided with a crude stereotype of the Scot which was widespread in
England. Scots were frequently regarded, for instance, as verminous and
diseased. "Set a louse upon a table and it will point north to its native
country" was one crude racial joke, while calling scabies 'the Scotch itch'
was another. There was a vein of anti-Scottish sentiment in educated
English circles, which can be seen in the works of leading writers from
Swift to Johnson, and turned ugly in crises like the Forty-five. Some
Englishmen, including Henry Fielding, accepted that the rebels were not
typical of all Scots. James Ray protested "that though the flame of rebellion was kindled and raised in Scotland to a very high pitch, yet it is very
unjust (as some ignorant people are apt) to brand the country in general
with the infamous name of rebels, since from what I have already said, it
plainly appears, that there are no people better attached to his Majesty's
person and government than many of the Scots."[14] Others, however,
allowed crude nationalism to shape their perception of reality. The earl of
Chesterfield, for instance, when he heard that loyal Highlanders were
being armed to fight the rebels, would not allow the distinction: "the
proverb indeed says 'set a thief to catch a thief', but I beg to except
Scotch thieves", he wrote to the duke of Newcastle, and even advised
him to "forbid provisions of any kind being sent upon any pretence
whatever (unless directly to the Duke's army) into Scotland, and I would
starve the loyal with the disloyal."[15] "Has Scotland an exclusive privilege
to be the seat of rebellion with impunity and not to be treated as an
enemy's country?" he protested to Sir Everard Fawkener, while condoling

with him and Cumberland for being "obliged to stay so long in that in-
fernal country, where the only laurels...are Scotch furrs."[16] "You seem
not to like the accounts from Scotland," the duke of Richmond replied to
a letter from the duke of Newcastle, " 'tis vain to think any government
can ever root out Jacobitism there...I hope and believe the Duke [of
Cumberland] will paint that whole nation in their right colours when they
come home; and he will certainly find now, what he has often called
national prejudice in me, prove to be pure naked truth."[17] Cumberland
undoubtedly acquired what has been called "sustained Scotophobia",
which he shared with the man he left in charge of the country, Lord
Albemarle, who referred to Scots as "the worse people I ever knew", and
preferred "the soil to the inhabitants, for more malice, falsehood, cunning
and self interest was never met with in any country whatsoever."[18]

Loyal Scots in London suffered much from this lack of discrimination.
"I need not describe to you the effects the surrender of Edinburgh and
the progress the rebels made had upon this country," one of them wrote
to the lord president, "I wish I could say that they were confined to the
lower sort of people; but I must fairly own, that their betters were as
much touched as they. The reflections were national; and it was too
publickly said, that all Scotland were Jacobites." "I am really in deep
distress," he confessed later, "already every man of our country is looked
on as a traitor, as one secretly inclined to the Pretender, and waiting but
an opportunity to declare. The guilty and the innocent are confounded
together, and the crimes of a few imputed to the whole nation."[19]

The myth that the Scots were all inclined to rebellion reinforced an
attitude widespread in England, that the Forty-five was an alien intrusion
into the country, a challenge more to English than to British liberties.
Charles Edward tried to present himself as the son of a true-born Englishman, who represented the native tradition of liberty, against a German
born tyrant. His manifestos emphasised the dependence that George II
had on Dutch and Hessian support, and the fact that his cause was upheld
by British subjects. The government turned the tables on him by stressing
the help he received from France and Spain and by sending home the
Dutch, while the duke of Cumberland was careful not to employ any
Hessians against the rebels at Culloden. "It adds to his Highness's glory,"
thought the lord justice clerk, "that he has done the business without
the help of foreigners."[20] The duke was even relieved when Lord Loudoun
and his Highlanders could not join him before the battle, since he considered "it much more for the honour of his Majesty's troops and of the
nation to finish this affair without any further use of the highlanders than
plundering and sending out parties."[21] At Culloden the few Highlanders in
his army were deliberately left behind the lines in charge of the baggage,
except for those Campbells who were sent ahead to break down the

enclosure walls for the cavalry. Apart from a few Lowlanders and a handful of French, whom the Young Pretender placed in his second line, the two armies that faced each other on Drummossie moor were overwhelmingly drawn from very different parts of Great Britain. A band of Highlanders clad in tartan, many of whom only spoke Gaelic, faced a body of Lowland Scots and above all Englishmen dressed in uniform. John Prebble put his finger on this vital distinction, when he observed that the officers of Cumberland's army could have felt no more kinship with the Highland host "than an officer of Victoria's army would later feel when surveying a Zulu impi or a tribe of Pathans."[22] Something of Cumberland's attitude towards them comes through an anecdote related in later life by Lord George Sackville, when he had become Lord George Germaine, "that when the General officers complimented the duke...on the line of march, order of battle and consequent victory, he disclaimed all praise, saying 'it is what Konigsegg taught me; it is what he used against the Turks'."[23] The tactics which the Austrian commander had employed against the infidels invading Christendom were singularly appropriate for the suppression of rebels whom the English regarded as barbarian invaders of civilisation. "Did you not land in a part of the island inhabited by wildmen and savages?" the Young Pretender was asked in print by a writer with the significant pen name 'John English'.[24] "Have you not with an army of these barbarians...invaded the civilised parts of this Kingdom? Have you in that civilised part found any number of abettors considerable enough to give you any hopes, or even worth your mentioning? How unfairly then do you pretend to represent your cause as favoured by this nation, when you know, [that] was it to be decided by an election, you would not have one vote in a thousand from those who have any vote for the Legislative?"

The rebellion was also seen as a disease entering the blood stream of a previously healthy patient. Initially it was neglected. "What vexes me," exclaimed one exasperated observer, "is that things have been so managed that a slight scratch has by inattention come to a mortification."[25] Then it seemed to become terminal. According to the archbishop of York's diagnosis "we are now, as to the health of the body politic, in the condition of a man who does not ask his doctor whether he may recover, but how long he thinks he can hold out."[26] Eventually, however, the body's own defences were roused, first to contain and then to eliminate what was referred to as "the cancer of our isle".[27]

This rallying to the regime during the course of the rebellion demonstrated that it was far more firmly based than its opponents had imagined. It even appears to have taken its more committed supporters by surprise. At the outset of the uprising the lack of support for the rebels seemed to indicate more a negative aversion to the Stuarts than a positive inclination to the house of Hanover. "Whatever disaffection there is to the present family," Horace Walpole wrote to Sir Thomas Mann on 29 September 1745, "it plainly don't proceed from love to the other."[28] During the first few weeks before the fall of Edinburgh ministers were nervous and pessimistic, wondering which way people would incline. Reactions from most parts of the country were lethargic and even apparently indifferent, while Scotland was collapsing, and Wales, the west country and Lancashire seemed to be on the verge of rebellion.

Then after the battle of Prestonpans all was transformed. The English woke up to their danger and began to organise resistance to it. Addresses, Associations and subscriptions pledged military support for the regime, and raised considerable sums to underwrite that commitment with cash. Court whigs were not surprisingly prominent in this movement. If beneficiaries of the Hanoverian succession such as the dukes of Bedford, Devonshire and Newcastle, and those they had rewarded in the central administration or in the localities with either lucrative or prestigious places, had not been prepared to defend George II, then his throne was very unstable indeed. These oligarchs, however, were joined by people to whom, until very recently at least, they had deliberately denied patronage. Country whigs, whose rhetoric denounced the government as an incipient tyranny bent on depriving Englishmen of their liberties, rushed to protect it from the Pretender. Tories, some of whom had flirted with Jacobitism, joined in the rush. As the wife of a former tory MP put it in a letter written to another tory in October:[29]

> I have been in dreadful frights about the rebellion, but the zeal and unnanimey (sic) that has appeared in all ranks of people in supporting our happy constitution in Church and State has given me inexpressible satisfaction and dissipated all my fears; and hope when we have recovered this shocking sceane a more pleasing one will present it self to our view which will be lasting, and hope make the king's crown sit easier upon his head many, many years. For he must now see t'was not him we cavelled att, but his ministers and I hope a mutual confidence will for the future be t'wixt king and people...

The minister they had most cavilled at had been Walpole. He had systematically kept tories from preferment, and ruthlessly purged the administration of any whigs who crossed him. Had the Young Pretender landed in 1741 he would have been able to tap a much deeper well of dissatisfaction with the government than he could in 1745. In the intervening years Walpole had fallen, and had been replaced by a ministry under Henry Pelham which at least gave the appearance of being willing to reconcile dissident whigs and even tories with the regime. Pelham's Broadbottom administration brought tory politicians into central government for the first time since the death of Queen Anne. Perhaps more important, Lord Chancellor Hardwicke agreed to include tories in the commissions of the peace in the localities, which probably did more to soothe the ruffled feathers of tory country gentlemen than the offer of a place at Court to the likes of Lord Gower. Pelham's achievement should not be underestimated. One of the men whom he reconciled to the administration was the writer Henry Fielding, an inveterate opponent of his predecessor. It is true that he was ripe for conversion. Fielding's zeal for opposition had flagged in the last year of Walpole's ministry, and he was to show himself susceptible to the allurement of patronage from the duke of Bedford. But when he began to write *The True Patriot* in response to the rebellion he had not succumbed to its charms. Unlike Walpole, therefore, Pelham had an able and unbribed pen to write for him. *The True Patriot*'s reaction to the Pelhamite manoeuvres of February 1746, when they forced the king to drop Granville and give them his support, was to back them up to the hilt. When they were re-established Fielding extolled the ministry as one which finally reconciled Court and Country, and which only Jacobites and traitors could oppose.

The battle of Culloden and its consequences set the seal on the Pelhamite victory. Relating the arrangements for settling a sum of £25,000 on the duke of Cumberland for his triumph over the rebels, Henry Pelham informed him that the king's goodness to his son "has its influence extended to your faithful servants, for I have perceived a visible alteration in His Majesty's behaviour ever since this affair has been in agitation."[30]

The chord which was struck in the autumn of 1745 was not just in harmony with recent political changes. By relentlessly hammering on the notes of 'Popery' and 'France' government propagandists touched strings which were still vibrating after registering the major themes of British history many years before. As Lord Hardwicke emphasised "representing the Pretender as coming (as the truth is) under a dependence upon French support; I say, stating this point, together with Popery, in a strong light, has always the most popular effect."[31]

The threat from an allegedly intolerant and persecuting Roman Catholicism was stressed remorselessly, the adjective 'popish' being almost invariably annexed to the word Pretender. In the early stages of the

(Opposite) George II depicted as Saint George slaying the dragon of Popery in the War of the Austrian Succession. This print, engraved in 1745 before the Jacobite Rebellion, illustrates the popular anti-Catholicism upon which the government was to draw by emphasising that James Edward, father of Bonnie Prince Charles, was a "Popish Pretender".

GEORGE's COMBAT

From Papal Power and Papal Rites,
From Relicks, Saints and Romish Rites,
Our Church secur'd by GEORGE's Hands,
Now on a Rock triumphant stands.

Religion sits beneath at Rest,
Smiles on the Prince in whom she's blest,
Justice exulting breaths Applause,
On Him defending Britain's Laws.

His conqu'ring Arm makes Envy sigh,
His virtuous Breast bids Malice die,
The Arts of Rome, the Pride of Gaul,
Prostrate before their Victor fall.

NASSAU with British Thunder arm'd,
Old Lewis and the World alarm'd,
Great GEORGE improving NASSAU's Plan,
Shall end the Work which he began.

Published according to Act of Parliament
1745

191

rebellion there was a concerted effort by several bishops, encouraged but not directed by the government, to warn their clerical colleagues of the dangers from popery in circular letters which received wide publicity.[32] The bishop of London spoke out particularly strongly, urging the clergy "to raise in your people a just abhorrence of popery, by setting yourself on this occasion to shew in your discourses from the pulpit, the grossness and perniciousness of the manifold errors and innovations of the church of Rome."[33] He also warned them "to guard your people against a delusion...that the person whose cause they [the Jacobites] espouse, will content himself with the exercise of his own religion, and that no change in our religion will be attempted." Charles Edward, of course, denied the accusation that his father would force his faith on his subjects, but he had to contend with long historical memories and myths, going back to the reign of his grandfather James II and beyond to that of Mary Tudor. A tract which was "read in country churches reprinted in different parts of the Kingdom, and many thousands given away by noblemen, gentlemen and others," asked *The question, Whether England can be otherwise than miserable under a Popish King?*[34] Its answer was emphatically "No; we have tried it under Q. Mary and K. James II and were brought by both to the brink of destruction." The bishop of Worcester invoked these legends at a public meeting held in Worcester town hall on 4 October 1745.[35] "There may be and certainly is humanity and good breeding in some papists," he conceded, "but 'tis their cruel religion, and not their natural temper, which must regulate their conduct and oblige them to join in promoting our destruction. That merciless religion, which has martyred so many of our pious ancestors, and but in the last century, massacred in cool blood, in the most inhuman manner, with all the shocking circumstances of the utmost barbarity, more than a hundred thousand of our innocent unguarding unoffending fellow subjects." 'Montanus' drove the same message home to the readers of several newspapers with an incredibly bigoted diatribe against the Roman Catholic church.[36] "She damns all who are not of her horrid communion, and murders, or would murder, all that she damns; witness her universal practice and constant massacres at Paris, in Ireland, her crusades against the best Christians, the daily fires of the Inquisition and the burning in Smithfield, especially under Queen Mary. Be warned, O Protestants; continue what ye are; Christians and freemen; your all is at stake, Liberty, Property, Conscience; abhor the Harlot and oppose the tool of the harlot."

Such bloodcurdling bigotry seems to have struck home, especially with the less educated. "Poor Nanny cried about the rebels in Scotland," Ann Worsley informed her brother in Vienna, "and advised us seriously to turn Papists before they got into Yorkshire."[37] One of the more violent manifestations of popular sentiment during the rebellion took the form of attacks upon Catholic chapels and private houses. The last of these occurred in Liverpool after the battle of Culloden had been fought and the rebellion was effectively over.[38] On 30 April "a very great and formidable mob of people" demolished the Roman Catholic chapel and burned its furniture, defying the magistrates who tried to suppress the riot. On 20 May "another mobb gather'd together and assembled before, demolished and burnt the house and furniture of Mrs Anne Palmer...a Roman Catholic lady...who maintained a priest in this her house." When the town clerk tried to read the Riot Act the paper was taken from him and burned. Next day they threatened the gaol until a few of their number who had been apprehended were released. The mayor then requested military assistance. Elsewhere the magistrates actually connived at anti-Catholic demonstrations. When some boys in Stokesley, North Yorkshire, pulled some tiles off the roof of "Mr Pearson's Mass house", one was taken before a magistrate by some Catholics, whereupon his accomplices appeared too.[39] The magistrate "could not forbear laughing at them; however, after giving them a gentle reprimand, he dismissed them, recommending it to the papists to put up with the damage". The boys then went back and, emboldened by the impunity they had virtually been guaranteed, gutted the building and burned its contents. As if to emphasise the legitimacy of their action, one of them put on a fine vestment and cap, and granted absolution for all his accomplices' past sins, "in consideration of the great service they had done to their King and country, in destroying the mass house that day".

Popery was inseparably linked with arbitrary power in government propaganda, and the most arbitrary regime in western Europe was held to be the French monarchy. That France was hand in glove with the rebels was taken for granted. " 'Tis as needless to attempt to prove that after the success in Scotland our enemies should intend an invasion," asserted the bishop of Worcester, "as it is absurd to question, whether French policy, which is always but too watchful for its own interest, will neglect an opportunity so favourable to the pernicious designs of that enterprising Court." In fact the French invasion plans of 1743—44 were not revived in 1745—46. Apart from enough behind-the-scenes aid to get his expedition to Scotland, and to keep it alive, France did not give Charles Edward any significant assistance. Fears that they might kept the British navy busy watching the Channel and Atlantic ports, and led to the panic on 12 December when it was believed that 15,000 Frenchmen were landing in Pevensey Bay. Although the alarm broke in London at three o'clock in the morning, and was "contradicted at eleven", it was enough to stop the duke of Cumberland in his tracks, and to hold up his pursuit of the rebels for twenty four hours. It is possible that the French deliberately raised a false alarm in order to give the Young Pretender time to get to

Scotland. If so it was the only occasion on which their assistance was a major asset. Otherwise they got the best of both worlds: they helped to create the maximum disturbance in Britain, one which led the British to withdraw virtually all their forces from the continent, with the minimum of effort on their part.

There can be no doubt that ministers took the threat of a French invasion seriously, and indeed were more apprehensive about it than they were about the rebels. Nevertheless they also exploited it for propaganda purposes. To remind his subjects that he was at war with foreign powers, as well as with the rebels, the king issued a Proclamation on 7 November to announce a general fast on 18 December for God's "special blessing on our arms both by sea and land". In the celebrations on his birthday the link between France and the rebellion was driven home. Thus the procession at Deptford was led by "a highlander in his proper dress carrying on a pole a pair of wooden shoes with this motto, *The newest mode from Paris*".[40] This symbolised the notion that popery and arbitrary power kept their subjects in poverty and slavery. It had been first used by the whigs in the Exclusion crisis, and invoked historic memories of Louis XIV and his alleged aim at universal monarchy. Just as popery was accused of seeking to destroy the liberties of Englishmen, so the French king was charged with planning the destruction of the liberties of Europe.

A handbill printed by "a loyal gentleman" at his own expense, for distribution to churches and handing out in the streets, neatly summarised the situation as the government liked people to see it:[41]

G. R.

| Liberty and Property with the Free Exercise of our Religion under a Protestant King and Parliament. | Slavery and Bigotry, Idolatory and Superstition, under a Popish Arbitrary Power sent from Rome. |

Chuse you this day whom ye will serve.

All this was fine public rhetoric. How far it echoed genuine beliefs is another question. The tory attitude towards a French invasion, to give the most obvious example, is so difficult to document that historians will probably always disagree about it. Velters Cornewall, when he heard that one had been prevented, thanked God "that the most Christian rascal of Paris cannot load his 12,000 well-booted and bucram'd troops...upon us", which indicates one tory MP's views on the subject.[42] On the other hand several others had intimated to the Pretender that they would rise on his behalf if a successful invasion were launched. Attempting to document attitudes from the fragmentary and even contradictory evidence of contemporary correspondence, therefore, can only be impressionistic.

In the absence of a reliable test of opinion, the only method of gauging inclinations is to deduce them from the way in which people behaved. And this leaves very little room to doubt that the most widespread response was not only the negative one of refusing to assist the rebels, but was also the positive one of supporting the government.

This is why in the end analogies between the Forty-five and previous attempts to change the dynasty by force are misleading. It was possible for a small number of determined men to effect a change of government by forcible means in the conditions of the time, provided the regime had alienated the majority of the political nation. Nor was it necessary for that majority to give them their active support; all that was needed was for it not to lift a finger in defence of the established order. The classic case was the Revolution of 1688. James II forfeited the allegiance of the aristocracy and gentry. Yet instead of declaring for William of Orange when he landed, most of them retired to their country houses to ride out the storm. That nevertheless created a truly revolutionary situation, since it left James abandoned and virtually helpless, and gave William an opportunity to succeed. Had the opposition to George II been similarly alienated in 1745, as the Young Pretender clearly thought that it was, then the fact that they did not join him need not have mattered. If they had simply refused to help the king it might have been enough. Instead they flocked to the assistance of the regime, and did all that they could to help defeat the rebellion.

It is true that most did not actually fight the Young Pretender, and that he got from Carlisle to Derby and back without any serious opposition apart from a skirmish at Clifton. Yet this in itself is no measure of his acceptability to people in England. He had defeated Cope's regular troops at Prestonpans, and rumours were rife that they had been horribly butchered and mangled by rebel broadswords. It is not altogether surprising that the amateur garrison at Carlisle, hastily scratched together from the local militias, capitulated when they learned that they could not expect any help from Wade's army, and were threatened with fire and sword if they refused. Although Wade himself blamed them for not holding out, he later instructed the Lancashire militia and the troops and companies raised by county subscriptions not to try to stop the rebels directly, but merely to harass them and thereby impede their progress. He himself was responsible to some extent for the fact that they progressed so far. His extreme caution, and the seeming inertia of his army, exasperated even his own fellow officers. When he arrived in Durham on his way south in November Dr Thomas Sharp, who helped to accommodate some troops, wrote to his son "you might possibly expect from me much more news being as it were in the midst of the army. But if you knew how little the officers themselves are apprized (such is the wisdom and wariness of the Marshal in the management of his intelligence and occultation of his designs) which way they are to march from hence, or when, you would cease to expect any intelligence from me."[43] In fairness to Wade he does seem to have encountered the worst of the severe weather which set in about the middle of November. We do not know enough about metereological conditions in different parts of the country to do more than guess about this, but people in the south of England were marvelling at the summery weather at the beginning of November, while when the rebels arrived at Carlisle they complained of the dense fog, so thick that they could not see their horses' ears in front of them. It was Wade who got bogged down in snow at Hexham on his way from Newcastle upon Tyne, and it seems possible that it was thicker on his side of the Pennines. But when all due consideration is given to this factor, the various forces involved had to endure a winter's campaign in very hard conditions. Both the rebels and the duke of Cumberland showed that it was nevertheless possible to move men about the country with more dispatch than the veteran Marshal. Unfortunately Wade was simply not up to the job of stopping the progress of the rebel army.

By the time they got to Derby it was perfectly obvious that the rebels were traversing hostile territory. A few people coming to gape at them, wearing white cockades, no doubt to avoid arousing hostility, might persuade James Maxwell of Kirkconnell that "from Manchester to Derby the country seemed pretty well affected", but it did not fool Lord George Murray.[44] He concluded that "the counties through which the army had pass'd had seemed much more enemies than friends", and that, even if they evaded the armies arrayed against them and managed to get into London, they would have the mob to contend with there. As they made their way back to Scotland the fact that the country was hostile to them began to tell. A dire fate awaited stragglers who fell into the hands of "the country people", as contemporaries called them. The duke of Cumberland tipped them the wink that they should simply kill any rebel they caught. His own troops felt the advantages of a friendly population, being provided with fresh horses, food, drink and accommodation as they travelled, and, when they caught up with them, clothes supplied by the Guildhall committee. At Preston they were joined by troops under General Oglethorpe, who included newly-raised companies of cavalry, paid for by subscription. When the two forces neared the border these considerations told more and more. The duke of Perth's attempt to get to Scotland ahead of the main body of the rebel army was stopped by local levies in Westmorland and Cumberland. Breaking up roads slowed down the Young Pretender's progress, until the duke of Cumberland's advance guard caught up with the rebels' rear guard at Clifton. As he waded across the river Esk on his twenty-fifth birthday Charles Edward might have pondered how seriously he had misjudged the situation in England, when he thought that tories and Country whigs would welcome him with open arms.

The Young Pretender's basic mistake was that he mistook opposition for disaffection. As *The Old England Journal* put it "there is the same difference betwixt opposition and rebellion as there is betwixt wholesome medicine and deadly poison".[45] Having lived in places where the open expression of views contrary to those held by the governors was circumscribed, and where critics to the regime were regarded as potential revolutionaries, Charles Edward could not appreciate that in Britain expressing such views was jealously guarded not so much as a privilege as a right. In this sense the idea that the rebellion was fundamentally a struggle between two different concepts of government, an arbitrary and a constitutional monarchy, was not merely whig rhetoric. One of the strengths of the eighteenth-century British political system was that, at the height of the rebellion, the earl of Westmorland could get up in the House of Lords and object to a vote of thanks to the king which did not recommend reforms of abuses.[46] "The spirit which, upon the present occasion, has appeared so generally without doors, could not but be agreeable to every man who has a regard for our present happy establishment," he declaimed. "But my Lords if we consider from whence that spirit arose, we must conclude that its continuance is not to be depended on unless a beginning, at least, be made in giving satisfaction to the people with respect to those grievances they have so long, so loudly and so generously exclaimed against." He then proceeded to attack the ministry, asking "is it not apparent that our constitution is in the most imminent danger of being undermined and blown up by ministerial corruption?" Just in case any Jacobites took heart from his speech, he concluded it by asserting that "revolution principles are those I have always professed, and upon these principles I must think it my duty, at such a dangerous conjecture, to talk freely as well as sincerely to my sovereign."

It is hard to imagine James Edward, had he by some miracle become James III, allowing such freedom of expression, or permitting himself the luxury of a formed opposition to his government. Of late there has been a tendency to deride the previously much vaunted Constitution of Hanoverian England. Certainly the more extravagant praise bestowed on it by some contemporaries must be qualified. Their assertion, for instance, that Englishmen were equal before the law might have been true in theory, but certainly was not in practice. Yet there was a rule of law, one which the lord justice clerk upheld against the duke of Cumberland's concept of 'Military execution' in Scotland. When the Privy Council ordered the requisition of provisions from farmers, so that they would not fall into rebel hands, they had to be reminded that there was no machinery for implementing such arbitrary decisions even in the middle of a rebellion. Lord Cholmondley thought that all that could be done was to assess the quantity of provisions available, "considering the nature and temper of the farmers in England, and the little power or authority either the justices of the peace or the Deputy Lieutenants have by Law or Usage to inforce the obedience of them."[47]

Critical contemporaries could show, as the Country opposition never tired of demonstrating, that the political system was shot through with abuses and riddled with corruption. But when it was put to the test, as it was in 1745, it showed itself to be preferable, for the vast majority of George II's subjects, to anything which the Pretender to his throne had to offer.

The mass of the people above all demonstrated that Jacobitism did not appeal to them. Again the Pretender and later historians misread the signs of popular disaffection. The heyday of anti-Hanoverian riots was over by the early 1720s. Even at their height they indicated more a zeal for high church toryism than for the Pretender, the main target of the attacks of the rioters being dissenting chapels. Walpole's belief that demonstrations at the time of the Excise crisis and the Gin Act were fomented by Jacobites was pure paranoia. The Pretender failed to exploit his chances in 1733, while in 1736 the chief victims of the mobs were Irish workmen. Attacking Catholics was scarcely a distinguishing mark of Jacobitism. On the contrary, in the Forty-five it was the chief characteristic of popular demonstrations of loyalty to the regime.

That the mass of the population should demonstrate its acceptance of the government despite penal laws and heavy indirect taxation was a phenomenon which appears to have taken even ministers by surprise. It has recently been attributed to favourable social and economic trends.[48] By 1720 at the very latest the population of England and Wales stopped growing, and might even have started to decline before the rapid demographic growth which occurred after 1760. During the 1740s, therefore, the level of population was unusually stable. At the same time between 1730 and 1750 most years witnessed bountiful harvests. Although a serious outbreak of cattle disease, which coincided with the rebellion, adversely affected meat prices, the price of bread, a staple of the labourer's diet, was relatively low in these years compared with those before and after. The resultant rise in real wages meant that the majority of wage earners were enjoying unprecedented prosperity, with a marked rise in their standard of living. The equation of popery and wooden shoes in government propaganda consequently exploited an assumption that their newfound affluence was attributable to the English political system. It asserted that economic improvement was a concomitant of a liberal constitution, and that conversely arbitrary regimes were detrimental to growth. Whether or not such crude symbolism had a real psychological impact on the mass of the population, the fact remains that they gave overwhelming support to the government during the rebellion.

While the Forty-five administered a therapeutic shock to the nervous system of the body politic which it was strong enough to withstand, for the Jacobites it was a blow which proved fatal. Jacobitism died a bloody death on the battlefield of Culloden and in the surrounding countryside. The brutality with which the British army destroyed it was no abberation, as the sequel to their victory was to show. Where they had killed rebels in warm blood during the battle and the ensuing pursuit, they executed others in cold blood in a calculated reign of terror in the Highlands.

The justification for the carnage and depredations was that the highlanders had inflicted rebellion on the rest of the country once too often. After 1715, the duke of Cumberland argued, the government had treated the Jacobites too leniently, and for its pains had been confronted with another rebellion thirty years later. The lesson was obvious. This time Jacobitism must be crushed once and for all. Cumberland's conviction was shared by most of those whose job it was to suppress the Forty-five, not just fellow officers like Hawley, Lockhart and Scot, but also politicians such as Henry Pelham, his brother the duke of Newcastle and the urbane, sophisticated earl of Chesterfield. And judging by the language employed by hosts of others below these, theirs was a common attitude. The rebels were widely regarded as subhuman, as animals or vermin, fit only to be hunted down and destroyed. Such sentiments found expression at the outset of the rebellion, but grew during the rebels' retreat from Derby, when the pursuit was frequently likened to a chase after hunted animals. This callousness came from a shared feeling that the rebels represented not an internal danger but an external threat. An expression which became a cliché during the Forty-five was "this unnatural rebellion". The idea that a claimant to the throne by divine hereditary right, who was thereby the father of his people, was interfering in the natural order of things, has an odd ring about it; but it sprang from the fact that the regime, at least in England, was so stable that it could claim not only the sanction of parliament but the blessing of Providence. By 1745 it seemed as though George II was the natural ruler of the country. How far Jacobitism in England was regarded as an unnatural phenomenon is indicated by the fate of the regiment which the Young Pretender recruited in Manchester. This was singled out for severe treatment, for a far higher proportion of the Englishmen captured at Carlisle was executed than of the Scottish rebels taken prisoner during the Forty-five. Indeed once the victorious forces had expiated their vengeance on the battlefield and in the glens, the actual

199

The duke of Cumberland at the battle of Lauffeld, 1747, where he was defeated by Marshal Saxe, a far more formidable adversary than the Young Pretender.

treatment of the rebels by the government was mild in contrast with the earlier threats of severity. There were even protests that too few had been executed.

The cooling of resentment turned to qualms of guilt, which people projected onto the duke of Cumberland, calling him 'the Butcher'. This was unfair. He had, undeniably, authorised butchery in the campaign in Scotland. But then he had been the mouthpiece of the whole political establishment. He was a young commander, much influenced by older men whom he respected, both in the high command and in the Cabinet. They gave him no reason to expect that his behaviour would meet with disapproval, but on the contrary he received every encouragement from them. When some withdrew in horror he became the scapegoat.

And yet Culloden was the crowning point of his career. He returned from Scotland as the conquering hero, while his later campaigns ended in defeat and even humiliation.

By the time he went back to the continent in February 1747 the French advance across the Low Countries had made them masters of the Austrian Netherlands. The only relief for the allies in 1745 had been the Treaty of Berlin, signed in December, whereby Prussia withdrew from the war. Otherwise it appeared as though Marshal Saxe would carry all before him, including the Dutch Republic. Cumberland tried to stop his eastward advance at Lauffeld, but had to admit defeat and order his troops to retreat after five hours of fighting. This was his last major engagement in the war of the Austrian Succession, for peace was signed at Aix-la-Chapelle in 1748. When war broke out in Europe again in 1756, the duke set out once more at the head of an army to fight the French. Unfortunately he failed to save his father's electorate of Hanover after his disastrous defeat at Hastenbeck in 1757. He then negotiated the convention of Klosterseven. Since this was virtually a capitulation, George II repudiated it, and dismissed Cumberland, who returned home in disgrace. His reception in London was far different from that afforded him as the victor of Culloden eleven years earlier, when honours and rewards were showered upon him.

Among the rewards he obtained in 1746 was the post of ranger of Windsor Forest, which the king gave him on 12 July. After the peace of Aix-la-Chapelle he employed hundreds of demobilised soldiers to construct the lake which became known as Virginia Water.[49] If this was to show sympathy for the men who had helped him to achieve victory over the rebels, he showed none to the common people who had displayed conspicuous loyalty during the rebellion. On the contrary he exploited the rangership just as ruthlessly as the whigs who had suppressed unwelcome hunters in the royal forests during the 1720s. He attempted to revive the swanimote courts, which they had used to enforce the forest laws far more rigorously than had their predecessors. He even prevented

Cumberland no longer "the martial boy" but a portly veteran, as seen by the caricaturist George, Lord Townshend.

people from entering the Great Park to collect firewood, though this was an immemorial custom, on the grounds that it disturbed the game.[50]

For the mass of Englishmen, indeed, their support of the regime in the Forty-five made no difference. The repressive legislation remained on the Statute book. The number of capital offences continued to rise. But then so did standards of living, at least until the reign of George III.

For the opposition the Forty-five proved to be a setback. The government cashed in on the wave of loyalty unleashed by the rebellion by dissolving parliament in 1747, a full year before a general election was due under the Septennial Act. The Court won a decisive victory at the polls, which reduced the tories and opposition whigs to their lowest strength for twenty years. During the election campaign government propagandists, taking their lead from Henry Fielding's *Jacobite Journal*, even depicted the tories as Jacobites despite their behaviour during the Forty-five. This was a gross libel, for in fact most tories looked not to the Pretender for salvation, but to Frederick, Prince of Wales. Cumberland's elder brother had returned to opposition following his uneasy truce with the king, and it was partly to forestall his electoral preparations that parliament was dissolved in 1747 rather than in 1748. Frederick realised that one of the main victims of the rebellion was Jacobitism itself. The tories had shown their loyalty to his family, and had he succeeded his father they would have reaped their reward. Unfortunately for them he died in 1751, while George II lived until 1760, making his the longest reign since Queen Elizabeth's.

The Forty-five had not seriously threatened to remove George from the throne. Instead of revealing that the dynasty was essentially unstable, it demonstrated as nothing else could have done just how firmly established the Hanoverian regime was. The stability of early eighteenth-century politics was not that of moribund stasis, but of dynamic tension. It was held together by the forces of Court and Country. Some contemporary observers and later historians observing the tension thought that these opposing forces would tear it apart. Instead they were a source of strength rather than of weakness. They made the English political system not only stable, but flexible enough to absorb the shock of an invasion aimed at overthrowing the regime, to expel it, and finally to crush it at Culloden.

Notes

ABBREVIATIONS USED IN THE NOTES

B.L. Add MSS	Additional manuscripts in the British Library.
Garnett	R. Garnett, 'Correspondence of Archbishop Herring and Lord Hardwicke during the Rebellion of 1745', *English Historical Review* (1904), xix, 528–53, 719–42.
H.L.LO	Loudoun papers at the Huntington Library.
H.M.C.	Reports of the Royal Historical Manuscripts Commission.
H.W.C.	W. S. Lewis, W. Hunting Smith and G. L. Lam, editors, *Horace Walpole's correspondence with Sir Horace Mann* (1955), volume three.
R.A.CP (M)	The duke of Cumberland's papers in the Royal Archive, Windsor Castle (microfilm copy in Cambridge University Library).
R.O.	Record Office.
S.P.	State papers in the Public Record Office. N.B. The State papers domestic series 36 have been foliated four times. Although the latest foliation is apparently the number stamped on the *verso* of each leaf, the one cited in the notes is that written in pencil within a diamond on the *recto* of each leaf, which corresponds with the foliation cited in the manuscript lists of contents at the Public Record Office.
W.W.M.	Wentworth Woodhouse Manuscripts in Sheffield City Libraries.

INTRODUCTION

1   V. H. H. Green, *The Hanoverians* (1948), p. 160.

2   B. Lenman, *The Jacobite Risings in Britain 1689–1746* (1980), pp. 231–59.

3   Eveline Cruickshanks, *Political Untouchables: The Tories and the '45* (1979); Linda Colley, 'The Tory Party 1727–1760' (Univ. of Cambridge Ph.D thesis, 1976); E. P. Thompson, *Whigs and Hunters* (1975).

4   W. A. Speck, *Stability and Strife* (1977).

5   E. Charteris, *William Augustus Duke of Cumberland* (1913), p. 132.

6   B. L. Add MS 5832, f. 145.

7   W. Coxe, *Memoirs of Sir Robert Walpole* (1816), iv, 342–3. cf. H.W.C., p. 20.

CHAPTER 1

"The whole Nation was ripe for a revolt"

1   *London Gazette*, 20—23 July 1745.
2   The discussion of ministerial changes, here and elsewhere, owes much to J. B. Owen, *The Rise of the Pelhams* (1956). Although John, Lord Carteret, did not become earl of Granville until 1744, to avoid confusion he is referred to by the latter title throughout this book.
3   Bodleian MS Don. c. 107, f. 69: John to Richard Tucker, 12 Jan. 1746.
4   See Rosalind Mitchison, 'The Government and the Highlands, 1707—1747', N. T. Phillipson and R. Mitchison, eds, *Scotland in the Age of Improvement* (Edinburgh, 1970), pp. 24—46.
5   B. L. Add MS 47098, ff. 9—10.
6   L. Stephen, *English Literature and Society in the Eighteenth Century* (1963), p. 82.
7   B. Williams, *Carteret and Newcastle* (Cambridge, 1943), p. 165.
8   The best account of the French invasion preparations is in Eveline Cruickshanks, *Political Untouchables: The Tories and the '45* (1979), chapter four.
9   Garnett, p. 535.
10 N. Tindal, *Continuation of Mr. Rapin's History of England* (1753), xviii, 314.
11 B. Lenman, *The Jacobite Risings in Britain 1689—1746* (1980), pp. 223—30.
12 Glamorganshire R.O.D/DKT.1/47: T. Prowse to Sir Charles Kemys Tynte, 25 Dec 1744.
13 G. Holmes, *British Politics in the Age of Anne* (1967), p. 279.
14 R. Patten, *The History of the Late Rebellion* (1717), pp. 93—4.
15 Cambridgeshire R. O. Cotton of Madingley MSS:588/0/8.
16 SP/36/82, f. 242: Revd G. Kelly to Colonel Strickland, 1 Dec. 1745: "Sir John H. Cotton should lay down his employment and this demission in the Gazette should be the signal of the embarkation."
17 Cambridgeshire R. O. Cotton of Madingley MSS:588/0/18; copper plate.
18 I do not share the cynicism about the independence of such independent country gentlemen which Derek Jarrett expresses in 'The myth of 'Patriotism' in eighteenth-century English politics', J. L. Bromley and F H Kossman, eds, *Britain and the Netherlands* (The Hague, 1975), v, 120—40.
19 James Maxwell of Kirkconnell, *Narrative of Charles Prince of Wales Expedition to Scotland in the Year 1745* (Edinburgh, 1841), pp. 9—10.
20 Cruickshanks, op. cit., pp. 47—9.
21 *A Full Collection of the Proclamations and Orders published by the Authority of Charles Prince of Wales* (Glasgow, 1746), pp. 28—45.
22 E. P. Thompson, *Whigs and Hunters* (1975).
23 P. Langford, *The Excise Crisis* (Oxford, 1975), p. 54.
24 G. Rudé, *Paris and London in the Eighteenth Century* (1970), p. 218.
25 C. Winslow, 'Sussex smugglers', D. Hay, P. Linebaugh and E. P. Thompson, eds, *Albion's Fatal Tree* (1975), pp. 119—66.
26 SP/36/72, f. 354: Anon to Newcastle, 30 Oct 1745.

CHAPTER 2

"This impotent attempt"

1   *London Gazette* 3–6 August 1745.
2   SP/36/67, f. 51.
3   SP/55/13, p. 204.
4   SP/54/25, ff., 159, 161.
5   R.A.CP (M) 4/136
6   SP/54/25, f. 174.
7   R.A.CP (M):4/136. The story of Cope's expedition is definitively discussed in Rupert C. Jarvis, *Collected Papers on the Jacobite Risings* (1971), i, 3–24.
8   R.A.CP (M):4/201.
9   Ibid. 4/116.
10 Ibid. 4/204.
11 *Culloden Papers* (1815), p. 218. There is a copy in the Loudoun papers. H.L.LO 7641.
12 B.L. Add MS 32705, f. 57.
13 R.A.CP (M):4/204
14 W.W.M.2, p. 219.
15 R.A.CP (M):4/225.
16 Ibid. 4/247.
17 Ibid. 4/201.
18 W. Sussex R. O. Goodwood MS 107/678: Edmund Martin to the duke of Richmond, 17 Sept 1744.
19 SP/54/25, f. 310.
20 W.W.M.2, p. 216.
21 SP/54/25, ff. 232, 234.
22 SP/54/25, f. 183.
23 SP/54/25, f. 199; SP/55/13, p. 216. Many details of Cope's march have been derived from *The Report of the Proceedings and Opinion of the Board of General Officers on their Examination into the Conduct, Behaviour and Proceedings of Lieutenant General Sir John Cope* (1749), hereafter *Cope Examination*.
24 See Jarvis, op. cit., pp. 48–74: 'Army transport'.
25 Garnett, p. 535.
26 R.A.CP (M):5/29.
27 W. Cobbett, *Parliamentary History* (1812), xiii, 1310: Henry Fox to Sir Charles Hanbury Williams, 5 Sept. 1745. Wade is sometimes taken to have been implying that the English would welcome the Pretender if he came first. It appears, however, that he was merely appraising the military, as distinct from the political, situation.
28 R.A.CP (M):5/29.
29 Cobbett, loc. cit.
30 Garnett, p. 534.
31 B.L. Add MS 32705, f. 187.
32 R.A.CP (M):5/67
33 W. Sussex R. O. Goodwood MS 106/528.
34 R.A.CP (M):5/68.

35   SP/36/68, f. 153.

36   *Culloden Papers* (1815), p. 219.

37   Sir James Fergusson, *Argyll in the 'Forty Five* (1951), p. 33.

38   SP/36/67, f. 128.

39   See Jarvis, op. cit., pp. 97—119: 'The Lieutenancy and Militia Laws'.

40   Carlisle R.O.D/Lons/W/Letters 43: D.Ls of Cumberland to Sir James Lowther.

41   SP/36/67, f. 199.

42   *London Gazette*, 3—7 Sept. 1745.

43   Garnett, p. 535.

44   W.W.M.2, pp. 222—3. Apparently the duke of Newcastle dismissed his French cook. W.W.M.1, p. 327.

45   Lancs R.O.DDHo/475/13.

46   SP/36/72, f. 394; /73, f. 61.

47   SP/36/75, f. 184.

48   W.W.M.1, p. 327.

49   Carlisle R.O.D/Pen. Acc. 2689. 17.

50   Northants R.O. Fitzwilliam Corr. box. 23. JPs to Fitzwilliam, 25 Sept. 1745.

51   Staffs R.O.D798/3/1/1: R. Baldwyn to ———, 20 Sept. 1745.

52   SP/36/70, f. 329. This did not prevent Norfolk's house at Worksop being searched with no result. W.W.M.2, p. 271.

53   W.W.M.2, pp. 217, 218.

54   Cited in E. Cruickshanks, *Political Untouchables: The Tories and the '45* (1979), p. 81.

55   This narrative of events in Edinburgh is based mainly on 'The examination of Provost Stewart, 7 Dec. 1745', SP/36/76, ff. 245—257; 'The Trial of Archibald Stewart', T. B. Howell, ed, *A Complete Collection of State Trials* (1813), xviii, 863—1070; and *Cope Examination.*

56   SP/54/26, f. 42.

57   SP/54/26 ff. 47—50, extracts from minutes of the Council of the City of Edinburgh, 23 Aug.—13 Sept. 1745.

58   SP/54/26, f. 79.

59   W.W.M.2, p. 254.

60   R.A.CP (M):5/260.

61   W.W.M.2, pp. 250—254. Andrew Wilkinson and Captain Singleton to Lord Malton, 26 Sept. 1745.

62   *Gentleman's Magazine* (1745), xv, 520.

63   *Culloden Papers* (1815), p. 224; W. A. S. Hewins, ed., *The Whitefoord Papers* (Oxford, 1898), p. 58.

64   The battle was over so quickly that Dr Alexander Carlyle, who was staying close by, missed it, even though he rose as soon as he heard the first cannon fire, and rushed out to observe the action. *The Autobiography of Dr Alexander Carlyle* (1910), p. 15.

65   *The Woodhouselee MS* (1907), pp. 35—6.

66   A. Henderson, *The History of the Rebellion* (1753), p. 87.

67   B.L. Add MS 35451, f. 10.

68   *Culloden Papers* (1815), p. 224.

69   W.W.M.2, p. 253.

70   R.A.CP (M):5/163.

71   Katherine Tomasson and F. Buist, *Battles of the '45* (1967), p. 48.

72   Henrietta Tayler, ed., *The History of the Rebellion in the Years 1745 and 1746* (Oxford, 1944), p. 64.

CHAPTER 3

"This thing is now grown very serious"

1   R.A.CP (M):5/174.

2   Garnett, p. 546.

3   B.L. Add MS 32705, f. 213.

4   SP/36/69, f. 206. Newcastle was informed that Charles Edward was going to summon a Convention of the Scottish Estates to Edinburgh. Had he in fact done so, on a programme of declaring Scotland an independent country, with an appeal for international recognition and support, he might have succeeded, as the American colonists were to do thirty years later. At least this would have stood a better chance of success than his ill-fated decision to invade England.

5   H.L.LO 12814.

6   W.W.M.2, p. 219; Garnett, p. 531.

7   *Gentleman's Magazine* (1745), xv, 501.

8   SP/36/69, f. 213.

9   H.M.C. Trevor MSS, p. 131.

10   Lancs R.O.DDHo/474/9: Pelham to Hoghton, 7 Sept. 1745.

11   W.W.M.2, pp. 220, 224.

12   Henrietta Tayler, ed., *The History of the Rebellion in the Years 1745 and 1746* (Oxford, 1944), p. 68.

13   W.W.M.2, p. 228.

14   Leeds Archive Dept. Temple Newsam MSS TN/PO/3c/13.

15   For a full discussion of the Yorkshire response see C. Collyer, 'Yorkshire and the 'Forty-five', *Yorkshire Archaeological Journal* (1952—5), xxxviii, 71—95.

16   Leeds Archives Dept. Newby Hall letters 2830/13.

17   H.W.C., p. 126.

18   *Gentleman's Magazine* (1745), xv, 471—2.

19   *An Exact List of the Voluntary Subscribers* (York, 1747).

20   Garnett, pp. 545—7.

21   W.W.M.1, p. 311.

22   *Newcastle Journal*, 5 Oct. 1745.

23   W. Cobbett, *Parliamentary History* (1812), xiii, 1353.

24   Herts R.O.D.EPF.266.

25   Linda Colley, 'The Tory Party 1727—1760', (Univ. of Cambridge Ph.D thesis, 1976), pp. 237—8.

26   SP/36/72, f. 253. Bath himself did not subscribe "one farthing in any place where, from his property, more than his generosity, it might have been expected". W.W.M.2, p. 324.

27 Swansea University Library Mackworth MSS: T. Peplow to H. Mackworth, 23 Oct. 1745.

28 Huntingdon R.O.DDM. 49/8/1—5.

29 SP/36/70, f. 38.

30 *London Gazette*, 1—5, 5—8, 15—19 Oct. 1745.

31 SP/36/70, f. 38.

32 W.W.M.2, p. 276.

33 W. Le Hardy, ed., *Hertfordshire County Records* (Hertford, 1931), vii, 575—83.

34 H.M.C. Ancaster MSS, pp. 253—4.

35 Lancs R.O.DDHo/475/18/, 32; SP/36/69, f. 126.

36 Cheshire R.O.D.CH/X/9/A/4.

37 SP/36/69, f. 233.

38 W.W.M.1, p. 308; SP/36/76, f. 97: SP/36/71, f. 93.

39 Staffs R.O.D. 1413/1: R. Hurd to Littleton, 18 Dec. 1745.

40 W.W.M.2, p. 272.

41 SP/36/71, f. 213.

42 Northants R.O.S(T)5; 10.

43 R. Sedgwick, ed., *The Commons 1715—1754* (1970), ii, 394.

44 SP/36/72, f. 190.

45 Staffs R.O.D798/3/1/1: F. Eld to J. Eld, 12 Oct. 1745. Eld continued "I wish some that signed it did apply it to K — — — G — — — — —."

46 SP/36/71, f. 32.

47 SP/36/70, f. 74.

48 SP/36/71, f. 96.

49 SP/36/71, ff. 129, 181.

50 W.W.M.2, p. 286: Lady Finch had picked up a story that Lords of manors in the West were promising to give life tenure gratis to the heir of any tenant who should die in the service of his country during the rebellion.

51 SP/36/74, ff. 31—3.

52 SP/54/26, f. 453; SP/36/70, f. 242.

53 R.A.CP (M):7/13.

54 SP/36/74, f. 179. For the abortive inquiries into an alleged Jacobite Club organised by the rector of Hawarden see SP/36/73, ff. 316, 427; SP/36/75, ff. 89, 160, 164, 181.

55 J. P. Jenkins, The Social and Political History of the Glamorgan Gentry, 1660—1760' (Univ. of Cambridge Ph.D. thesis, 1978), p. 274; J. P. Jenkins, 'Jacobites and Freemasons in Eighteenth-century Wales', *Welsh History Review* (1979), p. 394.

56 W.W.M.2, p. 302.

57 B.L. Add MS 32705, f. 198.

58 *London Gazette*, 26—30 Nov. 1745. It appears that Catholics in Ormskirk and its neighbourhood had been subjected to a rigorous implementation of the Order in Council authorising the seizure of their horses a short time before the demonstration. SP/36/73, f. 225. It nevertheless made Henry Pelham uneasy that more risings were to be expected from other Catholics, though he was adamant that "if they do give trouble I am certain they deserve no mercy; for

they have had great favour from this government, perhaps to a degree of delusion." R.A.CP (M):7/212.

59 R.A.CP (M):7/163.

60 B.L. Add MS 47098, f. 11.

61 Staffs R.O.D 798/3/1/1: F. Eld to J. Eld, 12 Oct. 1745.

62 W.W.M.1, p. 327.

63 *A Full Collection of the Proclamations and Orders published by Order of Charles Prince of Wales* (Glasgow, 1746), p. 27.

64 B.L. Add MS 47098, f. 13.

65 SP/36/69, f. 139.

66 "To Friends at their ensuing Quarterly Meetings", printed half sheet signed Jos Besse and dated 20th of the 7th month 1745.

67 A. Henderson, *The Life of William Augustus, Duke of Cumberland* (1766), p. 160. James Ray, a volunteer with Cumberland's army, recorded an extempore verse "spoken by a soldier the day after he received a flannel waistcoat, thro' the bounty of the Quakers", expressing how, kept warm by "this friendly waistcoat", he would "fight for those whose creed forbids to fight". J. Ray, *The Acts of the Rebels* (1746), p. 32. Quakers in Hertfordshire, although "very wealthy", withstood the "most pressing solicitations" to associate and subscribe. Le Hardy, op. cit., p. xi.

68 SP/36/73, f. 138. John Wesley himself was in Newcastle upon Tyne in October and wrote to the mayor expressing his distress at the cursing and swearing of the soldiers, offering his services to reform those "to whom our lives are intrusted". He also expressed his "love of my country and the zeal I have for his Majesty King George". Northumberland R.O.ZRI.27.5.

69 *A Full Collection of the Proclamations*, p. 29.

70 Bodleian MS Don. c. 107, f. 131.

71 Garnett, p. 546.

72 SP/36/72, f. 291. A sour note was struck in Somerset, however, where Lord Poulet noted "a strange indifference among the middling people". SP/36/74, f. 33.

73 *Newcastle Journal*, 19 Oct. 1745. The letter was apparently 'syndicated', for a version was published in the *Gentleman's Magazine* (1745), xv, 531—2.

74 *Newcastle Courant*, 8—15 Feb. 1745.

75 *True Patriot*, 26 Nov. 1745.

76 SP/36/68, f. 45.

77 W.W.M.2, p. 221.

78 SP/36/69, f. 274; Northants R.O. Fitzwilliam Corr: Malton to Fitzwilliam, 11 Nov. 1745.

79 Staffs R.O.D 798/3/1/1; SP/36/71, f. 16.

80 SP/36/71, f. 104.

81 *Newcastle Journal*, 9 Nov. 1745.

82 W.W.M.2, p. 296.

83 Staffs R.O.D 798/3/1/1: F. Eld to J. Eld, 6 Oct. 1745.

84 *Gentleman's Magazine* (1745), xv, 513.

85 W.W.M.2, p. 296.

86 Northants R.O. Fitzwilliam Corr: W. Strong to Fitzwilliam, 3 Nov. 1745.
87 SP/36/71, ff. 173, 286.
88 SP/36/69, f. 233.
89 Northants R.O. Fitzwilliam Corr: Malton to Fitzwilliam, 14 Oct. 1745.
90 Garnett, p. 722.
91 SP/36/70, f. 200.
92 W.W.M.2, p. 278; Northants R.O. Fitzwilliam Corr: Malton to Fitzwilliam, 12 Oct. 1745.
93 *Gentleman's Magazine* (1745), xv, 554.
94 SP/36/70, f. 243.
95 Carlisle R.O.D/Pen. Acc. 2689/18.
96 B.L. Add MS 47098, ff. 7—8.
97 H.L.LO 12819.
98 SP/36/72, f. 213;/74, f. 60. Edgecombe to Newcastle, 19 Nov. 1745: "They all express great readiness to defend their country, but they mean their county."
99 Cobbett, op. cit., pp. 1310—12.
100 W.W.M.1, p. 340.
101 L. Dickens and M. Stanton, eds, *An Eighteenth-century Correspondence* (1910), p. 113: Lord Deerhurst to Sanderson Miller.
102 H.W.C, p. 153.
103 Lord Hartington to Devonshire, 29 Oct. 1745. I am grateful to Dr Eveline Cruickshanks for the loan of photocopies of letters in the Chatsworth correspondence.
104 W.W.M.1, p. 340.
105 Ibid. p. 353. Lady Isabella claimed that the regiments were worth £10,000 each to their Colonels.
106 Bodleian MS Don. c. 107, ff. 158—9.
107 SP/36/72, f. 382.
108 R.A.CP (M):7/229.
109 Garnett, p. 548.
110 H.W.C., p. 105.
111 B.L. Add MS 47098, f. 8v.
112 R.A.CP (M):5/214.
113 B.L. Add MS 47098, ff. 9—10.
114 J. B. Owen, *The Rise of the Pelhams* (1956), p. 281; SP/36/69, f. 220.
115 B.L. Add MS 47098, f. 9v.
116 H.M.C. Onslow MSS, p. 523.
117 H.M.C. Hastings MSS, iii, 53.
118 *Newcastle Journal*, 26 Oct. 1745.
119 Northants R.O. Fitzwilliam Corr: Malton to Fitzwilliam, 23 Oct. 1745.
120 SP/36/72, f. 177.
121 R.A.CP (M):6/160.
122 SP/36/73, f. 131.

CHAPTER 4
"Flushed with success these lawless vagrants come"

1   SP/36/73, f. 192.
2   For a fuller description of the fall of Carlisle see G. G. Mounsey, *Carlisle in 1745* (1846).
3   Leeds Archive Dept. Temple Newsam MS TN/PO/3c/88.
4   H.W.C., p. 165.
5   Carlisle R.O.D.Sen/Acc.259: "some general hints concerning the late affair at Carlisle."
6   Carlisle R.O.D/Pen. Acc. 2689/22, 23 and 24.
7   SP/36/74, ff. 54, 55.
8   Cheshire R.O.DCH/X/9/A/11.
9   W. Le Hardy, ed., *Hertfordshire County Records* (Hertford, 1931), vii, p. xi.
10   SP/36/75, f. 1.
11   W.W.M. 1, p. 371.
12   H.M.C. Temple Newsam MSS, p. 128.
13   R.A.CP (M):5/214.
14   Ibid. 6/30.
15   H.W.C, p. 174; Staffs R.O.D 798/3/1/1: F. Eld to J. Eld, 23 Nov. 1745.
16   A. Henderson, *The History of the Rebellion* (1753), p. 177.
17   Halifax Central Library Shibden Hall MSS.SH7/FL/10: F. Fawkes to J. Lister, 9 Nov. 1745. Cf. above, p. 77.
18   Lancs R.O.DDHo/475/60.
19   Ibid./163.
20   Ibid./86. Derby wrote to the duke of Richmond that he was going to London "not seeing how it is in any way in my power or of any other friends to the Government to be longer serviceable to the country in which my fortune lies, or the nation in general, and therefore think I am at liberty to save myself from the hands of those whose religion of course makes them enemies to the Constitution under which they live, with which sort of persons this county does but too much abound." Carlisle R.O.D.Pen/Acc 2689/32 (copy).
21   Carlisle R.O.D.Sen/Acc 259.
22   Cheshire R.O.DCH/X/9/A/28.
23   Staffs R.O.D/413/1: R. Hurd to Sir E. Littleton, 29 Nov. 1745.
24   Leeds Archives Dept. Newby Hall MSS Letters 2830/13.
25   R.A.CP (M):7/164.
26   SP/36/75, f. 1.
27   Cheshire R.O.DCH/X/9/A/9, 13.
28   R.A.CP (M):7/38.
29   SP/36/73, f. 435.
30   see R. C. Jarvis, *Collected Papers on the Jacobite Risings* (1971), i, 75—93: 'The Mersey bridges'.
31   H.M.C. Underwood MSS, p. 287.
32   R.A.CP (M):7/261.

33 Swansea University Library, Mackworth MSS: T. Peplow to H. Mackworth, 4 Dec. 1745.

34 SP/36/76, f. 58.

35 R.A.CP (M):7/262.

36 Ibid. 7/195.

37 Ibid. 7/287.

38 SP/36/76, f. 155.

39 B.L. Add MS 32705, ff. 405, 409.

40 R.A.CP (M):7/287.

41 H.W.C., p. 177.

42 Herts R.O. 6879b: D. Gautier to W. Lee, n. d.

43 That London was loyal rather than the reverse is the conclusion of N. Rogers, 'Popular disaffection in London during the 'Forty Five', *London Journal* (1975), i, 1—26.

44 W.W.M.2, pp. 322—3.

45 A. and H. Tayler, *1745 and After* (1938), p. 95.

46 Bodleian MS Don. c. 107, f. 174.

47 *London Gazette Extraordinary*, 12 Dec. 1745. "But", it continued, "they have plundered the country in their retreat."

48 Chevalier de Johnstone, *A Memoir of the '45* (1958), p. 62.

49 SP/36/76, ff. 197, 205.

50 H.M.C. Lothian MSS, p. 154; H.W.C., p. 180.

51 A. and H. Tayler, op. cit., pp. 101—2.

52 H.W.C., p. 180.

53 W.W.M.1, p. 403.

54 H.M.C. Du Cane MSS, p. 85: J. Henshaw to Vice-Admiral Medley, 7 Jan. 1745.

55 J. Ray, *A Compleat History of the Rebellion* (1749), p. 152.

56 W.W.M.2, p. 302.

57 H.W.C., pp. 179—80. How right Walpole was to include Dr. Burton here depends upon whether the accounts of his activities put out by such enemies as Jacques Sterne or his own protestations of innocence are believed.

58 Northants R.O. Fitzwilliam Corr: Malton to Fitzwilliam, 2 Dec. 1745.

59 E. Charteris, ed., *A Particular Account of the Affairs of Scotland in the Years 1744, 1745 and 1746 by David Lord Elcho* (1907), p. 337.

60 SP/36/74, f. 100. Charles Edward sent the same message to the north of England. His messenger was arrested in Newcastle, however, and, though he tried to commit suicide, was resuscitated in expectation of "making great discoveries of the persons with whom he is to traffique." Although it was alleged that there were "not a few in this town and county", none were ever identified. *Culloden Papers* (1815), p. 226.

61 Ray, op. cit., p. 155.

62 B.L. Add MS 32705, f. 421.

63 R.A.CP (M):7/324.

64 E. Hughes, *North Country Life in the Eighteenth Century* (1952), pp. 87—8. As Professor Hughes commented, "so much for the myth of Derby!"

65 SP/36/76, f. 165.

66   Ibid. f. 159.

67   Northants R.O. Fitzwilliam Corr: Malton to Fitzwilliam, 7 Dec. 1745.

68   SP/54/26, ff. 211—14, 217, 219, 237.

69   Ibid. f. 240.

70   Charteris, op. cit., p. 187.

71   R.A.CP (M):7/325.

72   SP/36/76, f. 337.

73   Ray, op. cit., p. 187.

74   R.A.CP (M):7/369.

75   R.A.CP (M):7/324.

76   Essex R.O.D/DM.22. "The report of the committee appointed for making a... distribution of the money subscribed at the Guildhall for the relief and encouragement of the soldiers employed in suppressing the late unnatural rebellion", 23 Jan. 1747.

77   Ibid. The army was being inundated with pailliasses at this time, the Middlesex and Westminster Association having agreed to supply Cumberland's army with 3,000, while the parish of St James's supplied Wade's with 3,000 too. R.A.CP(M): 7/222.

78   R.A.CP (M):7/271, 342.

79   R.A.CP (M):8/6.

80   Swansea University Library Mackworth MSS: Peplow to Mackworth, 16 Dec. 1745.

81   R.A.CP (M):8/6.

82   R.A.CP (M):8/9: Pelham to Fawkener, 12 Dec. 1745. "The irregular, sudden and unusual marches which these extraordinary animals have taken could not be foreseen." The word 'animals' has been inserted in the sentence.

83   B.L. Add MS 32705, f. 458.

84   *Gentleman's Magazine* (1745), xv, 664. The Hunters consisted of young "bucks ...listed under a mad General, Oglethorpe." H.M.C. Du Cane MSS, p. 77. Oglethorpe the first Governor of Georgia, also formed a company known as the Georgia rangers, and even diverted a ship carrying arms for the colony to Hull to help suppress the rebellion. W.W.M.2, p. 256.

85   SP/36/76, f. 263. Doddridge, who was an admirer of Colonel Gardiner, the dragoon officer killed at Prestonpans, believed the accounts of the alleged atrocities committed by the rebels at that battle: *Some Remarkable Passages in the Life of the Honourable Colonel James Gardiner* (1778), p. 206.

86   Ray, op. cit., p. 188. Lady Isabella Finch called the rebels "beasts in confusion", W.W.M.1, p. 425.

87   Staffs R.O.D 798/3/1/1: F. Eld to J. Eld, April 1746.

88   *A Journey through part of England and Scotland along with the Army* (1746), p. 20.

89   *Newcastle Gazette*, 29 Jan. 1746.

90   R.A.CP (M):8/91.

91   R.A.CP (M):7/346; 8/6, 24, 25.

92   R.A.CP (M):8/44.

93   W.W.M.2, p. 325.

94 SP/36/76, ff. 426, 429.

95 R.A.CP (M):8/32.

96 Ibid. 50; H.M.C. Fitzherbert MSS, p. 176.

97 R.A.CP (M):8/50.

98 For a full account of the following events see Chancellor Ferguson, 'The Retreat of the Highlanders through Westmorland in 1745', *Transactions of the Cumberland and Westmorland Archaeological and Antiquarian Society* hereafter *T.C.W.A.A.S.* (1889), x, 186—228.

99 Although Sir Everard Fawkener could not "remember anything had been done towards breaking the roads" when he wrote to Lord Lonsdale from Carlisle on 25 Dec. (Carlisle R.O.D/Pen. Acc 2689/42), the Deputy Lieutenants of Westmorland informed Cumberland that they had implemented his orders, R.A.CP (M):8/46.

100 A. and H. Tayler, op. cit., p. 106.

101 Carlisle R.O.D/Pen. Acc. 2689/18.

102 J. P. Dalton, 'Cumberland and the '45: some Letters', *T.C.W.A.A.S* (1947), xlvi, 111; Carlisle R.O.D/Lons/L/CL16/39.ii; D/Pen/Acc 2689/34.

103 Carlisle R.O.D/Sen/Addl letters: Bishop of Carlisle to H. Senhouse, 15 Dec. 1745.

104 Ferguson, op. cit., p. 225; SP/36/77, ff. 178—9.

105 W.W.M.1, p. 421. 'The Sheffield Messenger's Account'.

106 R.A.CP (M):8/190.

107 Ibid. 8/80.

108 Ibid.8/110.

109 *T.C.W.A.A.S* (1889), x, 222.

110 G. G. Mounsey, *Carlisle in 1745* (1846), p. 149.

111 SP/36/77, f. 85.

112 Ibid. ff. 121, 123.

113 Ibid. f. 170.

114 Ibid. f. 10.

115 Ibid. ff. 26, 35.

116 Ibid. f. 189.

117 Ibid. f. 102.

118 H.M.C. Du Cane MSS, p. 84.

119 SP/36/78, f. 232.

120 SP/36/80, ff. 70, 350.

121 R.A.CP (M):8/109, 152, 155.

122 R.A.CP (M):8/162.

123 W.W.M.1, p. 427.

124 R.A.CP (M):8/138, 161.

CHAPTER 5

"Go, glorious Youth, belov'd of Britain, go"

1 Sir Richard Lodge, ed., *Private Correspondence of Chesterfield and Newcastle* (1930), pp. 91, 93.

2   B.L. Add MS 32705, f. 403: "For God's sake let this be private."
3   Lodge, loc. cit.
4   R.A.CP (M):7/286.
5   SP/54/26, f. 259.
6   H.W.C., p. 201.
7   *Culloden Papers* (1815), p. 270.
8   SP/36/78, f. 78.
9   SP/36/78, f. 211; SP/54/27, f. 22.
10   SP/36/78, f. 247.
11   R.A.CP (M):5/157.
12   SP/36/78, f. 176.
13   R.A.CP (M):8/168.
14   SP/54/26, f. 284. Lord President Forbes's dealings with Lovat, which began by offering him a commission in one of the independent companies, and ended by acquiescing in his arrest, are amply documented in the *Culloden Papers* (1815). They deteriorated when some Frasers attacked Forbes's house at Culloden on 16 Oct., and were irreparably damaged when Lovat's son came out in open rebellion, though Lovat himself all the while protested his own innocence.
15   SP/54/27, ff. 67, 69.
16   *Culloden Papers* (1815), p. 265; R.A.CP (M):9/81; SP/54/27, f. 28.
17   R.A.CP (M):9/43.
18   Ibid. 9/66.
19   Ibid. 9/81.
20   Hawley admitted to having "two thousand more than them." R.A.CP (M):9/99. Another estimate was that "our army was about 9,000 strong and the rebels only 6,000 in number." Northumberland R.O.ZRI.27/4/53. The numbers here are taken from K. Tomasson and F. Buist, *Battles of the '45* (1967), pp. 108—9.
21   H.M.C. Underwood MSS, p. 440.
22   H.M.C. Hastings MSS, iii, 54.
23   *Culloden Papers* (1815), p. 271; Northumberland R.O.ZRI.27/4/53.
24   H.M.C. Underwood MSS, p. 441.
25   Carlisle R.O.D/Hud/A4.
26   SP/36/80, f. 342.
27   R.A.CP (M):9/99.
28   H.M.C. Hastings MSS, iii, 54.
29   SP/54/27, f. 117.
30   Ibid. ff. 115, 128, 130.
31   B.L. Add MSS 32706, f. 18.
32   R.A.CP (M):9/141.
33   Northumberland R.O.ZRI.27/4/53.
34   R.A.CP (M):10/18.
35   *Newcastle Courant*, 8—15 Feb. 1745.
36   SP/36/80, f. 430.
37   Ibid. f. 479; /81, f. 25.
38   Herts R.O.D/ENa.F61.

39   SP/36/81, f. 25.

40   E. Charteris, *William Augustus Duke of Cumberland* (1913), p. 247.

41   *An Address to the Army*, 30 Jan. 1746.

42   H. Tayler, ed., *The History of the Rebellion in the Years 1745 and 1746* (Oxford, 1944), p. 161.

43   R.A.CP (M):10/28.

44   B.L. Add MS 35354, f. 179.

45   R.A.CP (M):10/49.

46   Ibid. 11/15.

47   Ibid. 10/43.

48   B.L. Add MS 35354, f. 185.

49   R.A.CP (M):10/74.

50   Ibid. 168.

51   Ibid. 74.

52   B.L. Add MS 47098, f. 11.

53   W.W.M.1, p. 410.

54   J. B. Owen, *The Rise of the Pelhams* (1956), pp. 285—6, 292—3.

55   Lord Ilchester, *Henry Fox, first Lord Holland* (1920), i, 126.

56   Lodge, op. cit., p. 97.

57   Ibid. p. 109.

58   B.L. Add MS 47098, f. 17.

59   Bodleian MS Don. c. 107, f. 226: J. Tucker to R. Tucker, 11 Feb. 1746.

60   B.L. Add MS 32706, f. 140.

61   H.W.C., p. 213.

62   R.A.CP (M):10/161.

63   B.L. Add MS 32706, f. 157.

64   When Lord Cholmondley's son, Sir Robert Walpole's grandson, was made a Captain, Cumberland wrote "I was very glad of this occasion to oblige you and to show any mark of regard to a descendant of Lord Orford's, to whom I had great obligations, and shall always be rejoiced to return them to any of his family." Cheshire R.O.DCH/X/9/A/1.

65   R.A.CP (M):10/221.

66   B.L. Add MS 32706, f. 233.

67   B.L. Add MS 35354, f. 191.

68   R.A.CP (M):12/71.

69   Ibid. 11/41.

70   Ibid. 10/131; 11/12.

71   Ibid. 10/250; 11/12.

72   Ibid. 10/233; 11/12.

73   Ibid. 11/62.

74   Ibid. 11/64, 65.

75   Ibid. 11/87.

76   Ibid. 12/58.

77   Ibid. 11/236.

78   Ibid. 13/6.

79   Ibid. 12/135.

80   Ibid. 12/154.

81   Ibid. 12/168.

82   Ibid. 13/88.

83   James Maxwell of Kirkconnell, *Narrative of Charles Prince of Wales Expedition to Scotland in the year 1745* (Edinburgh, 1841), p. 130.

84   "Anent the march of the Highland army...February 1746", R.A.CP (M):10/220.

85   Ibid. 11/139; 12/177.

86   Ibid. 12/142, 198, 200, 240, 260; 13/88.

87   Ibid. 11/277; 12/31, 196, 198, 231, 351: H.L. LO 9503, 9504, 11183.

88   R.A.CP (M):11/198, 239.

89   Maxwell, op. cit., p. 92.

90   R.A.CP (M):12/163.

91   Ibid. 12/292.

92   Ibid. 12/353.

93   Ibid. 12/28.

94   Ibid. 12/14, 76.

95   Ibid. 12/75.

96   Ibid. 12/108.

97   B.L. Add MS 35354, f. 203.

98   R.A.CP (M):12/108.

99   Ibid. 12/179.

100   Ibid. 12/226.

101   B.L. Add MS 32706, f. 325. Connoisseurs of Newcastle's handwriting will appreciate his own acknowledgement of its illegibility. Despite his injunction to Cumberland to burn the letter he kept a copy, clearly written by his under-secretary.

102   B.L. Add MS 32707, f. 13.

103   R.A.CP (M):13/74, 75.

104   Ibid. 12/209.

105   Ibid. 12/182.

106   Ibid. 12/353.

107   Ibid. 13/45, 104.

108   Ibid. 13/152.

109   Ibid. 13/145.

110   A journal of the siege was published in the *Gentleman's Magazine* (1746), xvi, 205—7.

111   R.A.CP (M):12/198. Smith sent his log book to the duke's secretary to account for his movements. Ibid. 13/254.

112   Ibid. 13/125, 250.

113   Ibid. 13/269.

114   Essex R.O.D/DM.22., f. 5.

115   B.L. Add MS 35354, f. 229. The king also sent four additional regiments to Scotland, but these did not arrive to reinforce Cumberland's army until after the battle of Culloden. R.A.CP (M):13/186.

116   *The History of the Rebellion in 1745 and 1746 extracted from the Scots Magazine* (1755), p. 179.

117 A. Henderson, *The Life of William Augustus, Duke of Cumberland* (1766), p. 236.

118 R.A.CP (M):13/149, 152, 179.

CHAPTER 6

"So many butchers"

1 J. C. Leask and H. M. McCance, eds., *The Regimental Records of the Royal Scots* (Dublin, 1915), p. 149; J. Ray, *The Acts of the Rebels* (1746), pp. 32—3.

2 R.A.CP (M):13/279.

3 A. Henderson, *The Life of William Duke of Cumberland* (1766), p. 245.

4 R.A.CP (M):13/294.

5 Leask and McCance, loc. cit.

6 R.A.CP (M):13/281, 294.

7 A. and H. Tayler, *1745 and After* (1938), p. 155.

8 Henderson, op. cit., pp. 149—50.

9 Leask and McCance, loc. cit. Cf. Henderson, op. cit., p. 251; "He [Cumberland] ordered every soldier a glass of brandy, a biscuit and a little cheese."

10 Leask and McCance, loc. cit. Accounts of how often the columns were formed into lines on the march to Culloden differ. "A description of the order of the march" in Cumberland's papers states that there were three such manoeuvres, the first occurring after marching between five and six miles, when the army had the Loch of the Clans on its right, and Kilvarock wood on its left. R.A.CP (M): 14/4. Captain Thomas Buck also wrote that they "formed in order of battle three different times". W.W.M.2, p. 392. The duke of Cumberland himself, however, reported only two occasions, the first after marching eight miles. H.M.C. Underwood MSS, p. 442. Private Taylor also recorded two such formations, though he thought that the first had occurred after only four miles. Such discrepancies in the record, even on such a totally non-controversial point, shake confidence in some accounts of the battle which purport to reconstruct the sequence of events almost minute by minute, with scarcely any recognition of such documentary difficulties.

11 *Gentleman's Magazine* (1746), xvi, 271; Henderson, op. cit., p. 253.

12 J. Ray, *A Compleat History of the Rebellion* (1749), pp. 356—7; Henderson put a curious version into his *History of the Rebellion* (1753), pp. 324—5, which he altered for his *Life* of Cumberland.

13 R. Chambers, ed., *Jacobite Memoirs of the Rebellion of 1745* (1834), p. 82; J. Keegan, *The Face of Battle* (1976).

14 Northumberland R.O.ZAN.M12/C39/55: Hugh Ross to Thomas Davidson, 30 April 1746; M. Hughes, *A Plain Narrative or Journal of the Late Rebellion* (1746), p. 44.

15 *An Authentic Account of the Battle Fought...on the 16th of April 1746.*

16 W. B. Blaikie, ed., *Origins of the 'Forty-five* (Edinburgh, 1975), pp. 213—14.

17 James Maxwell of Kirkconnell, *Narrative of Charles Prince of Wales Expedition* (Edinburgh, 1841), p. 150.

18 E. Charteris, editor, *A Short Account of the Affairs of Scotland...by David Lord Elcho* (1907), p. 431.
19 Hughes, op. cit., p. 46; Northumberland R.O.ZAN.M12/C39/55.
20 Ibid.
21 R.A.CP (M):14/6, 7.
22 Blaikie, op. cit., pp. 212—13.
23 K. Tomasson and F. Buist, *Battles of the '45* (1967), p. 150.
24 R.A.CP (M):14/63.
25 *Newcastle Journal*, 26 April 1746.
26 W.W.M.2, p. 393: Captain Thomas Buck to Lord Malton, 20 April 1746.
27 H.M.C. Underwood MSS, p. 443.
28 Northumberland R.O.ZAN.M12/C39/55.
29 Northumberland R.O.ZRI/27/4/66.
30 Carlisle R.O.D/Sen/corr/2.
31 Ray, *Compleat History*, p. 334. Even the time when the fighting began differs from one eye-witness account to another. According to Michael Hughes "the battel began at twelve o'clock", while Alexander Taylor claimed that the action commenced "about ½ an hour after 2 o'clock." Hughes, op. cit., p. 44; Leask and McCance, loc. cit. Most accounts agree, however, that it was about one o'clock.
32 R.A.CP (M):2/289. The French also alleged that Cumberland "gave orders for no quarter to be given".
33 Hughes, op. cit., p. 41.
34 H.M.C. Underwood MSS, p. 443.
35 W.W.M.2, p. 392.
36 Carlisle R.O.D/Sen/corr. 2.
37 W. A. S. Hewins, ed., *The Whitefoord Papers* (Oxford, 1898), p. 78.
38 *Newcastle Journal*, 26 April; *Newcastle Courant*, 26 April—3 May, 1746.
39 Henderson, op. cit., p. 256.
40 Greater London R.O. WSP.1746.Ju/15.
41 Henderson, loc. cit.
42 *Newcastle Journal*, 10 May 1746.
43 W.W.M.2, p. 393.
44 *Newcastle Journal*, 26 April; *Newcastle Courant*, 19—26 April; 26 April—3 May 1746.
45 B.L. Add MS 35451, f. 34.
46 *Newcastle Journal*, 26 April; 10 May 1746.
47 H.M.C. Trevor MSS, p. 145.
48 A. Henderson, *History of the Rebellion* (1753), pp. 332—3.
49 *Newcastle Journal*, 26 April 1746.
50 *The Second Book of Dathan's Account of the Rebellion: being also the Third Book of the Chronicle of William the Son of George* (1746), p. 12.
51 Henderson, *History of the Rebellion*, pp. 330—1.
52 R.A.CP (M):10/275.
53 Leask and McCance, op. cit., p. 150.
54 Scottish R.O.GD1/322/1.

55   E. Charteris, *William Augustus Duke of Cumberland* (1913), p. 278.

56   *Newcastle Journal*, 3 May 1746.

57   H.L.LO 10882.

58   H.M.C. Hastings MSS, iii, 56.

59   *Newcastle Journal*, 26 April 1746.

60   Greater London R.O.WSP.1746.Ju/15.

61   Hughes, op. cit., p. 50.

62   Northumberland R.O.ZRI/27/4/65.

63   R.A.CP (M):14/385.

64   Northumberland R.O.ZAN.M12/C39/55.

65   *Newcastle Journal*, 26 April 1746.

66   *Gentleman's Magazine* (1746), xvi, 220.

67   James Maxwell, op. cit., p. 169. Cf. J. Prebble, *Culloden* (1961), p. 132: "the phrase about no quarter was a crude forgery added afterwards."

68   B.L. Add MSS 35889, f. 95v; R.A.CP (M):13/404; H.M.C. Athole MSS, p. 74.

69   R.A.CP (M): 13/405. See page 154.

70   Some of them are discussed in Henrietta Tayler, ed., *The History of the Rebellion in the Years 1745 and 1746 from a Manuscript now in the Possession of Lord James Stewart-Murray* (Roxburgh Club, Oxford, 1944), pp. xvii—xix. She reproduces the genuine orders of Lord George Murray, and those in the Cumberland papers box 13/405, though not entirely accurately. Her conclusion agrees with her assertion on page xvii that "it is now admitted by all unprejudiced historians that the copy of the order of the day so often quoted has had the passage added by another hand". Thus she claims that the version in R.A.CP (M):13/405 is "the faked order", p. xix.

71   SP/36/82, ff. 234—44.

72   A. and H. Tayler, *1745 and After* (1938), p. 154.

73   *The Lockhart Papers* (1817), ii, 508.

74   *A Particular Account of the Battle of Culloden*, April 16, 1746.

75   A. Henderson, *The Life of William Duke of Cumberland* (1766), p. 274.

76   A. Henderson, *The History of the Rebellion* (1753), p. 343.

77   R.A.CP (M):14/114.

78   H.W.C., p. 249.

79   *Newcastle Journal*, 10 May 1746.

80   *General Evening Post*, 3 May 1746.

81   Henry Paton, ed., *The Lyon in Mourning* (Edinburgh, 1895), ii, 260—1. Cf. Prebble, op. cit., pp. 134—5.

82   R.A.CP (M):43/286.

83   Scottish R.O.GD1/322/1.

84   H.L.LO 10882: Brodie to Loudoun, 29 April 1746.

85   H.M.C. Polwarth MSS, v, 179.

86   H.W.C. p. 288.

CHAPTER 7
"They in rebellion shall arise no more"

1   B.L. Add MS 32707, f. 110.
2   R.A.CP (M):14/303.
3   Ibid. 144.
4   Ibid. 234.
5   Ibid. 58.
6   Ibid. 57.
7   H.L.LO 9505. Cumberland erased from the initial draft an instruction to take prisoners. R.A.CP (M):14/123.
8   R.A.CP (M):14/354. Ancram added "Major Lafouselle would have been pleased with the blaze."
9   H.L.LO 12056. McKenzie to Loudoun, 29 May 1746. "I own my fingers itched for more," McKenzie confessed "but was afraid of misrepresentations."
10   R.A.CP (M):15/78.
11   *The History of the Rebellion in 1745 and 1746 extracted from the Scots Magazine* (1755), p. 232.
12   W. A. S. Hewins, ed., *The Whitefoord Papers* (Oxford, 1898), p. 79.
13   *History of the Rebellion...from the Scots Magazine*, p. 236.
14   R.A.CP (M):14/274.
15   Ibid. 15/388; 16/170.
16   Many parochial lists survive in the papers of the duke of Cumberland, and some in the Loudoun papers, e.g. H.L.LO 10839, 10840.
17   Hewins, loc. cit.
18   R.A.CP (M):15/16.
19   Ibid. 129.
20   W. Sussex R.O. Goodwood MSS 111/203.
21   M. Hughes, *A Plain Narrative or Journal of the late Rebellion* (1746), p. 54.
22   R.A.CP (M):15/78.
23   James Maxwell of Kirkconnell, *Narrative of Charles Prince of Wales Expedition to Scotland in the year 1745* (Edinburgh, 1841), p. 170.
24   H.L.LO 10882, Brodie to Loudoun 29 April 1746.
25   R.A.CP (M):18/20.
26   Ibid. 15/101.
27   Ibid. 369.
28   Ibid. 396.
29   Ibid. 221.
30   *History of the Rebellion in 1745 and 1746*, p. 232.
31   R.A.CP (M):15/389. Fawkener erased this sentence in the draft of the letter.
32   Ibid. 271.
33   J. Prebble, *Culloden* (1961), pp. 203—29.
34   R.A.CP (M):16/10.
35   Ibid. 15/302, 417.
36   H.L.LO 11199, 7354.

37 *A journey through Part of England and Scotland along with the Army* (1746), p. 179.
38 R.A.CP (M):16/59.
39 W. Sussex R.O. Goodwood MSS 111/204.
40 Hughes, op. cit., p. 54; W. Sussex R.O. Goodwood MSS 111/259.
41 *History of the Rebellion in 1745 and 1746*, pp. 133—4.
42 *A Journey...along with the Army*, p. 179. Another observer wrote of being surrounded "by clusters of prodigious, high, barren rocky mountains that seem thrown upon one another as boys heap up stones, and shew us poor Dame Nature in a much worse sight than I ever yet met with her, even in Westmorland; or indeed than I believe she has ever appear'd in anywhere else, since the Chaos." Goodwood MSS 111/259: R. Meggott to Richmond, 20 May 1746.
43 *Gentleman's Magazine* (1746), xvi, 382.
44 W. Sussex R.O. Goodwood MSS 106/477: Albermarle to Richmond, 13 July 1746.
45 Ibid. 111/261: R. Meggott to Richmond, 1 Aug. 1746.
46 R.A.CP (M):15/373.
47 Ibid. 16/339.
48 19 George II c. 39.
49 R.A.CP (M):17/51.
50 *Culloden Papers* (1815), pp. 286, 289.
51 19 George II c. 38.
52 *Culloden Papers*, p. 286.
53 R.A.CP (M):17/51.
54 W. Cobbett, *Parliamentary History* (1812), xiii, 1416—18.
55 B. Lenman, *The Jacobite Risings in Britain 1689—1746* (1980), p. 278.
56 See T. B. Howell, ed., *A Complete Collection of State Trials* (1813), xviii, 338—850.
57 R.A.CP (M):17/22, 20/365.
58 Ibid. 20/365.
59 A. Henderson, *The History of the Rebellion* (1753), pp. 355—9.
60 H.M.C. Kenyon MSS, p. 478.
61 H.M.C. Du Cane MSS, p. 128.
62 Sir Bruce Seton and Jean Gordon Arnot, eds., *The Prisoners of the '45* (Edinburgh, 1928), 3 vols, i, 3. All work on the prisoners is indebted to these volumes.
63 R. C. Jarvis, 'Carlisle trials', 'Trial proceedings', *Collected Papers on the Jacobite Risings* (Manchester, 1972), ii, 255—302.
64 *York Courant* 14 Oct. 1746.
65 Ibid. 7 Oct. 1746.
66 H.W.C., p. 296.
67 *Gentleman's Magazine* (1746), xvi, 302—5.

CHAPTER 8

"King George reigns in the Hearts of all"

1 B. Lenman, *The Jacobite Risings in Britain* (1980), p. 255.

2   *York Courant* 11 Feb. 1746.

3   R.A.CP (M):6/67.

4   Northumberland R.O.ZA1.84/20.

5   R.A.CP (M):14/99.

6   *Newcastle Journal*   5 Oct. 1745.

7   R.A.CP (M):16/204.

8   R. Fitzroy Bell, ed., *Memorials of John Murray of Broughton* (Edinburgh, 1898), p. 244. *Pace* Dr Cruickshanks, *Political Untouchables: The Tories and the '45* (1979), p. 88, the fact that some of the tenants of the duke of Somerset bore "the historic names of Northumberland" was purely coincidental. The heads of the leading families, such as Sir Walter Blackett, Sir Henry Liddell and Matthew Ridley, were conspicuous in their support of the government.

9   J. Ray, *A Compleat History of the Rebellion* (1749), p. 113.

10   *Gentleman's Magazine* (1745), xv, 547.

11   Ibid. xvi, 16.

12   *A Letter to the Archbishop of York...15 Oct 1745*, p. 2. (MS copy in Gloucs R.O.D 1086 F196: Cf.SP/36/71, f. 221.)

13   G. G. Mounsey, *Carlisle in 1745* (1846), p. 165.

14   J. Ray, op. cit., p. 378.

15   Sir R. Lodge, editor, *Private Correspondence of Chesterfield and Newcastle 1744—6* (1930), pp. 93, 123.

16   R.A.CP (M):12/341.

17   B.L. Add MS 32706, f. 278.

18   Ibid. f. 257; Lenman, op. cit., p. 289.

19   *Culloden Papers* (1815), pp. 253, 426.

20   R.A.CP (M):14/107.

21   Ibid. 12/198.

22   J. Prebble, *Culloden* (1961), p. 34.

23   *Observations on Mr Home's Account of the Battle of Culloden* (Exeter, 1802), p. 32.

24   *York Courant* 31 Dec. 1745.

25   L. Dickins and M. Stanton, eds., *An Eighteenth-century Correspondence* (1910), p. 117.

26   Garnett, p. 533.

27   *Newcastle Journal*, 23 Nov. 1745.

28   H.W.C., p. 110.

29   Hereford R.O.AD 30/176: Elizabeth Boteler to Thomas Penoyre, 11 Oct. 1745.

30   R.A.CP (M):14/397.

31   Garnett, p. 535.

32   SP/36/67, ff. 162, 166, 203.

33   *Gentleman's Magazine* (1745), xv, 482.

34   Ibid. p. 522.

35   Worcs R.O. Bellomont MSS 899:169.

36   Montanus's article appeared in the *General Evening Post* 5 Oct. 1745 and the *Newcastle Journal*, 12 Oct. 1745.

37   Leeds Archives Dept. Newby Hall MSS 2830/12.

38 SP/36/83, f. 341, James Bamfield, mayor of Liverpool to Newcastle, 23 May 1746.

39 *Gentleman's Magazine* (1746), xvi, 40.

40 Above, p. 69.

41 SP/36/70, f. 135.

42 Hereford R.O.AD 30/177: Velters Cornewall to T. Penoyre, "Christmas Eve".

43 Gloucs R.O.D3549: box 15a; T. Sharp to J. Sharp, 22 Nov. 1745.

44 J. Maxwell, *Narrative of Charles Prince of Wales Expedition to Scotland* (Edinburgh, 1841), p. 72; E. Charteris, editor, *A Short Account of the Affairs of Scotland...by Lord Elcho* (1907), pp. 337—9.

45 *Gentleman's Magazine* (1745), xv, 545.

46 W. Cobbett, *Parliamentary History* (1812), xiii, 1319—26.

47 SP/36/74, f. 1.

48 G. Holmes, 'The achievement of stability: The social context of politics from the 1680s to the Age of Walpole', J. Cannon ed., *The Whig Ascendancy: Colloquies on Hanoverian England* (1981), pp. 1—22.

49 E. Charteris, *William Augustus, Duke of Cumberland* (1913), p. 292.

50 Royal Archives, Windsor, Cumberland papers 70/93, 161 (not microfilmed).

Index

Firth of Murray

Culloden